SECOND EDITION

Introduction to Casino and Gaming Operations

Denis P. Rudd, Ed.D., CHA, FMP

Lincoln H. Marshall, Ph.D.

Prentice Hall
Upper Saddle River, NJ 07458

Library of Congress Cataloging-in-Publication Data

Rudd, Denis P., 1944–

    Introduction to casino and gaming operations / Denis P. Rudd,
Lincoln H. Marshall. — 2nd ed.

      p.   cm.

    Rev. ed. of: Introduction to casino and gaming operations /
Lincoln H. Marshall, © 1996.

    Includes bibliographical references and index.

    ISBN 0-13-979568-5 (case)

    1. Gambling.   I. Marshall, Lincoln H.   II. Marshall, Lincoln H.
Introduction to casino and gaming operations.   III. Title.

GV1301.M27   2000

795—dc21   99-30911

                                                        CIP

Acquisitions Editor: *Neil Marquardt*
Director of Manufacturing and Production: *Bruce Johnson*
Production Liaison: *Denise Brown*
Manufacturing Buyer: *Ed O'Dougherty*
Managing Editor: *Mary Carnis*
Editorial Assistant: *Susan M. Kegler*
Creative Director: *Marianne Frasco*
Senior Design Coordinator and Cover Design: *Miguel Ortiz*
Marketing Manager: *Shannon Simonsen*
Printer/Binder: *R.R. Donnelley & Sons/Harrisonburg*
Cover Printer: *Phoenix Color*

©2000, 1996 by Prentice-Hall, Inc.
Upper Saddle River, New Jersey 07458

Printed in the United States of America

10 9 8 7 6 5 4 3 2 1

ISBN 0-13-979568-5

Prentice-Hall International (UK) Limited, *London*
Prentice-Hall of Australia Pty. Limited, *Sydney*
Prentice-Hall Canada Inc., *Toronto*
Prentice-Hall Hispanoamericana, S.A., *Mexico*
Prentice-Hall of India Private Limited, *New Delhi*
Prentice-Hall of Japan, Inc., *Tokyo*
Pearson Education Asia Pte. Ltd., *Singapore*
Editora Prentice-Hall do Brasil, Ltda., *Rio de Janeiro*

Contents

Preface

Casino gaming around the world is growing at a phenomenal rate. As more jurisdictions and venues add new forms of gaming, the total population of gamblers increases. In the United States, there has been an expansion of gaming activities. Lotteries have evolved from small, state-run operations to multi-state, multi-million-dollar operations. In addition, race tracks around the country have instituted slot and VLT (video lottery terminal) operations to increase their revenue base. As more people are made aware of and participate in gaming activities, they look to the established gaming centers around the world. This expansion, instead of it being the demise of the industry, has become its savior.

Introduction to Casino and Gaming Operations is a book designed to introduce readers to the history of the gaming industry from its inception to the present time and to familiarize them with possible gaming trends and areas of future expansion. To successfully achieve these objectives, the reader must understand the operation and management of the casino industry.

People gamble for a variety of reasons, and the easiest to understand is their desire to be winners. However, some experts contend that the urge to gamble is a much more complicated process than the prospect of easy gain. One school of thought on the subject suggests that gambling is a relief from the boredom of everyday life. Others believe that gambling is exhilarating in and of itself, whether the gambler wins or loses. Still others argue that gambling is an indication of virility. Given that almost half of those who gamble are women, this theory is currently given little credence. No matter what the reason, people have always made wagers on outcomes. This passion for gambling is primarily responsible for the proliferation of gaming establishments around the world. The other major reason for the growth of the gaming industry is, of course, much easier to understand: the profit generated by this expansion.

The structure of the text material will enable the reader to understand the fascinating and intricate operations of the casino and gaming industry. The brief history of gambling from the beginning of time to the present acquaints the reader with the background necessary to understand the potential that exists for casinos today. The prolific growth throughout the world that has taken place in the casino and gaming industry from the 1970s until now emerges as a pattern of needs for state, province, and federal governments.

Three major developments took place in the United States that enabled casino gaming to establish the basis for its phenomenal growth: first, the acceptance and endorsement of lotteries by state governments and the general population; second, the approval of hybrid forms of gaming and casino operations throughout the United States (charities, bingo, etc.); third, the passage of the Indian Gaming Regulation Act by Congress. The acceptance of lotteries, numbers games, riverboat gambling, charity gambling, and Native American casinos has affirmed the legitimacy of gaming and provided a training ground for future casino expansions. According to a Harrah's Survey of U.S. Casino Entertainment, acceptance of casino entertainment among Americans remained high in 1998. Fifty-one percent of the adults surveyed found casino entertainment "acceptable for anyone," and 35 percent considered it "acceptable for others, but not for me." In addition, a 1996 CNN-Gallup Poll shows that over two-thirds of Americans surveyed believe that gambling has a positive effect on the economy.

The domestic market is still growing significantly, but the international market is ready for an expansion at the speed of light. Casinos are springing up in every country around the world. According to International Gaming Technology, one of the largest makers of slot machines in the world, sales are expected to quadruple over the next five years. Growth is expected in the Canadian market as well as the European market, Pacific Rim market, and the potentially untapped Asian markets. It appears that states, as well as countries, are experiencing the domino effect as their next-door neighbors receive the benefits of casino and gaming activities. For example, the Windsor, Ontario, casino, one of the most successful in the world, depends solely on the Detroit market for its profit. Detroit, realizing this, is frantic to stop the flow of American dollars into Canada by instituting its own casino. Niagara Falls, Canada, has opened one of the most successful casinos in the world, and Niagara Falls, New York, is attempting to cash in on this lucrative market.

From the evolution of gambling to pari-mutuel lottery operations, from horse racing to dog racing, this book transports you from the pyramids of Egypt to the royal court of Elizabeth I of England. Slot machines and video lottery terminals are investigated from the viewpoint of the gaming public as well as from that of the gaming establishments. Rules, regulations, and events that have shaped the development of gaming in the United States are brought into perspective. Games of chance and games of skill and their economic and social impact are explored. Marketing and customer relations, accounting and finance, and the procedures involved in gaming operations as they relate to profitability within the industry are investigated and analyzed. America's relationship with Canada, her most significant trading partner, and other international gaming markets are studied.

Acknowledgments

Dr. Denis P. Rudd would like to take this opportunity to thank his daughter, Helen, and his wife, Julia, for putting their time and effort into this endeavor. In addition, he would like to thank Ms. Cindy Kaiser Murphey, Executive Vice President, MGM Grand Hotel and Casino; Mr. Albert Lacle, Vice President of Sales and Marketing, Taj Mahal Resort; Paul Speirs, Director of Public Relations, Excaliber and Luxor Hotel and Casino; Ms. Kimberly Wilson, Director of Public Affairs, Claridge Hotel and Casino; Ms. Kathy Driscoll, Director of Public Relations, Bally Gaming; Rachel Bogitan, Vice President, Hilton Casino; Allen Hopper and Mr. R. Burton, Director of Public Relations, Circus Circus Enterprises, Reno and Las Vegas; and Mr. Rick Sorenson, Director of Public Relations, IGT. He would especially like to thank his mentor, Dr. Thomas Casesse, from the University of Nevada at Las Vegas.

Dr. Lincoln Marshall thanks his his wife, Megan, and daughter, Dominique, for their continued support and understanding on this and other projects. He also thanks Marilyn Gleason and Demtria Noisette for their diligent help with proofreading and giving suggestions for the book.

Both Dr. Rudd and Dr. Marshall would especially like to thank the CEO of Tiffany Design, Frank Gresser, for the use of his image entitled "Las Vegas from 4000 Feet" on the cover of this book. Tiffany Design is located at Tiffany Design Poster, P.O. Box 71895, Las Vegas, NV 89170.

Chapter 1

The Evolution of Gaming

OBJECTIVES

- Trace the ancient origins of gambling.
- Provide a brief history of gambling up to the present time.
- Examine the development of modern forms of gambling.
- Explore various attempts at gambling reforms.
- Discuss current trends in gambling.

INTRODUCTION

Gambling is a cultural event that is present in almost all societies, in all periods of time, and is participated in by all members of the social strata. People have been gambling, in one form or another, for over four thousand years (Abt, Smith, and Christiansen, 1985; Bolen and Boyd, 1968). Gambling is predetermined: it does not matter what is said or done by its advocates or opponents. It is an activity that is practiced, or implicitly sanctioned, by a considerable majority of people (Enforceability of Gambling Laws, 1976).

Gaming is as ancient as time itself. A game similar to lotto began in prerecorded history. Archeologists have found evidence of gambling games initiated by the pharaohs of Egypt. In the Old Testament 26:55–56, it is recorded that ". . . the Lord instructed Moses to take a census of the people of Israel and to divide the lands among them by lot" ("Lottery," 1994–1998). Around 100 B.C., Chung-Lung introduced a game similar to keno to raise money for his armies. The Great Wall of China was constructed from the profits of gaming. Some believe that the history of modern casinos began in ancient Rome as a method of entertainment for the Roman emperors. Nero, emperor of Rome from 54 to

68 A.D., held lotteries to celebrate the eternity of the empire in which thousands of prizes consisting of land, jobs, ships, and slaves were awarded ("History of Lotteries," 1999).

Gambling, in various forms, is permitted in many countries; it is increasingly regarded as a legal method of fund raising in the United States and Canada. However, it certainly has not met with universal approval. Many are still convinced it is a vice, even while they condone its existence. What is it about gambling that creates this paradoxical viewpoint? Perhaps an examination of gambling through the ages will provide some helpful insights.

ANCIENT ORIGINS

The origins of gambling are obscured in antiquity. The consensus, however, is that games of chance probably evolved out of primitive people's captivation with religion. Pagan priests cast lots to coerce the deities they worshiped into revealing the future, thereby increasing certainty in decision making (Bolen, 1968). Modifications of gambling and gambling equipment were used by witch doctors in primitive medical practice to determine whether a person in danger of dying would recover or to appeal to the gods to bring about a cure (Reid and Demaris, 1963).

Original papyrus casting lots for the soul.

Even though the ancient Greeks considered gambling to be a grievous sin, they incorporated gambling ceremoniously into their religion, and worshiped a goddess of gaming and fortune named Tyche. Fortuna was the Roman equivalent of Tyche. The Greeks expressed the relationship of gambling and religion in a number of their myths. In one myth, three brothers shot dice to split up the universe among themselves. Zeus won the upper world, Poseidon won the oceans, and Hades lost and became master of the underworld (Wagner, 1972; Puzo, 1977). In yet another myth, Palamedes invented the dice and taught his companions how to play craps during the long, boring siege of Troy. He eventually learned the art of trick dice-throwing and was later stoned to death for cheating (Reid and Demaris, 1963).

Evidence of the existence of gambling is verifiable through mention in ancient texts and through archeological endeavors. In ancient Egypt, those with addictive gambling habits were sent to the quarries to work off their debts. Archaeologists have excavated dice used by the pharaohs, who supposedly were inveterate gamblers (Wagner, 1972). An Egyptian myth tells the story of Rhea, the Earth, and Saturn, who had a torrid love affair; Rhea became pregnant. The Sun was savagely angry with her and decreed that she could not deliver the baby on any day of the year. Mercury, who secretly admired Rhea, came to her rescue. He played a game of dice with the Moon and won some of her light. He made five new days out of his winnings and, during that time, Rhea gave birth to Osiris and Isis. Those five days were added to the existing 360 days in the year and were celebrated by the Egyptians as the birthdays of the two deities (Messick and Goldblatt, 1976).

Although the ancient Jews disapproved of gambling for financial gain, there are many stories in the Bible involving wagers of one kind or another. The soldiers of Pontius Pilate gambled for Christ's clothing while they were crucifying Him (Messick and Goldblatt, 1976). In the Old Testament, God commanded Moses to divide Canaan by casting lots (Puzo, 1977; Messick and Goldblatt, 1976). The Lord ordered Aaron to cast lots to ascertain which of two goats was to be sacrificed to Him (Messick and Goldblatt, 1976).

One particularly lurid Bible story involves Samson, the son of Manoah, who met and married a Philistine woman. On his way to the wedding, he saw a dead lion that was covered with bees who were in the process of making honey. At his wedding celebration, he bet thirty guests that they could not guess the answer to a riddle he had for them:

Out of the eater came forth meat

And out of the strong came forth sweetness

The guests had seven days to guess the answer to the riddle or lose thirty changes of clothing to Samson. After a few days had passed, the guests began to worry. They told Samson's wife to wheedle the riddle's answer out of her husband or they would burn down her father's house. She wept so long and so bitterly that Samson finally told her the solution; she, in turn, passed it along to the guests. On the seventh day, the guests answered the riddle:

> *What is sweeter than honey?*
>
> *And what is stronger than a lion?*

Samson had bet without the means to pay off the debt, so he killed thirty men for their clothing and gave them to the guests (Messick and Goldblatt, 1976).

During the early days of the Roman Empire, there were strict laws forbidding gambling. However, when the Roman Empire was at its peak, gambling became a favorite pastime of the citizenry (Messick and Goldblatt, 1976). Even Roman children were taught to gamble. The Roman Emperor Caligula lost his entire treasury in a dice game. To continue playing, he went out into the street, accused two passing noblemen of treason, seized their wealth, and then continued the game. Emperor Claudius owned carriages that were specifically designed to allow dice games to be played inside. Whenever he did not care for the throw, he ordered his driver to increase the carriage's speed and overturn the dice. Even Aristotle wrote a remarkable treatise on how to cheat at dice (Puzo, 1977).

GAMBLING IN EUROPE AND ENGLAND

Although little is written about gambling from the fifth through the ninth centuries, it is known that the Germanic hordes who brought down the Roman Empire played dice; the losers became the slaves of the winners (Puzo, 1977). During the first Holy Crusades, gambling became so prevalent that Richard the Lion-Hearted and King Philip of France decreed that any soldiers beneath the rank of knight could not gamble. The exceptions were clerics, knights, and servants of the kings; however, they could not lose more than twenty shillings during the course of a day. The punishment for disobeying the law was severe; those who did so were stripped naked and publicly whipped for three days. The two kings, of course, could gamble whenever and for whatever stakes they chose (Messick and Goldblatt, 1976; Puzo, 1977).

Throughout the centuries following the Crusades, gambling was widespread in Europe, and many ancient games evolved into the games that are well-known today. **Hazard,** the forerunner of craps, was invented during the Crusades by English soldiers who held the Arabian castle called Hazart under siege. Variations were made to the game throughout the next seven hundred years. The name craps is derived from the name given to a throw of two aces in hazard, craps (Asbury, 1969).

The roots of **faro,** a very popular game in Europe during the sixteenth and seventeenth century, lie in the German game Landsquenet, a game played by German soldiers around 1400. In the middle of the seventeenth century, faro, or pharaoh, was extremely fashionable in Paris. The *ph* spelling was used because the backs of the French cards had a picture of an Egyptian king on them. The game was banned by Louis XIV but later regained favor under the rule of the Duke of Orleans who controlled the throne after the death of Louis XIV in 1715. Faro was probably introduced in England by noblemen who shared the exile of Charles II in France. It became a favorite diversion of the ladies and gentlemen of Charles II's court and was often played for extraordinarily high stakes. Faro was ultimately prohibited by an Act of Parliament in 1738 (Asbury, 1969).

Other games popular in Europe and England after the Middle Ages were roulette, vingt-et-un, loo, all-fours, lotto, casino, monte, and several forerunners of poker (Asbury, 1969). **Roulette** originated in Egypt but became a favorite of the French people, and is still one of the best-known games in gambling casinos. The game changed from its original version of three zeroes on the wheel to a wheel with one and sometimes two zeroes. The odds are heavily with the house (Puzo, 1977).

Vingt-et-un is known as van jon in England and in the United States as twenty-one and blackjack. It is considerably older than the evolved game of roulette and was a favorite of Napoleon. Loo is a game of seventeenth-century England and was especially popular with the ladies who attended social gatherings in the evening. All-fours, whose name derives from the four points of high, low, jack, and the game, has generated many variations since it first appeared in the seventeenth century. The final edition, which is still very popular, is called pitch. Casino is an extremely old game of Italian origin. Like loo, it is associated with respectability and gentility (Asbury, 1969).

Lotto, which evolved into keno, consisted of balls numbered from one to ninety, a large round receptacle to hold the balls, and a deck of lotto cards, also numbered from one to ninety. The operator of the game released the balls one by one and called the number off. The players covered the corresponding number on the lotto card with a button or similar object. The first person to cover a row of five numbers won after the operator had taken a certain percentage (Asbury, 1969).

Monte is an old game of Spanish origin and is somewhat similar to faro. It was usually played with a forty-card deck that had no eights, nines, or tens. Two cards were drawn from both the top and the bottom of the deck and exposed to the players. The deck was turned face up and if the exposed card matched any of the four cards already drawn, all the players' bets were paid out, usually in silver coins. This game eventually became very popular in Cuba, Mexico, and other Hispanic countries (Asbury, 1969).

The ancient Persian game of as nas, or dsands, is thought by some historians to be the basis for the modern types of poker (Asbury, 1969). However, a great many more experts believe that the current variations of poker originated not in one game of chance, but in several. Poker has been directly traced to the old Italian game of primero and the French game of gilet. A combination of the two games evolved into the game of brelan between 1550 and 1574, during the reign of Charles IX. Brelan metamorphosed, during the French Revolution, into the game of bouillotte, which introduced betting techniques. Out of a game called ambigu came the draw feature, and from the English game brag came the concept of bluffing (Lorrimore, 1992b).

Lotteries, over the centuries, were organized for a number of purposes. In a **lottery**, participants purchase a ticket, usually numbered, and the winning tickets are picked randomly. A portion of the revenue realized from selling the tickets is the prize. Sometimes governments used lotteries to raise monies that would otherwise have been generated through taxation. The first recorded state lottery took place in France in 1520 (Lorrimore, 1992a). Queen Elizabeth I of England held a lottery in 1596 to raise enough money to fund a fleet of ships. In the 1770s, England also ran a lottery to fund the army that fought in the American Revolution against the colonists (Doocey, 1994).

National lotteries were banned in England in 1826. In 1992, however, Britain endorsed the use of lotteries to help fund a number of worthy causes. The new national lottery will supposedly be the largest of its kind (Doocey, 1994).

Policy is another form of gambling that originated in the lottery shops of London during the early part of the eighteenth century. **Policy**, now known as **numbers** in the United States, is the illegal offshoot of the lotteries. For a significantly smaller sum than a lottery ticket cost, players chose a number and bet that their selections would be drawn in a particular lottery. This pastime was particularly popular with members of the upper class (Asbury, 1969).

In addition to those already mentioned, other prominent members of the royalty were addicted to gambling. King Henry VIII of England was an imprudent gamester. He lost the Jesus Bells of St. Paul's Cathedral to Sir Miles Partridge. Henry IV of France was not only a dissolute gambler, but also a thief. He hired professional gamblers to cheat members of his own court. When King Charles V of France held the city of Orange in a siege, the commanding officer of his army gambled with and lost the soldiers' pay. Charles was forced to surrender. Afterward, members of the French cavalry were forbidden to gamble; the punishment for disobeying was death (Puzo, 1977).

Gambling in Europe gained and lost popularity periodically during the eighteenth century and the first half of the nineteenth century until the advent of the great gambling houses that became so fashionable with royalty and the polite society. Francois Blanc, a crooked stock market player, built a successful casino in Luxembourg and later built the magnificent casino in Baden-Baden, Germany. The wealthy from all over Europe flocked to the city to gamble and to enjoy the curative waters of the spa.

In the early 1860s, gambling was prohibited in Italy and France; on the advice of his mother, Caroline, Prince Charles III of Monaco decided that the only way he could earn money from the 368 rocky coastline acres was to build a

Prince Charles the Third, Monte Carlo Casino.

casino. In 1863, Blanc was commissioned by the Grimaldi family to build a casino in the principality of Monaco, all that was left of the great Grimaldi family holdings. In Monte Carlo, Blanc built both an opulent casino and a hotel. The casino was an overnight success. The Prince of Wales gambled there often, as did Emperor Franz Josef. Czar Nicholas and Leopold II of Belgium were frequent visitors as well. Wealthy Americans traveling in Europe discovered Monte Carlo, and their enthusiasm for this stylish type of gambling establishment was responsible, in part, for John Morrissey's decision to build the **Saratoga** Club House in Saratoga Springs, New York (Messick and Goldblatt, 1976).

Gambling casinos are still permitted in Europe today, most notably in Germany, Monte Carlo, Austria, and Great Britain. Britain legalized gambling in the 1960s so that churches could raise funds through games like bingo. But loopholes in the law allowed private clubs to offer games of chance. By the end of the decade, there were over a thousand gambling casinos in Great Britain. Gambling proved to be so lucrative an enterprise that bookie joints were legalized. Gambling had become an established and acceptable way to earn revenues (Messick and Goldblatt, 1976).

GAMBLING IN THE UNITED STATES

The first games of chance brought to the New World were probably played by the sailors who crewed Columbus's three ships. The Spanish and the Portuguese, in addition to bringing dice and cards with them to the Americas, also brought horses and subsequently introduced horse-race betting. Some of the horses escaped captivity and eventually found their way into the Great Plains. After a time, their progeny became the property of the Plains Indians who were excellent riders and loved to gamble for herds of ponies and horses. Those who lost often raided neighboring tribes, which led to wars over the ownership of the animals (Longstreet, 1977). Indians also gambled with dice made from pear and plum pits (Messick and Goldblatt, 1976).

The colonial Americans loved to gamble in one form or another, probably a passion acquired from some of their European forebears. The early colony of Virginia was funded mostly by proceeds from English lotteries. In the same spirit, by the end of the 1600s, almost every county seat held a lottery. Revenues from lotteries were responsible, in part, for the founding of many institutions of higher learning: William and Mary, Yale, Dartmouth, Harvard, Princeton, and Columbia, to name a few (Plesser, Siege, and Jacobs, 1986).

Besides lotteries, other forms of gambling caught on quickly. Cockfighting was popular, especially in the southern colonies, as were bearbaiting and dog-fighting. Cards and dice were brought over by the Dutch and English. Horse racing caught on quickly, but was generally limited to the more well-to-do colonists (Plesser et al., 1986).

Almost every household in colonial America owned decks of playing cards. George Washington was a confirmed card player and Benjamin Franklin both printed and sold playing cards. Decks of cards sold so well that the British passed the infamous Stamp Act; the act, in addition to taxing tea, imposed a tariff on every pack of cards sold (Plesser et al., 1986).

Not all colonists embraced gambling so enthusiastically. The New England colonists considered gambling a sin and imposed fines and physical punishments on unfortunate transgressors (Plesser et al., 1986). This attitude was reflected in the antigambling bias promulgated by the American judicial system after the Revolutionary War. Gambling statutes were largely under the jurisdiction of each state, however, and most states adopted a live-and-let-live attitude regarding gambling. This acceptance sprang from economic necessity among the colonies while they were still under English rule. Gambling was allowed for financing both public and private works such as buildings, roads, dams, colleges, hospitals, and churches (Abt et al., 1985).

Lotteries were probably the most popular method of raising monies for specific projects. Ben Franklin promoted a lottery to raise funds for supplies to defend Philadelphia from the French and Indians. All manner of people bought lottery tickets despite their official illegal status (Plesser et al., 1986). This attitude prevailed during and after 1776 to the point where state-franchised lottery companies were formed, despite statutes against gambling in any form (Abt et al., 1985).

Lotteries were not without their problems. The Continental Congress devised a five-million-dollar lottery to finance the Revolutionary War in 1777. All winners who held winning tickets for amounts in excess of fifty dollars were told they would be paid in the future and received promissory notes. Due to fraud and mismanagement, most of those who purchased winning tickets never received their money and the lottery was a disaster (Plesser et al., 1986).

Gambling was condoned and even encouraged without opposition during the fifty-odd years after the Louisiana Purchase in 1803. Gambling houses and halls were built, the old games from Europe and England were imported and expanded on, and crooked gambling practices became prevalent (Asbury, 1969). This widespread acceptance of gambling continued until the pre–Civil War era. Big businesses conducted a number of fraudulent lotteries and offended the population. As part of a reform movement that swept the country, antigambling sentiments developed. This campaign was directed against all forms of gambling, but especially against lotteries. Some members of the reform movement, however, did not endorse the campaign against lotteries. Labor reformers continued to support lotteries even though a significant amount of revenue gained came from the workers who purchased tickets. The labor leaders believed that this was a relatively inexpensive way for the workers to have a chance at becoming wealthy. Despite this attitude, the reformers were successful in their efforts to ban lotteries in most states. By the time the Civil War began, only three states still allowed them: Delaware, Missouri, and Kentucky (Plesser et al., 1986).

The lottery again reared its head in 1865. An eastern gambling syndicate received permission from the state of Louisiana to operate a lottery at a cost of $40,000 a year for twenty-five years. Politicians and legislators were bribed and elections were manipulated to insure the continuation of the Louisiana Lottery. Soon, lottery tickets were sold all over the country and the system grew even more corrupt. The Lottery's charter was voided in 1879, but the syndicate again bribed officials to force an extension. Several bills to halt the Lottery were introduced in Washington, D.C., but were unsuccessful until 1890. Legislation was passed that banned the use of the postal service to mail any Lottery paraphernalia. The Louisiana legislature voted down a charter renewal in 1892, and the syndicate moved the operation to Honduras to avoid the postal regulations. In 1895, however, Congress prohibited the importing of any lottery material, effectively ending the Louisiana Lottery. A significant legacy of the Lottery is that it created in people's minds a lasting image coupling gambling with political corruption (Plesser et al., 1986).

One region largely unaffected by the antigambling movement was that of the Mississippi and Ohio Rivers and the states that bordered them. Professional gamblers earned their living riding up and down on the riverboats (Plesser et al., 1986). Unfortunately, **riverboat gambling** attracted many cheaters and sharpers (con artists). Some of them spent an extraordinary amount of time and money in setting up their victims from among the passengers. One infamous passenger, however, was known to turn the tables on dishonest gamblers: the inventor of the bowie knife, James Bowie, who died with Davey Crockett defending the Alamo in 1836. Bowie often traveled on the Mississippi River and routinely beat professional cheaters at their own game and returned the money to the hapless victims.

Mississippi riverboat gambling.

Before returning the money, however, he demanded that the victim swear never to gamble again (Asbury, 1969). One of the best-known tales of Bowie's knight-errantry apparently involved a young couple on their honeymoon. Bowie came aboard the steamboat New Orleans in Vicksburg. A gang of sharpers were in the process of fleecing a young planter and his new wife out of $50,000 owed to various friends and relatives. The planter lost all the money and was about to kill himself when Bowie stopped him. Bowie went into the bar and let it be known that he also had a large amount of money and was willing to while away the time in a friendly game of cards. After winning and losing a few hands, Bowie was dealt an almost unbeatable hand. The pot eventually reached a total of $70,000; only Bowie and one other player were still in the game. The remaining sharper reached into his sleeve to pull out the card he needed to win when Bowie grabbed his hand and pulled out his knife at the same time. Caught in the act, the sharpers had no choice except to let Bowie take the pot. Bowie returned $50,000 to the young man and his wife and kept the rest (Messick and Goldblatt, 1976).

New Orleans, one of the largest cities on the riverboat run, became a gambler's haven and had numerous formal and informal gambling casinos (Plesser et al., 1986). A very fashionable game in the casinos and on the riverboats was faro, almost certainly brought to America by the French colonists who settled in Alabama and Louisiana in the first half of the eighteenth century. Faro spread to the east and north through travelers and sailors. It gained even more popularity after the Louisiana Purchase and was played more widely than any other game until the twentieth century (Asbury, 1969).

Poque, or poker, was also a favorite in New Orleans and on the riverboats. This game spread through America in much the same way faro spread. However, poker never declined as did faro (Asbury, 1969).

Three-card monte, an offshoot of the old game of monte, was played often, especially by the riverboat gamblers. The gamblers usually worked in pairs to cheat their victims. The prey was shown three cards, usually a king, queen, and jack, which were then placed face down and moved around rapidly. The player had to pick the queen in order to win the bet. The dealer's partner won several games to demonstrate to the sucker how easy it was to win. While the victim's attention was engaged elsewhere, one of the gamblers marked the queen. When the victim bet to win, often heavily, the dealer slipped the marked card off the table and replaced it with another king or jack. It is obvious why this game was favored by the riverboat sharpers: it was a simple matter to dupe the victims into thinking they could win easily (Messick and Goldblatt, 1976).

As riverboat traffic increased, the cities bordering the Mississippi River swelled in population. Unfortunately, as the towns expanded, they drew unsavory characters as well as law-abiding citizenry. Prostitutes, thieves, and sharpers flocked to such cities as Louisville, Natchez, Memphis, and Cincinnati. At first, the townspeople ignored this influx of criminals. By the 1830s, however, even hamlets far from the river were subjected to scandalous and violent behavior from the criminal element. From this lawless territory sprang the **Clan of the Mystic Confederacy** (Messick and Goldblatt, 1976).

The Clan was very much like the organized crime syndicates of modern times. The leader of the Clan was John Murrell. He established this group of criminals in 1832 and determined that a slave revolt that he had planned would take place in December of 1835 throughout the river valleys. His gang of thugs, in the midst of this revolt, were to plunder the river towns. The Clan, ruled by a Grand Council of one hundred criminals, consisted of fifteen hundred outlaws. Some of the gang incited unrest among the black slaves. The Clan bought weapons and whiskey with funds contributed by the riverboat sharpers (Messick and Goldblatt, 1976).

A man named Virgil Stewart posed as a gambler and successfully infiltrated the Clan. While he was at Murrell's headquarters in Randolph, Tennessee, he learned about the planned revolution. With Stewart's information, charges of slave-stealing were brought against Murrell, and he was sentenced to ten years in prison. Stewart capitalized on his heroic role by writing a best-seller named *The Western Land Pirate* (Messick and Goldblatt, 1976).

After Murrell's trial, Tennessee made it illegal to play faro within its borders. Some cities ran gamblers out of town after they had been tarred and feathered, but most of the river valley residents felt safe because the Clan's leader was in jail. Their complacency was shattered, however, when they learned that the revolt had only been postponed to July 4, 1835. Alarmed citizens authorized lawmen to arrest every gambler they could lay their hands on. One of those arrested was a member of the Clan's Council; he was persuaded to divulge where the Clan's weapons were hoarded before he was hanged. Arrests escalated and the revolt was terminated. Even so, on July 4, towns all along the river had to combat looting and burnings engineered by the Clan members. The river town residents were mostly successful in their efforts to quell the riotous outbreaks and only encountered substantial resistance in Vicksburg. The outlaws intended to burn down the city but were driven back to their gambling hells. The citizens gave them twenty-four hours to get out of town, an edict that the gamblers ignored. The civilian army assaulted every gaming house and confiscated all equipment. One physician was killed when the volunteers were fired upon. The citizens dragged several sharpers out of their sanctuaries, hanged them, and burned all gambling apparatus. By the next morning, every gambler had fled (Messick and Goldblatt, 1976).

Natchez also ordered gamblers to vacate; after the incident at Vicksburg, they were only too happy to comply. In Cincinnati and Newport, Kentucky, bands of citizens burned gambling houses. Most of the exiled fugitives migrated to New Orleans, where they remained for almost twenty years. Gambling again became commonplace on the Mississippi only after the passage of several years. The new breed of gamblers took care to dress in dashing clothes and to treat their victims with a modicum of respect (Messick and Goldblatt, 1976).

Riverboat gambling resumed after the hiatus caused by the Civil War, but it never regained the popularity of the antebellum era (Plesser et al., 1986). Very few riverboats were making scheduled trips. The slave owners and cotton planters who had widely traveled on the boats no longer existed. In addition, professional gamblers were not looked upon with the same tolerance they had enjoyed before the Civil War. Several states through which the Mississippi and Ohio Rivers flowed passed laws making it difficult for the gambler to earn a living, and by the late 1860s, it was unusual to see a riverboat gambler plying his trade. Many of them wandered to the larger cities, joined the settlers moving to the West, or traveled on the trains that ran throughout the settled territories in the South and Southwest just as they had traveled on the riverboats. However, gambling on the trains was not as lucrative or as long-lived as river gambling had been; the train crews barely tolerated the sharpers and the journeys were over too quickly for the gamblers to set up their victims properly (Asbury, 1969).

In the North, New York City developed as one of the primary gambling centers of America both during and after the Civil War despite the antigambling sentiments of the time. By 1850, the gambling houses numbered an astounding six thousand (Plesser et al., 1986). William Tweed and his crooked Tammany Hall crew ravaged the city more than any other politician in American history. The dishonest police force turned a blind eye to the operation of the gambling houses, following the lead of the country's politicians and business leaders. Even women began gaming in halls built solely for them (Asbury, 1969).

In this corrupt city, one name stood out: John Morrissey. Morrissey was the undisputed king of gambling in New York for over twenty years. He was a Tammany Hall politician and heavyweight fighter of some repute whose nickname was Old Smoke. He was a member of the New York Senate and the United States Congress. He fleeced his customers ruthlessly in the gambling houses he built all over the city (Asbury, 1969).

Morrissey was born in Ireland but came to the United States with his parents in 1834, when he was three years old. His family settled in Troy, New York;

Morrissey roamed the streets of Troy until young adulthood and didn't learn to read or write until he was nineteen. He became the leader of a street gang called the Downtowns and had frequent brushes with the law. He moved to New York City and worked as a boardinghouse runner and a bouncer; he also engaged in several bloody brawls with other fighters. He managed to save enough money to pay his passage to San Francisco in 1851, where he opened a faro game with a partner and soon earned a considerable amount of money. In addition, he made his debut as a professional prize fighter, winning sizable purses. He fought professionally until 1858, when he announced his retirement from the ring. With all his earnings, he returned to New York and opened two gambling saloons, which he later sold at a profit. Thereafter, he followed a pattern of buying gambling saloons, running them efficiently, and selling them at a profit. During this time, he amassed a considerable personal fortune (Asbury, 1969).

One of Morrissey's most famous achievements as a professional gambler was the development of gambling and horse racing in Saratoga Springs, New York. Prior to Morrissey's arrival on the scene in 1861, Saratoga Springs housed several moderate gambling establishments. Morrissey built a gambling house on Woodlawn Avenue and operated it successfully for about six years; he was careful to build a reputation as an honest gambler who contributed heavily to the community. In 1867, he built the Saratoga Club House and a horse-racing track to go with it. The Club House was Morrissey's crowning achievement and remains so even today. It was compared to the great European gambling spas of the time. Morrissey established two rules for his Club House, which were rigidly adhered to even after he sold it: the residents of Saratoga were not allowed to gamble there and women were not permitted in the gaming rooms (Asbury, 1969).

Morrissey was as successful a politician as he was a gambler. He dominated New York politics because of his great power among the gamblers and became a congressman for two terms. He broke with the Tammany Hall gang in 1875 and was elected to the State Senate over opposition from Boss Tweed's gang of thugs. He successfully ran for a second term but contracted pneumonia during the campaign and died in 1878 (Asbury, 1969).

Chicago emerged as another important gambling center during and after the Civil War era, and there was no more prominent a player than Mike McDonald. By the time McDonald was in his early twenties, he was already a well-known gambler and politician. He had several run-ins with the police over the operation of his gambling house, but his big chance came after the great Chicago fire in 1871. The existing political system was destroyed along with over three acres of Chicago, and Mike became the new political force to be reckoned with. He opened a gaming establishment called The Store, which offered all types of gambling; the games of roulette and faro were the most popular. He paid off the authorities and staged planned police raids on The Store to appease the honest element of the city's residents (Messick and Goldblatt, 1976).

When a new mayor was elected in 1887, Mike decided it was time to retire from the gambling house business. He became a businessman and invested in several honest ventures; he also retained his power in the political arena. When he retired, none of his associates was able to run the rackets as he had and the city of Chicago divided itself into four separate segments: the East Side, the South Side, the West Side, and the Loop. Mike died a wealthy but dejected man in 1907 after his second wife shot and killed her lover (Messick and Goldblatt, 1976).

Many of the gamblers who did not flock to the cities of New York and Chicago followed the pioneers who traveled to the West. The climate was ideal for gambling; there was little interference of any kind, especially on the part of the authorities. Frontier life was lonely and difficult, and gambling became one of the few forms of entertainment available to the miners, trappers, homesteaders, ranchers, and cowboys who populated the West (Plesser et al., 1986).

Gambling in the western frontier was decidedly different from that in the East. The great majority of all kinds of people living in the West gambled in one form or another. Women dealers were often preferred because they were a rarity in this man-dominated land. Gambling establishments were much more primitive than those in the East, and the suckers weren't nearly as wealthy. The favored games were, for the most part, the same: faro, roulette, and, later, poker. In some parts of the West, the game of monte was also popular (Asbury, 1969).

San Francisco became the gambling capital of the West during the first Gold Rush. Her first gambling establishment, the El Dorado, opened as a tent, though it was later rebuilt of more substantial material. By the early 1850s, there were well over a thousand gaming houses (Longstreet, 1977). Other prominent gambling houses were the Bella Union, Parker House, Mazourka, Ifontne House, Alhambra, and Verandah. Free bar food and entertainment were provided to lure the customer into playing the popular games of the time: roulette, vingt-et-un, (later called blackjack), three-card monte, and faro. Poker didn't become popular until the 1870s. Most of the games were dishonest, but that didn't deter the players (Hicks, 1978).

Denver became another prominent gambling city of the West. The gambling houses in that town went a step further than those in San Francisco; they offered, in addition to games of chance, saloons, dance halls, and a type of bawdy theater. Card sharps like Soapy Smith flocked to Denver; Soapy dominated the scene until his brother murdered another gambler and Soapy and his associates were forced to leave town (Longstreet, 1977). Soapy sailed up to the Klondike in 1897 with his gang and opened a gambling saloon in Skagway, where he commanded the scene for six months. He was shot by a city engineer when he tried to interfere with a meeting of town residents who were discussing how to rid Skagway of Soapy (Asbury, 1969).

Kansas City, Missouri, was a smaller gambling town and boasted 40 gambling halls by the 1870s. By 1881, however, Missouri passed a strong antigambling law and gamblers were forced to play in social clubs, a euphemism for places housing high-stakes poker games. Those gaming establishment owners who didn't convert to clubs moved across the river into Kansas City, Kansas, where they were allowed to operate by bribing political officials (Longstreet, 1977).

Southern Texas also had its share of gambling establishments in the cities of San Antonio, Fort Worth, and Austin. Players who wished to indulge were welcome to play in a game of three-card monte or poker. One of Texas's most famous gamblers was Ben Thompson, a notorious gunslinger who owned a gambling house, but was so clumsy a card sharp that he killed over twelve men who accused him of cheating. He was murdered while he attended a theater show in San Antonio in 1884 (Longstreet, 1977).

Some of the most notorious towns in the West were Abilene and Dodge City in Kansas; Deadwood, South Dakota; Leadville, Creede, and Cripple Creek, Colorado; Tombstone, Arizona; Cheyenne, Wyoming; and Virginia City, Nevada. Of these towns, Dodge City, Deadwood, and Tombstone were the worst. Dodge City gained prominence as the shipping center for the herds of cattle from Texas during the 1870s. It attracted all sorts of grifters and criminals and was known for the number of murders committed there. Deadwood, after gold was discovered in South Dakota in 1874, was almost as bad. Deadwood is remembered as the town where Jack McCall murdered Wild Bill Hickok when he was holding a poker hand of aces and eights. Tombstone came into being in 1879 after silver deposits were discovered in southern Arizona. This tough mining town attracted all sorts of criminals; it earned a place in American history because it was the site of the gunfight between Wyatt Earp and his brothers and the Clanton and McLowery gangs. Tombstone dominated the Arizona territory as a center of gambling until its decline in the 1890s (Asbury, 1969).

After the turn of the century, both Arizona and New Mexico territories had over eight hundred gambling resorts that attracted frontier gamblers from all over the country. This happy state of affairs lasted until both territories applied for admittance into the Union. New Mexico passed extraordinarily rigorous antigambling laws in 1907 and Arizona quickly followed suit. Except for a few pockets of resistance, the era of wide-open frontier gambling was over (Asbury, 1969).

GAMBLING IN THE TWENTIETH CENTURY

America's thriving industrialism, together with the influx of immigrants during the latter half of the nineteenth century, restructured America into a largely urban society. Gambling reformers at the turn of the century were responsible for closing gambling establishments, race tracks, numbers, and bookmaking operations. By 1915, only seven states permitted horse racing. However, the public's desire to gamble persisted. Gambling syndicates developed in the city slums, and when the Prohibition era began, gambling evolved into an organized, national system (Longstreet, 1977; Messick and Goldblatt, 1976).

The creator of this nationwide business was Arnold Rothstein. Rothstein operated in Chicago and devised the practice of helping syndicates in other cities to cover risky bets; the system spread to encompass a loose conglomerate of organized crime. He was also the instigator of the 1919 World Series scandal during which the White Sox deliberately lost the Series to the Cincinnati Reds (Messick and Goldblatt, 1976).

Rothstein's heirs were among the more infamous citizens of the day: Al Capone, Frank Costello, Meyer Lansky, Frank Nitti, Bugsy Siegel, and others like them. These men were high-profile mobsters who dealt in misery and violence. Organized crime leaders eventually became more circumspect as time passed; they no longer wished to be in the limelight. Although they now operate mostly behind the scenes, they still exist (Plesser et al., 1986).

Colonel Edward R. Bradley is generally credited with being the first person to allow respectable women to gamble in his gambling club. This circumstance came about through Henry M. Flagler, who built a railroad that ran from the North to the South. He erected hotels, churches, and some gambling houses along the way. By 1894, his railroad reached Palm Beach, Florida; he built the Royal Poinciana Hotel and the Royal Poinciana Chapel and Beach Club (Longstreet, 1977; Messick and Goldblatt, 1976).

Flagler hired Colonel Bradley to run his gambling club. Bradley had been very much influenced by the elegant gambling clubs run by John Morrissey and Richard Canfield. To gain admittance to the Beach Club, gentlemen had to wear evening clothes, no one younger than twenty-five was allowed, and no free food was provided. Women and local residents were not allowed to enter. As a result, the Club did not show a profit in the first year of its operation. Bradley decided to permit society women, both young and old, to enter the hallowed halls, and was well pleased with the results. The female patrons were reckless and extravagant gamblers (Longstreet, 1977; Messick and Goldblatt, 1976).

Flagler did not approve of this new wrinkle; in fact, he came to disapprove of gambling altogether. He tried to oust the Colonel from his post after Bradley refused to change his policy, but to no avail. Bradley eventually built a much larger club in 1912 and hired renowned chefs to cook haute cuisine. The casino was only open in the winter when society people traveled to Florida. His wealthy patrons enjoyed playing a game somewhat like blackjack, chemin de fer, hazard, and poker for enormous stakes (Longstreet, 1977; Messick and Goldblatt, 1976).

Gambling was not legalized in Florida, but no successful attempt was made to close down Bradley's casino. His club was the main attraction enticing high society to Palm Beach until 1946, when Bradley died. In his will, he stipulated that the Beach Club was to be torn down and all the gambling equipment dumped into the ocean. Old-time patrons insist that Palm Beach has never been the same since (Longstreet, 1977; Messick and Goldblatt, 1976).

When Flagler's railroad reached Miami, Florida, it, too, became a gambling town. Gaming existed on a small-time basis until the 1920s when Al Capone's mob moved into town. He had interests in a large number of businesses and hotels where gambling was the greatest draw. He avoided trouble with the local law by bribing them. By the 1930s, Miami Beach casinos brought in first-class entertainers such as Helen Morgan, Jack Benny, and Sophie Tucker to dazzle the tourists. Capone's influence waned and his predecessors now ran the show. Race tracks and dog tracks were built and jai alai became prevalent when Cuban exiles moved into Miami after Castro's revolution. The authorities cracked down on organized crime in the 1950s, and Miami's mobsters either entered into legitimate businesses as a front for their gambling enterprises or made the move to Las Vegas (Longstreet, 1977; Messick and Goldblatt, 1976).

Las Vegas became a town on May 5, 1905, when the San Pedro, Los Angeles, and Salt Lake Railroad organized a land auction. The railroad told the thousands of Californians present that a train system would run through Las Vegas and throughout the Southwest. Over 1,200 lots were sold for $1,500.00 apiece. Wagon loads of settlers came to the town and erected hotels, a post office, a bank, and a number of gambling establishments. The railroad came through and the town slowly grew. In 1911, Las Vegas was chartered as a city. However, the year before, the Nevada state legislature made gambling illegal; that law stayed in place for twenty years (Longstreet, 1977; Puzo, 1977).

After the stock market crash in 1929, the Great Depression settled in, and in 1931 the citizens of Nevada finally voted legalized gambling back in. The need for electric power generated the construction of the Boulder Dam, later called Hoover Dam. The workers who built the dam sought diversion in the gambling halls of Las Vegas, bringing that city its first significant prosperity (Longstreet, 1977; Puzo, 1977).

Las Vegas's present-day prominence was brought about by a gangster named Benjamin "Bugsy" Siegel. He originally came West to become an actor but had no talent. He eventually became a director of Mob racing wire activities in California, and part of his job necessitated his traveling to Vegas frequently. By that time, Las Vegas boasted some fairly opulent gambling casinos, and Bugsy became interested in the little oasis in the desert. He decided to build a casino to rival all others and persuaded some of his Mob associates to invest with him in this venture. He hired the Del Webb Construction Company to build the casino he planned to name the Flamingo. The original projected cost for the casino was $1.5 million, but Bugsy wanted only the best materials and these were hard to come by in post–World War II America. He bought the materials on the black market and the casino ended up costing over $6 million (Longstreet, 1977; Puzo, 1977).

In December of 1946, Bugsy opened the Flamingo before it was completed and during the first two weeks of operation, the casino lost over $100,000. He closed it and his Mob investors tried to fire him, but he insisted that the Flamingo would make a profit. He reopened in March of 1947; the first few weeks brought more losses, but finally the casino began to show a substantial profit. His investors were still warring with him, however; in June of 1947, while he was staying in his girlfriend Virginia Hill's Beverly Hills home, Bugsy was shot to death (Longstreet, 1977).

Bugsy was followed by others of his kind who saw the enormous potential in this city of legalized gambling casinos that is just a few hours from Los Angeles. The Mob entrepreneurs were able to engage in gambling operations openly. They brought their families with them and settled down to become part of the community. Because they wanted nothing to jeopardize their gambling paradise, they brought a semblance of law and order with them. They forced thieves and muggers out of town and Mob killings were forbidden. They built churches and contributed heavily to community projects (Puzo, 1977). Over the last twenty-some years, however, Nevada officials have passed laws and organized commissions to reduce the influence of organized crime on gambling. Legitimate businessmen and conglomerates now own a substantial number of the gambling operations (Plesser et al., 1986).

Glamorous Las Vegas has become one of the largest, most honest, and most successful gambling centers in the world. People can gamble on slot machines, blackjack, roulette, craps, baccarat, poker, chuck-a-luck, keno, and less well-known games of chance. The gambling casinos cater to their customers, giving them free drinks when they gamble, providing inexpensive food, bringing in first-rate entertainers into the extravagant showrooms, and giving away free gambling tokens. Until recently, though, the city was not a place to bring children. Enterprising businessmen realized that they could construct Disney-like resorts that would provide entertainment for their customers' children while the customers themselves could gamble in peace. The Excaliber, MGM Grand, Circus Circus, and Treasure Island have all built casinos and provided a place for children to enjoy themselves. Las Vegas has become a true gambling Mecca.

On November 2, 1976, New Jersey passed an amendment to the State Constitution that allowed Atlantic City to operate gambling casinos. The purpose was to use the licensing fees and taxes from the gambling operations to lower taxes and help defray the expenses of the state's elderly and disabled population. Atlantic City was a decaying beach resort with very little industry of any sort. In May of 1978, Resorts International became the first casino to open, followed quickly by Caesars Boardwalk Regency, Bally's Park Place, the Sands, Harrah's Marina, the Golden Nugget, the Atlantic, Claridge, Tropicana, Trump's Casino Hotel, and Trump's Castle. Two of the hotels lost money. The Atlantic filed for bankruptcy in 1985, with a loss of 68.1 million dollars, and the Claridge had lost 91.5 million dollars as of 1986 (Plesser et al., 1986).

With the passage of the amendment, the Casino Control Act authorized the New Jersey Casino Control Commission to monitor gambling activities. Gambling is permitted only in Control Commission-approved hotels; the hotels must have at least five hundred guest rooms and must meet certain minimums of meeting and exhibition space. They must provide dining facilities, live entertainment, and indoor sports. Credit practices and the collection of winnings is stringently controlled by the Act (Plesser et al., 1986).

There are basic and very obvious differences between Las Vegas and Atlantic City. Visitors in Atlantic City have only one purpose: to gamble. Local retail businesses have not been revitalized by the influx of tourists. The hotels in Atlantic City are not often used by paying guests, except for conventioneers, because many of the gamblers are day-trippers. On the average, tourists lose less money in the casinos than those in Las Vegas; they are not big spenders by any means. Most of the tourists arrive in Atlantic City via car or bus, whereas most of the tourists arrive in Las Vegas via car or jet. Roughly more than twice as many people visit Atlantic City as visit Las Vegas each year, but the combined gaming and convention revenue is higher in Las Vegas (Plesser et al., 1986).

Part of the original rationale for allowing gambling casinos to operate in Atlantic City was the hope that the revenues would be used to improve the run-down housing of the city's large poor and elderly population. Although some improvement has taken place, it has not been as significant as had been hoped. Recently, there has been a casino-sponsored effort to build homes on city-owned lots and to refurbish others. Even with its problems and limitations, however, Atlantic City is still a significant gambling center (Plesser et al., 1986).

Charitable gambling has become increasingly popular in the United States. By 1993, forty-five states, Washington, D.C., and Puerto Rico had made bingo games legal (North American Gaming Report, 1994). This is probably because bingo games are sponsored by charitable organizations such as churches, though an increasing number of Native American tribes are allowing bingo on their reservations. Most people spend a relatively small amount for what they view as an evening's entertainment (Plesser et al., 1986). Other forms of charitable gambling are allowed in many states (North American Gaming Report, 1994).

More and more states are allowing various kinds of gambling because they see it as a way of augmenting local and state economies. In 1964, New Hampshire became the first state to legalize a lottery in the twentieth century. As of 1998, thirty-eight states and the District of Columbia allowed lotteries (North American Gaming Report, 1998).

New Jersey was the first state to legalize the numbers game in 1975 and other states followed. The most common form of the game involves betting on a three-digit number between 000 and 999. The winning number is determined by mechanical means. The legal numbers games are an attempt to stamp out the numerous illegal games popular in lower-income communities (Plesser et al., 1986).

Off-track betting (OTB) operated as a totally illegal form of gambling until New York legalized it in 1970 (Plesser et al, 1986). Thirty-two states now have OTB and race-track betting. Proponents say that OTB increases state and local funds and helps to create jobs. It may also have a positive impact on the decline of illegal gambling. Off-track betting is also legal in Australia, France, Japan, the United Kingdom, and New Zealand (Plesser et al., 1986).

Presently, the gambling business in North America is undergoing phenomenal growth. Only two states in the United States prohibit any form of legalized gambling, Utah and Hawaii. Ten provinces in Canada have legalized various forms of gambling, and hotels and casinos have been operating in Puerto Rico since 1948. The number of casinos, especially on Indian reservations and riverboats, is on the rise, as are the number of states that permit lotteries (North American Gaming Report, 1994). Even with the unprecedented growth in this industry, disputes are still raging in cities and states over whether or not gambling should be permitted within their limits. These and other dilemmas must be addressed in the future, but the prospect of anything but increased growth is not foreseeable.

HISTORY OF GAMBLING

The history of gambling is outlined in Table 1-1.

Table 1-1 Selected Important Events in the History of the Casino Industry

Unknown	Origin of gambling
2300 B.C.	Chinese recorded first account of gambling
1360 A.D.	French invented present-day cards
1387	John I banned card playing
1440	Johannes Gutenberg printed the first deck of cards in Germany
1765	Introduction of the game of roulette
1827	Jack Davis became America's first casino operator in Louisiana
1835	Gambling law in Louisiana overturned
1845	England permitted the recovery of gambling debts
1869	Gambling legalized in Nevada over the veto of the governor—five years after statehood
1895	Charles Frey invented the slot machine
1907	Slot machine refined by Mills—new symbols
1910	Nevada banned gambling and made it illegal
1920	First casino opened in the Bahamas
1931	Legalized gaming in Nevada passed by its state legislature—modern era of casino gambling
1933	Florida legalized jai alai
1935	Pappy Smith and Harold Smith opened Harold's Club in Reno
1935–1947	Reno was the center of casino activities

Table 1-1   Selected Important Events in the History of the Casino Industry (continued)

1936	Nevada introduced keno
1937	Bill Harrah opened his first bingo club in Reno
1940	El Rancho, the first major casino, was built in Nevada
1943	The Last Frontier Casino was built in Las Vegas
1945	"Bugsy" Siegel began the construction of the famous Flamingo Hotel Casino
1945	Nevada passed a gaming revenue tax
1946	Flamingo Hotel Casino opened—major disaster
1948	First casino opened in Puerto Rico
1950	Conclusion of a U.S. Senate Committee was that Nevada casino owners were associated with organized crime
1955	State of Nevada created a Gaming Control Division
1958	Women banned from becoming dealers
1959	Nevada Gaming Control Act was enacted
1959	Nevada Gaming Commission was formed
1959	Gamblers Anonymous was founded
1960	Gam-Anon was founded
1961	First junket was started
1964	Bally introduced the first electrical mechanical slot machine
1967	Nevada legislature adopted a bill requiring casinos to provide an audited financial statement
1967	Nevada enacted a Corporate Gaming Act
1969	Corporate Gaming Act was amended
1971	Women were allowed to become dealers
1971	First course in *Casino Management* was taught
1972	First *Nevada Gaming Abstract* was published
1975	International Gaming Technology was founded
1976	New Jersey residents approved the legalization of gambling in Atlantic City
1977	New Jersey Casino Control Commission and Division of Gaming Enforcement was created
1978	First casino opened in Atlantic City, New Jersey
1984	Lie detector tests were used at the Marina Hotel in Nevada

(continued)

Table 1-1　Selected Important Events in the History of the Casino Industry (continued)

1986	Money Laundering Act was passed
1988	Harrah's established an employee task force on compulsive gambling
1988	Indian Gaming Regulatory Act was enacted
1989	Riverboat gambling was legalized in Iowa
1989	Compulsive gambling toll-free line became active
1989	Gambling was legalized in South Dakota
1989	Legal age for drinking and gambling changed from 18 to 21 years in New Jersey
1990	Riverboat gambling was legalized in Illinois
1990	Riverboat gambling was legalized in Mississippi
1990	Gambling was legalized in Colorado
1991	Gaming was approved in Connecticut
1991	Riverboat gambling was legalized in Louisiana
1992	Legislation was passed for legalized riverboat gambling in Missouri
1993	Legislation was passed for legalized riverboat gambling in Indiana
1993	Slot machine was operated on the Indian reservation in Connecticut
1994	Casino opened in Windsor, Ontario, Canada
1994	MGM Grand Hotel and Casino, Las Vegas
1994	Casino De Quebec opened in Quebec
1996	Monte Carlo opened in Las Vegas
1996	Casino Niagara opened in Ontario, Canada
1998	New York, New York opened in Las Vegas
1999	Bellagio opened in Las Vegas

REVIEW TERMS

charitable gambling	monte
Clan of the Mystic Confederacy	numbers (policy)
faro	riverboat gambling
hazard	roulette
lottery	Saratoga Club House
lotto	three-card monte

REFERENCES

Abt, V., Smith, J., and Christiansen, E.M. (1985). *The business of risk: Commercial gambling in mainstream America.* Lawrence: University Press of Kansas.

Asbury, H. (1969). *Sucker's progress: An informal history of gambling in America from the Colonies to Canfield.* Montclair, New Jersey: Patterson Smith.

Bolen, D.W., and Boyd, W.H. (1968). Gambling and the gambler: A review and preliminary findings. *Archive General Psychiatry* 20:617.

Doocey, P. (1994). Camelot wins UK lottery. *International Gaming and Wagering Business* 15(7):1.

Enforceability of Gambling Laws. (1976). *Gambling in America: Final report of the commission on the review of the national policy toward gambling.* 1:551–64. Washington, D.C.: GPO.

Hicks, E. (ed.). (1978). The Gamblers. In *The Old West.* Alexandria, Virginia: Time-Life Books.

"History of Lotteries." (1999). Available at:
http://www.awii.com/AWIsite/LotHistory.htm

Longstreet, S. (1977). *Win or lose: A social history of gambling in America.* New York: Bobbs-Merrill.

Lorrimore, L. (ed.). (1992a). Lottery. In *Academic American Encyclopedia* 12:420. Danbury, Connecticut: Grolier.

Lorrimore, L. (ed.). (1992b). Poker. In *Academic American Encyclopedia* 15:386. Danbury, Connecticut: Grolier.

Lottery. (1994–1998). *Britannica Online.* Available at: http://www.eb.com.1994-98

Messick, B., and Goldblatt, B. (1976). *The only game in town: An illustrated history of gambling.* New York: Thomas Y. Crowell.

North American Gaming Report. (1994). *International gaming and wagering business.* Supplement.

Plesser, D., Siege, M., and Jacobs, N. (1986). *Gambling: Crime or recreation?* Plano, Texas: Information Aids.

Puzo, M. (1977). *Inside Las Vegas.* New York: Grosset and Dunlap.

Reid, E., and Demaris, O. (1963). *The green felt jungle.* New York: Trident Press.

Wagner, W. (1972). *To gamble or not to gamble.* New York: World Publishing.

Chapter 2

Pari-Mutuel and Lottery Operations

OBJECTIVES

- Develop an understanding of the operation and function of pari-mutuel wagering.
- Comprehend the operation and function of lotteries.
- Grasp the social and economic implications of pari-mutuel and lottery operations.

HORSE RACING

Horse racing is broken down into thoroughbred, harness, and quarter-horse racing and is the most popular form of racing. Dog racing is a distant second and is held in sixteen states, and jai alai is held in only three states. In Florida, jai alai is a major attraction, whereas in Connecticut and Rhode Island it is of minor interest to gamblers (Zacharia, 1994).

More money is wagered legally and illegally on horse racing (the sport of kings) and dog racing (the sport of queens) than any other sport in the United States. Pari-mutuel wagering is permitted in forty-four states within which 80 percent of the population of the United States lives (Zacharia, 1994).

The first recorded horse race occurred in Greece in 600 B.C., but racing is thought to be at least six thousand years old. About three thousand years ago, a rider who mounted directly on the back of a horse is thought to have begun **flat racing.** From the twelfth century to the seventeenth century, British royalty developed horse racing into the Sport of Kings. In the early part of the eighteenth century, scientific breeding of horse stock began and the first thoroughbreds were developed. In 1764, the first thoroughbred contests took place, and horse racing as we know it today had its beginning (Plesser, 1986).

Ancient chariot racing. *Illustration:* Kathy Rood.

America, true to its English heritage, developed horse racing into a sport for the aristocrats. It was known as the gentlemen's sport, and if lesser individuals engaged in it, they were fined and sentenced to jail. At Hempstead, Long Island, in 1665, the first racetrack, known as the New Market Course, was built. With the conclusion of the American Revolution, horse racing became a sport that was

Flat horse racing.

open to everyone. To raise an animal that could neither pull a cart nor plow a field was an expensive pastime, so this sport was limited to those individuals who could afford the luxury of feeding an animal that produced nothing in return. In the 1800s dozens of horse-racing tracks were built in Maryland, Virginia, and Kentucky. The Traveler's Stakes in Saratoga Springs, New York, a center offering gambling of all types, developed the first American stack race, which provided a purse or prize for the winner. By the nineteenth century, most horse racing occurred at county fairs and traveling tracks; unfortunately, dishonesty was commonplace. In 1905, Belmont Park in New York State was the first of the major racing tracks to open in the United States. In 1934, California's Santa Anita opened. In 1959, America's largest track, New York's Aquaduct, opened for business (Buck, 1971).

Pari-mutuel betting, the standard form of wagering on horses, was invented by a Frenchman in 1865 and made its first appearance in America in 1871 at New York's Jerome Park. **Pari-mutuel** betting consists of bettors wagering against one another rather than against an oddsmaker. Until this time, race-track betting was monopolized by bookmakers. (**Bookmaking** is giving odds and accepting wagers on the outcome of events.) In 1908, pari-mutuel betting became established in U.S. horse racing when it was successfully used at the Kentucky Derby. The newly appointed sheriff of Louisville, Kentucky, Scott Bullitt, charged that bookmaking was a violation of the law and that it would no longer be tolerated in Jefferson County, in which Churchill Downs is located. Mayor Grinstead of Louisiana, a violent foe of race-track gambling, upheld the sheriff's decision and threatened to send city police to the track to enforce this edict. This, of course, was a blow to the organizer and director of Churchill Downs, Colonel Matt Winn, because it meant no revenue from betting on the Kentucky Derby would be realized. Colonel Winn examined the local statutes and discovered that, although gambling was prohibited, pari-mutuel betting was not. On Kentucky Derby day, pari-mutuel betting was conducted on the largest scale ever in the United States. Colonel Winn's experiment was so popular that the Maryland Jockey Club at Pimlico tried the pari-mutuel system the next year, side-by-side with the regular bookmakers operating at the track. It was so successful that other racing associations began to adopt it, and pari-mutuel betting became unified throughout the United States (Buck, 1971).

Pari-mutuel betting is currently legal at more than one-hundred and fifty tracks in forty-two states and is the most popular form of betting in the United States. Eighty-two to 85 percent of the total amount wagered is returned to the winners in the form of payoff. The rest of the amount is legally deducted for operational costs and taxes. Straight ticket holders collect only if their horse wins. Holders of place tickets have two chances to collect, because the place pool is divided between holders of place tickets on the horses that finish first or second. Therefore, players are paid if their horse finishes either first or second. Show bettors have three chances to cash in their tickets. The money bet on a show pool is divided into three parts and is paid to the holders of show tickets on horses fin-

Sports betting. *Source:* Harrah's Casino, Las Vegas.

ishing first, second, and third. The payoff is, as a rule, smaller than both straight bets and place bets, primarily because the holders of show tickets have three chances to win on their tickets. All payoff prices in all three pools vary greatly, just as place prices are sometimes greater than win prices. An example of this would be when the winning horse is a favorite and the place horse is a long shot. The winning favorite horse would have a large number of bets on it, thereby making the payoff small. A long-shot horse would have a relatively small number of bets placed on it, thereby making the payoff large. Players can win on the first three horses in any given race as well as combinations of the three; first place is **win,** second place is **place,** and third place is **show.** Sometimes these combinations of the three take the form of a quiniela, the first and second of a race in any order; exacta, the first and second place in that exact order; and the trifecta, the first, second, and third in that exact order. These unusual bets are sometimes called **exotic bets.** At a race track, the starting wager is $2. Bets can be increased in increments of $5, $10, $50, or $100. Individuals may bet as high an amount as they wish; however, it must be in one of these denominations. The amount that is received in payoff is determined by the total amount wagered on each of the winners (win, place, show). When a heavily favored horse wins, the payoff would be much smaller than when a horse who is less favored wins. When a three-to-one horse wins, it means that for every dollar bet on that horse five dollars has been bet on other horses. In negative odds or odds-on favorite, a one-to-three horse means that for every dollar bet on all the other horses three dollars was bet on the one-to-three horse. At the track, bettors are constantly informed by a computerized tally sheet (similar to the old tote board), which flashes new bets, totals, and odds every thirty to sixty seconds. Pari-mutuel machines facilitate horse-racing betting. They are automated tallying systems that calculate and compute the odds two to three times a minute. At most tracks, the odds that flash automatically on the infield track display sign have the state taxes, the track breakage, and all expenses previously deducted. On the tote board, the horses are designated by number only, not name. The board indicates the odds for each of the horses (Silberstang, 1972).

The winners' purses and the state's take are known as the take-out percentage. This amount varies, but generally ranges from 15 to 18 percent. In general, the state receives about one-third to one-half of the total takeout, with the remainder divided between the track and the horse owners. In tic bets, the takeout is higher than in a normal bet. Examples of this are states such as New York and New Jersey, where 25 percent is taken off the top.

The bookmaker in some cases has a distinct advantage over legal track betting, because his takeouts will be much lower and the payouts will be much higher, because bookmakers don't pay the purse or the state taxes.

Racetracks within the United States operate for relatively short periods called meets. They are not open every day of the year, as are other forms of gambling activity. There might be a spring and fall meet at Belmont and just a summer meet at Saratoga. The meets are normally determined by the state regulatory agency, which approves the times for these meets and tries to arrange the times so that the meets do not conflict with nearby racing establishments. In 1993, there were 13,683 racing days in the United States. These were divided among harness and thoroughbred racing, with a small percentage on quarter-horse racing. Horse racing, like virtually all forms of legalized gambling, produces large amounts of revenue for the government. Although statistics vary from state to state, the total government takeout from the states is approximately 5 to 6 percent plus various licensing fees. Off-track betting (OTB) has increased this amount tremendously across the country.

Harness Racing

Harness racing, quarter-horse racing, and contests among Appaloosas, Arabians, and Paints fall a distant second to thoroughbred racing. Harness racing is probably about three thousand years older than flat racing. Most Americans have seen the famous chariot race in *Ben Hur* with Arab against Roman and the coffers of gold as the ultimate payout. Egyptian, Mesopotamian, and Babylonian temples and tombs depict the chariot races of the past. Throughout the United States, at county and local fairs and nonbetting horse tracks, which now number more than four hundred, harness racing is conducted much the same way it was fifty or more years ago.

Although harness racing existed in colonial America, the sport in America received its most important transfusion when a grey thoroughbred named Messenger was imported to the United States in 1788. This larger-than-life horse eventually became the patriarch of many of the finest trotting horses in the United States. In 1949, Hambletonian, a descendant of Messenger, was born and this began a new age in harness racing. Although racing only sporadically throughout his life, this animal became the greatest sire of all time; today, virtually all of the trotters and pacers can trace their lineage to Hambletonian (Plesser, 1986).

When the horse was dislodged by the automobile as the main means of transportation, harness racing began its decline. But in the 1940s, harness racing made a recovery. In 1941 at Roosevelt Raceway outside of New York City, a major innovation saved harness racing. Nighttime racing allowed the harness industry to acquire an entirely new market. The increased excitement of nighttime racing and the development of the mobile starting gate allowed a faster and even start. Thirteen states and four Canadian provinces have harness-racing tracks operating today.

The Triple Crown events of thoroughbred racing are the Kentucky Derby, held the first Saturday of May; the Preakness Stakes, held the third Saturday of May; and the Belmont Stakes, held the second Saturday of June. The Triple Crown was an imaginary title until 1987, when the three tracks created the Triple Crown challenge and offered a $5 million bonus to any horse that won the Triple Crown ("Triple Crown," 1998). A record crowd of over 80,000 people packed the Belmont Park in New York in 1998 and wagered a record $56 million on the outcome of this race. The Triple Crown effort has increased attendance and brought some of the former racing fans back to this exciting sport.

In thoroughbred racing, the jockey rides on the back of the horse. In harness racing, the jockey follows in a sulky behind the horse. The horses may be trotters or pacers, depending on their gait. A trotter's front left and the right rear leg move forward almost simultaneously, and then the front right and rear left leg move forward almost simultaneously. A pacer's left legs move forward in unison and then both right legs move forward in unison. Harness racing is usually conducted at night on small tracks; the longer races are one mile in distance.

One of the most important differences between flat racing and harness racing is the post position. The horses in harness racing have sulkies attached to them which make them slower and far less mobile. Trotters and pacers must run a certain gait, either a pace or a trot. This involves a special coordination of leg movement. If they gallop, they go off the gait and are said to break. The rider of a breaking horse must pull him back until he goes on the gait again; a break is usually costly and generally means that the horse will lose the race (Silberstan, 1972).

Quarter-Horse Racing

In colonial Virginia, native English horses were bred with Spanish thoroughbred horses, resulting in a swift hybrid good for short distances. This resulted in the development of the quarter horse; its name refers to the quarter-mile sprint it runs. The thoroughbred is strictly for racing, but the quarter horse was used for farm work or transportation as well. The majority of the quarter-horse races takes place at state and county fairs or other community functions. Pari-mutuel betting on quarter horses occurs in sixteen states, usually in mixed races within a thoroughbred program. Quarter-horse breeders are hoping that there will be an increased demand for their animals in the future because there has been such a tremendous increase in smaller tracks across the country. Quarter-horse owners are hoping to fill this demand (Siberstang, 1972).

Conclusion

One of the dreams of many racing fans is to own a racing horse. However, the costs involved are extremely high, limiting racing horse ownership to the wealthy. A new concept being introduced by Robert Goldberg, thoroughbred owner and president of Racing Concepts Inc., would allow the ordinary person to be part owner of a racehorse for a day, week, month, or year. One of the most common sentiments heard at the track is that the horse players would like to own a specific horse. Mr. Goldberg stated, "I felt it's always been a fantasy of the average horse player that one day he'd like to be a real owner and own a racehorse, but in most cases he doesn't have the finances to do that. That's the genius of this idea. The question was, is there a way to allow fans to act out that fantasy, and make it affordable to them, in a way that would also be of benefit to the industry as a whole?" The program is called Fan-A-Claim fantasy ownership program. This gives fans a new way to try and make money at the track and be part owners of racing horses. The concept is simple: a fan can buy any horse on any day that it is going to compete at a race track. The purchase price will be based on a percentage of the purse that the horse could win. The track would operate the program and pay the fan owner just as if he or she were an actual owner. According to Bill Finley of the *Daily News Sports* (Jan. 6, 1994) the fan owners would be treated just as normal thoroughbred owners are. They would be given free admission to the track, would have their picture taken in the winner's circle, and would be able to visit with the trainers and watch the thoroughbred work out. The horse-racing industry wants to bring people to the track and promote thoroughbred ownership. The more people are exposed to and involved in thoroughbred operations, the brighter the future of thoroughbred racing will be.

DOG RACING

The roots of dog racing can be traced to ancient Rome. The hunting sport called coursing seems to have evolved into the modern dog racing. A pair of greyhounds set out in pursuit of a hare that had been released. The race was judged on the dogs' performances as they raced down the hare and devoured it. During the rule of Queen Elizabeth I of England, coursing became very popular and was known as the sport of queens (Plesser, 1986).

In 1904, Owen Patrick Smith, who loved the sport of coursing but disliked the killing of the hare, developed the modern version of dog racing. Smith spent fifteen years perfecting a mechanical device to imitate and perform as the hare does. It took many years to iron out the rough spots in the mechanical hare; however, Smith's hare eliminated one of the more inhumane aspects of dog racing. Dog racing would have perished if it had not been for the introduction of pari-mutuel betting, which immensely helped the development of dog racing in America (Plesser, 1986).

In 1993, dog racing was legal in seventeen states. There are forty-eight dog-racing tracks in the United States. Florida has the most, followed by Arizona and Colorado. Over twenty-five million Americans went through the turnstiles at the nation's greyhound racing tracks in 1993 (Zacharia, 1994).

Purses in dog racing are generally half those of horse racing. The take-out percentages for greyhound pari-mutuel racing are similar to those for horse racing, with the takeout representing approximately 15 to 18 percent of the gross. Greyhound racing revenues to the states have increased even more than those of

Hounds to the hunt.

horse racing. However, greyhound racing revenue is declining from its high. In 1997 the pari-mutuel handle at forty-four U.S. greyhound tracks dropped to $2.6 billion from $3.2 billion five years earlier. Attendance during that same period fell to 18.4 million from 28 million. Yet this is nowhere near the decline being experienced in horse racing.

ADVANCEMENTS IN RACING

Gambling has flourished in the United States in one form or another throughout the nation's history. As new forms are introduced, older forms have a tendency to suffer. An example of this is apparent in Corpus Christi, Texas. A successful greyhound and thoroughbred track did a spectacular business until the advent of the Texas lottery. The effect of the Texas lottery on the Corpus Christi Race Track was immediate and drastic. According to the Texas Racing Commission, by the end of 1992, attendance had dropped by 174,000 people and the total handle had declined by roughly $11 million. Triplett, general manager of the track, realized that the lottery could cause as much as an 18 percent decline. Triplett stated that the track's revenue had fallen 38 percent. "We thought we had stumbled onto heaven, but then someone opened a trapdoor and sent us straight to hell" (Triplett, 1993). Triplett was not the only racing executive to have the rug pulled out from under him. Various race tracks around the state reported handle and attendance declines ranging from 12 to 38 percent. They blamed the lottery for this (Triplett, 1993).

Although racing might be suffering in Texas, other states have been able to compensate for the introduction of lotteries and other forms of gambling by developing and experimenting with unique racing concepts.

What started as a one-nighter in Birmingham, Alabama, has developed into a racing phenomena. The experiment involved a ten-horse, ten-greyhound card run on Memorial Day. It drew a crowd of over six thousand people who bet over $600,000. The event involved the alternate racing of dogs and thoroughbreds every fifteen minutes and was the first time that this had ever been done. This appears to have been an unqualified success. The most important thing gained from this success was the exposure of many customers who only play the dogs being exposed to horse racing. Executives at the racecourse believe the eclectic mix reflects a redefinition of racing in the United States, to witt, gives customers not only a variety of gambling opportunities but also a variety in the same venue (Triplett, 1993).

Taking a page from some of the more successful casino enterprises, the new Birmingham racecourse is considering a hotel constructed adjacent to its track that will provide piped-in races to the rooms. It appears from the results of this trial that the best results are obtained through integration of the various components of gaming operations. When bettors have all of their options available in one place, that place is where they will go to gamble (Zacharia, 1993). Racetracks cannot rely on tactics and procedures that have worked in the past. They must develop new and innovative concepts to stay on top.

Another advent in pari-mutuel betting is the ultimate in technology. It is a system that provides information, gives results, and allows the player to place a bet, either through a telephone or through the television. Officials at tracks using telephone betting systems are making the technology more efficient and consumer friendly. Capitol OTB, in Schenectady, New York, has automated its phone lines so that bettors can place wagers more quickly and easily. Customers can make telephone betting deposits or withdrawals from any of its branches and place wagers on its toll-free number from any location in the country where pari-mutuel wagering is legal (Zacharia, 1994).

With track revenue declining all over the United States and Canada, a glimmer of sunlight appears on the horizon. Canada's racetracks were full of negatives in 1998. No matter where you looked, the numbers were always down. There was one startling exception though, and it speaks loudly for current trends at racetracks in Canada and the United States. It involved simulcasting, the sending of one track signal to another facility. It has become the buzzword in the pari-mutuel horse industry. The Canadians' tracks are nowhere near as advanced as the Americans' and are unable to offer six full cards of racing a day, so many of the tracks are moving rapidly to simulcasting. There is an undeveloped market in Canada, ripe for simulcasting in the winter and possibly some additional summer action to round out the local live events. Simulcasting and Canadian racing have the makings of a match made in pari-mutuel heaven (Campbell, 1994).

The new wave of the future will offer the consumer a multiple gambling experience, whereby successive forms of gambling media are available in one central location. If anyone understands the importance of integrating, it's Jim Right, owner of Assiniboia Downs. His racing audience has been carved up by lotteries, video lottery terminals (VLTs), and the nearby Crystal Casino. To compete, he installed VLTs of his own as well as simulcasting. Tracks in the future are going to have to become a complete gambling center in order to succeed (Campbell, 1994).

JAI ALAI

Jai alai is as old as the Egyptian pharoahs. The Greeks called it Pailos and played it as a form of exercise. The Romans called it Pilatta. English and French monarchs played it in the fourteenth and fifteenth centuries. The Basque, who live in northern Spain and southern France, improved on this sport in the seventeenth century. Jai alai came to Cuba from Spain in 1898, and it was introduced in the United States in 1926 at the Miami Fronton.

Jai alai, which means merry festival, is an extremely fast-paced sport in which the players, using a large carved basket strapped to their arms, whip a small hard rubber ball against four walls of a huge playing court in much the same manner as hand ball or racquet ball. The ball travels at over 150 miles per hour, making jai ali the fastest game played with a ball, according to the Guinness Book of World Records. One of the unusual aspects of jai alai involves the grading of players into A or B players. The A grades play in later games (7–12) in the program. Those players with less ability, grade B, play in the earlier games (1–6). The importance of all this is that the better players are more consistent and can be expected to win with greater regularity. The lesser players are more erratic in their behavior, resulting in unpredictable results. It is to the house's advantage to have bettors bet on the earlier games, and it is to the bettor's advantage to bet on the later games (Adams, 1983). Observers bet two dollars or more on players or teams to win, place, or show. They may also bet on exotic bets. Jai alai is legal in only four states in America; it encompasses the third form of pari-mutuel betting. In the early 1980s it was tried in Las Vegas at the MGM Grand Hotel, but it could not compete with casino gambling and subsequently closed. Florida and Connecticut have developed a considerable following for jai alai. Jai alai is most popular in Florida, with an annual attendance of approximately 7.3 million. Jai alai is also played in Rhode Island (Adams, 1983).

THE FUTURE OF PARI-MUTUEL SPORTS

For pari-mutuel sports to continue, a new product line is needed that will include entertainment, casinos, horses, greyhounds, and jai alai. This utilizes the quality of entertainment that is found in Las Vegas, allowing for 24-hour-a-day national television coverage. This must be done in combination with at-home interactive betting. For racing in particular to continue, drastic changes are needed. The combination of different gaming activities under one roof is the wave of the future, and a number of states presently offer slots at race tracks.

LOTTERIES

Lotteries are as ancient as time itself. Although lottery-like games have been played for thousands of years, the modern lottery dates back only about five hundred years. The modern state-run lotteries are available in thirty-eight states and the District of Columbia. By 1998, state-run lotteries were giving away approximately $100 million every day; that translates into approximately $69,000 every minute, twenty-four hours per day (International Gaming and Wagering Business, 1998).

The modern form of state-run or organized lotteries was introduced in France in the 1420s in the city of L'Ecluse, which used the money to strengthen the town's fortifications. Many historians credit King Francis I of France with operating the first state lottery. Florence, Italy was struck by lottery fever in the 1530s, followed quickly by Venice and Genoa.

England's first lottery was organized by Queen Elizabeth in 1566. The money raised by this lottery was used "towards the reparation of the havens (harbors for ships) and strength of the Realme *(sic)* and towards such other public good works," according to the Queen ("History of Lotteries," 1999; *Financial History Magazine,* 1999).

A precursor of the modern-day lottery, keno, has been played in many forms for thousands of years. The most common form involves picking ten numbers from a selection of eighty, then the house or state picks twenty numbers. The players then observe if all ten of theirs were picked ("Lottery Facts," 1997).

The modern form of state-run or organized lotteries was introduced in France in the 1420s in the city of L'Ecluse, which used the money to strengthen the town's fortifications. Many historians credit King Francis I of France with operating the first state lottery. Florence, Italy, was struck by lottery fever in the 1530s, followed quickly by Venice and Genoa. England's first lottery was organized by Queen Elizabeth in 1566. The money raised by this lottery was used "towards the reparation of the havens (harbors for ships) and strength of the Realme [sic] and towards such other public good works," according to the Queen (Ashton, 1969).

The history of lotteries in the New World predates the United States. King James I of England used a lottery to raise money for the Virginia Company's expeditions to colonize America. He raised 29,000 pounds. Once established, the settlement of Jamestown funded almost 50 percent of its budget through the use

Colonial lottery ticket. *Source:* Collection of the Museum of American Financial History.

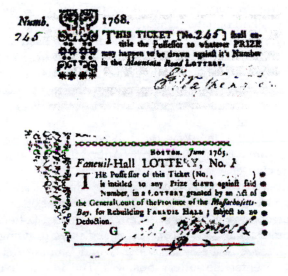

of lotteries. The Dutch in New Amsterdam, the predecessor of New York, utilized lotteries in the 1660s to raise money for the poor. In 1768, George Washington sponsored a lottery to build a road across the Blue Ridge Mountains. Although many of his projects were successful, this one was not. The Continental Congress used lotteries to help finance the American Revolution. (The Museum of American Financial History has on display two of these lottery tickets.) Funds from the Continental Congress lotteries provided the army with arms and clothes. After the Revolutionary War, a lottery was used to repair the damage done by the war. Washington and Jefferson depended on lotteries to fund the development of the new nation ("A Long History," 1997).

Even in these early times, at the birth of our country, controversy raged over how appropriate it was to utilize lotteries. Many citizens then and now consider lotteries to be a form of tax. Thomas Jefferson, on the other hand, stated, "A lottery is a salutary instrument and a (tax) . . . laid on the willing only, that is to say, on those who can risk the price of a ticket without sensible injury, for the possibility of a higher prize" ("Historical Overview of Lotteries," 1999). Colonial lotteries were modeled after the English lotteries and were used to fund public improvements. Lotteries have even been used by some of the foremost institutions of higher learning in the country. Between 1750 and 1772, revenues from lotteries were used to construct buildings on the campuses of Columbia, Harvard, Dartmouth, and Williams. However, all citizens of America did not believe that the lottery was an appropriate way to fund public works. "In 1762 the Pennsylvania Provincial Assembly denounced lotteries, declaring they were responsible for vice and idleness and were injurious to trade" ("Historical Overview of Lotteries," 1999). Lotteries continued to gain popularity in the 1800s mainly because this was the only form of gambling available to most people. However, problems arose in the early part of the nineteenth century as lotteries went nationwide with very little or no control. By 1830, most of the states in the United States had outlawed the use of the lottery system due to misuse. For several years following the Civil War, lotteries were used to fund the reconstruction of the South. By 1868, postmasters were banned from selling lottery tickets, and the mail system could no longer be used to transfer lottery material. The changes in the law did not stop one of the most successful lotteries ever in America from running. In many ways this lottery was an early form of the now famous Powerball.

Following the Civil War, the Louisiana Lottery company obtained from the state legislature a twenty-five-year charter, effective on January 1, 1869. The purpose of the charter was to raise money for a New Orleans charitable hospital. As the twenty-five years progressed, the company grew tremendously wealthy, politically powerful, and corrupt. The Louisiana Lottery was the last major lottery in this country for almost seventy-five years. Lotteries, however, started to make a comeback in 1934 when raffles and prize drawings were again legalized. With the passage of the Small Lotteries and Gaming Act of 1956, charities were permitted to enter the lottery business. The first state-operated lottery of the twentieth century began operating in New Hampshire in 1964. Congress then had to pass legislation allowing the states to run lotteries and to exempt them from the excise tax and the occupational tax stamps. In 1967, New York State initiated its own lottery but the results were disappointing. In 1971, New Jersey was the first state to introduce a 50¢ weekly lottery game, which was inexpensive enough that everyone could afford to buy a ticket. There are still federal laws regulating and prohibiting the sending of lottery information across state lines (Plesser, 1986).

By 1999, thirty-eight states and the District of Columbia permitted lotteries. In 1998, the gross receipts for lotteries exceeded $36.67 billion. It is interesting to point out that in almost every state that has placed a lottery on the ballot, voters have approved the ballot and instituted the lottery. Today most lottery tickets are sold in retail stores such as supermarkets, gas stations, convenience stores, liquor stores, and drug stores. Most lottery tickets sell for 50¢ to $1 and new superlotteries range from $2 to $100 dollars. The tickets are sold and receipts are picked up by state employees, who then give them to a central office. Those individuals who sell tickets (agents) earn a commission on their sales volume. The commission varies from state to state, but is normally around 5 percent. Some states offer a bonus to the retail outlet equaling a small percentage of the first-place winning ticket if sold at their location. Lottery laws in each state are different, but most states require a certain percentage of the handle to be returned to the state. This amount ranges from 25 percent in Vermont to 43 percent in New York. Most states return approximately 50 percent of every dollar bet back to the winners. This is relatively low when compared to horse racing, which returns 75 to 85 percent, or casino gambling, which is 80 to 90 percent. This makes lotteries the worst bet of all in the gambling arena. However, lotteries are the second largest division of gambling in the United States.

Most lottery revenue is designated for specific purposes. New York, New Jersey, Michigan, New Hampshire, and California funnel the lottery revenue into education. In Pennsylvania, it goes to senior citizen programs (tax and rent rebates as well as medical aid). In Oregon, it goes to the public for such works as school buildings, hatcheries, and the county fair system. Recreation and park facilities receive Colorado's revenue share. Massachusetts returns its lottery revenues to local municipalities, and a specific percentage goes to the development of the arts. In Arizona, the revenue goes to the general fund with a small amount set aside for transportation (Plesser, 1986).

Lottery Formats

There are many forms of lotto, policy, or lottery in the United States. The policy or number games are probably the easiest to understand. They came from England to the United States in the early 1800s and became part of the lottery themselves. Although governments and charities used lotteries to raise money, the policies or numbers were developed and used exclusively by the lottery companies for their own profit. The numbers have been illegally operated in the United States for years. The establishment of a daily number is an attempt by government to put a stop to illegal numbers. In 1975, New Jersey started the first legalized numbers game; a number of states soon followed. The numbers are drawn either daily or weekly; normally, a three- or four-digit number is used. The player picks a sequence of numbers from 1 to 999 or 9,999. The winning numbers are drawn nightly on television shows, using ping-pong balls and an air-filled tank and attractive young men and women. Across the United States, a number of states that have lotteries have instituted the numbers. It appears to be a popular form of gambling, and according to the Public Gambling Research Institute, it is profitable (Plesser, 1986).

Lotto is popular in the United States because it is a combination of player participation with the chance to win small as well as large prizes. It develops within the players a belief that they can win. Psychologists state that variable reinforcement is the strongest means available to enforce a behavior. By providing players with the potential of a large win and reinforcing their gambling behavior with small wins, gamblers' participation is ensured again and again (Connor, 1995).

The first lotto game was played in Massachusetts in 1978. In lotto, a player selects five or six numbers out of thirty to sixty-four numbers and bets from 50¢ to $4 on each set of numbers. There is a biweekly or weekly drawing during which the numbers are selected mechanically in a manner similar to that used for policies (numbers). If no one wins the game, the prize is carried over to the next drawing, allowing it to grow and, in some cases, reach levels of $100 million. When more than one player has the winning numbers, the pool is divided equally among the winners (Connor, 1995).

National Lotteries

The Coeur d'Alene Indian tribe in Plummer, Idaho, launched the nation's first Indian lottery game. The National Indian lottery is the only current national lottery and is offered in more states than in the history of the United States. Players can purchase lottery-style tickets with their credit card using a toll-free number. According to the press secretary for the tribe, Bob Bostwick, the tribe can operate the lottery game as an inter-state and intra-state lottery (Connor, 1995).

Instant Lotteries

The **scratch ticket,** used in **instant lotteries,** has become extremely profitable and popular as we enter the twenty-first century. It has been used in clubs and fraternal organizations for years to raise funds. In 1974, it was introduced in Massachusetts. For $1 bettors knew instantly whether they had won. Bettors purchased a ticket and either lifted the tabs or scratched off boxes to reveal a winning or losing combination. If the payout is small, they receive their winnings immediately; if the winnings are over $500, in most states they have to send the winning ticket to the lottery headquarters or go in person to collect their winnings. The first lottery the state normally institutes is an instant lottery because of the ease of introduction and the approval of immediate self-gratification by the general public.

Illinois has studied consumers and determined that they wanted something unique. Their instant lottery sales indicate this. For the first time ever, the Illinois lottery sales have surpassed their lotto sales. Better games with better graphics have brought this about. Today, Illinois offers eight instant categories of games at any given time, including such areas as sports, casinos, bingo, and specialty games. A new game they offer, called Win for Life, is the biggest addition to their weekly sales records. One thousand dollars a week for the rest of the life of the player is the ultimate prize. The prize pays one thousand every week, every month, every year for as long as you live, even if you live one hundred and fifty years. This unique game has sent the scratch sales in Illinois to record highs.

Another state using a unique technique is Massachusetts, which plans on using its lottery ticket to its fullest potential. Massachusetts is planning on creating a new advertising medium on the back of each lotto ticket and betting slip. This advertising space will be sold to prospective advertisers, and the funds will be used to revamp the computer system for the Massachusetts lottery. Other states, such as Kansas, are launching their first $2 or $5 scratch tickets.

Video Lotteries

Video lotteries are lotteries that are played on computerized terminals and allow the winner instant verification of win or loss. The player plays a video game for a set sum of money. This game is predetermined and preprogrammed, eliminating the chance of skill on the part of the player. Winning or losing is solely the result of chance. A number of these machines has been successful in arcades, bars, truckstops, and convenience centers around the country. In most states, these computerized terminals are considered entertainment and have no direct payout. Video lotteries in the United States have a handle in excess of $1.5 billion (Plesser, 1986).

Powerball

Powerball is played in twenty-one states. In Powerball, players pick five numbers from one to forty-nine, and then an additional number from one to forty-two. This means that five numbers are drawn out of a pool of forty-nine numbers and one number is drawn out of a pool of forty-two numbers; players must match all six numbers to win. The odds of winning Powerball are one in eighty million. The Powerball jackpots begin at $10 million, and the payouts are either annuities or cash options (the cash option is usually 50 percent of the jackpot). If no one has the correct numbers, the jackpot is rolled over to the next game. In May of 1998 the Powerball jackpot reached $100 million, and on August 1, 1998, Powerball set a new world record with a payout of $295.7 million to the lucky thirteen people who won it.

In an article in the *International Gaming and Wagering Business* magazine's December 1993 issue, a survey shows that $10 million is the magic number to develop consumers' interest in the lottery. However, the higher the jackpot, the more tickets are sold. In March 1995, Powerball had its first $100 million single winner. In August 1998 the Powerball jackpot was $280 million, and thirteen lucky people shared the gigantic windfall (McQueen, 1999).

Powerball has become so popular that the Powerball commission has decided to initiate a new game. The new game consists of a multiple-state raffle-type drawing that will award one hundred players $1 million each. Mr. Strautt of MUSL (Powerball) stated that "people are attracted to the larger jackpots but we also found that they want a better chance of winning more prizes; that is what this new game will address."

THE FUTURE OF LOTTERIES AND INSTANT GAMES

The immediate future for lotteries and instant games in the majority of the states in the United States looks promising. This is despite the fear expressed by states about the expansion of casino gaming and its possible effect on the lottery and instant game revenue potentials. As Karen Kerr-Pettigrew, Director of Marketing for the Illinois lottery, stated, "I think the industry as a whole has been successful in identifying and developing games that speak to different players and provide entertainment. That's the next challenge, to reinvent the game, make it more relevant, and have people come to play it earlier." Lottery sales are jackpot driven; the lotteries of the future will need to have a mechanism in place that will create gigantic jackpots from the beginning. To achieve this, the states will have to band together or the federal government will have to become involved.

REVIEW TERMS

bookmaking	pari-mutuel
exotic bets	place
flat racing	scratch ticket
harness racing	show
instant lotteries	video lotteries
jai alai	win

REFERENCES

"A Long History of Good Causes." (1997). Available at:
http://www.oregonlottery.org/general/1_hist.htm

Adams, E. (1983). *Handbook for gamblers.* Vienna, WV: Vienna Office Supplies, p. 28.

Ashton, J. (1969). *The history of English lotteries.* London: Leadenhall Press, Ltd.

Buck, F. S. (1971). *Horse race betting.* New York: ARCO Publishing.

Campbell, N. (1994). Spotlight on Canada. *International Gambling* 15:28.

Christiansen, E. (1993). Gross annual wagering. *International Gaming and Wagering Business* 15:31.

Connor, M. (1995). National Indian lottery. *International Gaming and Wagering Business* 16:4.

Financial History Magazine, issue 65 (1999).

"Historical Overview of Lotteries," *Financial History Magazine,* spring 1999.

"History of Lotteries." (1998). Available at:
http://www.awii.com/AWIsite/LotHistory.htm

International Gaming and Wagering Business. (1993). Power Ball. *International Gaming and Wagering Business,* 14:28.

International Gaming and Wagering Business. (1998). "Lottery." *International Gaming and Wagering Business* 19, no. 10 (1998).

"Lottery Facts." (1997). Available at: www.hitlotto.com/lottery_factoids

"Lottery Facts and Myths." Available at:
www.nmlottery.com/com/facts_myths.htm

McQueen, P. (1999). Florida debates Powerball entry. *International Gaming and Wagering Business* 20(1):53.

Plesser, D. (1986). *Gambling: Crime or recreation.* Texas: Informational Aids, pp. 13–27, 76–81.

Siberstang, E. (1972). *Book of games.* Chicago, Illinois: Playboy Press, pp. 392, 385.

"Triple Crown." (1998). HickokSports.com, sports history. Available at:
http://www.hickoksports.com/history/trpcrown.shtml

Triplett, J. (1993). Slow trot to the finish line in Texas. *International Gaming* 14:43.

Zacharia, M. (1993). Redefining Racing in America. *International Gaming and Wagering Business* 14:11.

Zacharia, M. (1994). North American Gaming Report. *International Gaming and Wagering Business,* July 5 (Suppl.).

Chapter 3

Slot and Video Operations

OBJECTIVES

- Develop an understanding of slot and video slot operations.
- Examine the financial procedures in slot accounting.
- Develop an understanding of marketing for slot clubs.

SLOT MACHINES

In the late 1800s, Charles Fay of San Francisco invented the first mechanical slot machine. It was used primarily in the city's bars, and it appears to be the only true American casino game. Slot machines have spread across the United States, North and South America, the Caribbean, and the rest of the world. They are rapidly becoming the casino game of choice for the majority of casino customers. Slot machines can be found wherever they are legal. When you get off the plane in Las Vegas or Reno, bank upon bank of slot machines await you. They are also located in grocery stores, gas stations, laundromats, and just about any place that people spend time waiting or standing in line.

Slot machines and other coin-operated gaming devices are mechanical or electronic machines in which the player deposits one or more coins or tokens for an opportunity or chance to win a prize, payoff, or jackpot. In most cases, prizes are based on the machine's ability to align similar symbols in rows of three or more. These symbols are located on rotating drums, called reels, or within the video machine's memory. The mechanical and electronic devices can simulate all types of games such as poker, roulette, blackjack, keno, bingo, or horse races. A typical three-reel slot machine contains over thirteen hundred parts that are required to operate in a sequential order to ensure proper functioning (Friedman, 1982).

The denominations that slot machines accept can range from pennies, which are played at some downtown Las Vegas casinos, to $100 tokens ($500 per chance), which are used in such casinos as the Mirage and Caesar's in Las Vegas and the Windsor Casino in Canada.

The layout of slot machines on the casino floor is not as haphazard as it might appear; it is generally the result of flow-and-motion studies done by casino management before the installation of the slots. The **slot mix** refers to the placement of the machines within the casino. The casino normally evaluates its drop (actual amount of money collected) and determines which machines produce the greatest benefits to the casino.

Atlantic City, Las Vegas, and Reno have shown increasing slot machine revenue in recent years. The growth of slot machines exceeds that of table games. The industry believes that this reflects increasing gambling by middle- and lower-income families. With the changes in basic slot machine forms, more and more companies are entering the slot machine business. In the 1930s, only a half-dozen companies built mechanical slot machines. Today, the field is dominated by such giants as Bally's and IGT, although numerous smaller companies are players within the game.

Slot machines have four qualities that make them appealing to potential gamblers. First, there is no human contact and they are self-taught, with only a limited number of rules. Those individuals who felt uncomfortable playing baccarat, blackjack, or craps because of the complicated skills needed to play the games have no fear of the slot machines. Second, slots can be played for a very insignificant investment: a nickel, dime, quarter, or dollar. Third, slot machines offer the potential for the highest payoff of any casino game. They often have mega-jackpots well over a million dollars. And last, from the casino's point of view, slots have a tendency to become addictive. Behavioral psychologists have stated that the most effective means of reinforcement is variable reinforcement, or the occasional win. This optimal conditioning provides the player with an occasional win, which encourages the player to continue playing the game (Ortiz, 1982).

Nevada's Slot Machine Payouts

The state of Nevada has gaming laws, as do other states, that require slot machines to pay out a minimum amount. The Nevada State Gaming Commission inspects these machines and licenses them to ensure that each machine pays out the minimum amount.

Recently casinos have adjusted their slots to offer a 98 to 99 percent payoff. These casinos normally operate under exceptionally high volume. Most casinos offer a variety of slot machines, from the standard three-cherry to progressive machines (or mega-machines). In a progressive or mega-machine, a certain amount of all money that is entered into the machine goes into the progressive or mega-jackpot. In some cases to receive the progressive or mega-jackpot, the customer must put in multiple amounts of coins. For example, a minimum $1000

Game Maker multi-game touch-screen machine. *Photo:* Bally Gaming.

might be obtained for the first quarter, and five quarters would be needed to obtain the progressive jackpot. In many cases, the jackpots are so large that only a small portion of the wins are paid by the machine. The change person or the slots manager is required to make payments above the normal limits of the machine jackpots. For example, if an individual won a $1,000 jackpot, four hundred quarters might be paid out by the machine, with the other $900 paid out by the change person.

Characteristics of Slot Players

Casino patrons who frequent the gaming tables have always looked down on slot players as being inferior beings. The telltale blackened hands are a sure indicator of a slot player. However, casinos themselves have been taking a new look at the slot players. They are a loyal, consistent, and highly prized commodity in today's competitive casino arena. The largest majority of slot players in the past have

Video poker machine. *Source*: International Gaming Technology.

been women. The traditional slot player was thought to be a wife or girlfriend of the male high roller, passing time aimlessly, plunking quarters and dollars into slot machines. However, with the introduction of video poker and other video gaming devices, the slot machine scene has changed drastically. This change is reflected in the balance sheet, as the winnings from slots and other video games become larger and larger. Slot machine players tend to be very territorial in nature; if they start playing a machine, they consider it *their* machine, no matter how many machines they start playing. When a slot player has to leave for any reason and is going to return, he or she will place a cup on the handle of the machine to indicate that the machine is in play and that other players should be wary. Many altercations have taken place over the legality of territorial marking of slot machines. On a recent trip to Windsor with over two hundred people in line outside, I noted on the third floor of the casino that one older gentleman had marked two machines by placing cups on the handles; however, to further ensure that no one would use these machines, he had placed a note on each of them that read "touch this machine and you die." He then proceeded to go to the men's room. Whether murder would be justifiable in this instance is questionable.

VIDEO LOTTERY TERMINALS (VLTS)

A **video lottery terminal (VLT)** is a slot machine that can play bingo cards, poker hands, or whatever type of game the manufacturer desires; it is known as adult entertainment, or adult amusement. It is the updated version of the one-armed bandit. These games are identical to the video poker games in Las Vegas and Atlantic City. Cities across the United States and Canada are looking at ways to finance their deficits. With most VLTs you don't feed the machine quarters, half dollars, and dollars. You feed dollars, fives, twenties, and hundreds. Your winnings are electronically tabulated and printed out on redeemable slips. These games have assisted the state lotteries during periods of slackened revenue. Thanks to the ability of state lotteries to make gambling appear respectable, they present to states and counties potential revenue for the environment, education, and economic development. One of the advantages that the VLTs have over a normal lottery is that they can offer the gambler instant gratification because the gambler knows the results immediately. Players can sit for hours before the video terminals playing interactive games with touch-control screens, providing them an avenue for turning their hard-earned cash into instant adrenaline (Cook, 1992). Another advantage to the casino is the lower labor costs of VLTs than for other consumer games. Floor and pit games are inherently labor intensive, whereas slot and VLTs are technologically oriented.

One of the most popular VLT games is video poker. The odds of winning are posted right on the machines, so no matter how we try to disguise the odds, the player knows what they should be. In casinos that try to tighten the odds, poker doesn't do well.

Several VLT manufacturers are taking on this profitable challenge of developing new VLT games. Most of these games use double, triple, and quadruple simultaneous games, requiring the player to bet ten, fifteen, or twenty coins at the same time. In the future, customers may have to play up to fifty coins instead of the present five coins to win the jackpot. The larger the gross wagering, the higher the eventual profit to the casinos (Grochowski, 1999).

Since the advent of VLTs a debate has been raging in the advertising and business circles as to the best approach to "sell" this product. Two theories have emerged. One side of the debate argues that an aggressive approach to marketing is necessary to the success of VLTs and the other believes that the soft-sell approach to marketing is needed. Both theories appear to be correct; however, an investigation of the VLT segment of the gaming industry indicates that the aggressive approach generates much higher profits. Some states live in fear of the antigaming lobbyists and therefore are afraid of the aggressive marketing approach to VLTs. With the removal by the FCC of bans on television promotion of gaming activities, it is entirely possible that the wrath of the antigaming lobbyists will descend on the casino industry. Some states limit number of machines to the small retailers, and other states, such as West Virginia, Rhode Island, and Delaware, concentrate machines at one location or several race tracks. This allows the track to develop a more casino-like atmosphere, allowing the player to play multiple games (Rzadzki, 1998).

SLOT OPERATIONS

To better understand the complicated and intricate details of slot operations, we interviewed Ms. Donna Cassese, Director of Casino Marketing for the Luxor Hotel Casino. Her job entails slot marketing, special events, and table game marketing. Ms. Cassese has been in the gaming business for twelve years. She began working at the Gold Coast, which is a casino geared toward local gamblers. She began organizing the slot club there and soon became involved in the marketing department. While in the marketing department, she did all of the advertising and promotions for slots. When the Mirage opened, Mr. Steve Winn from the Golden Nugget and Mirage asked her to come to his casino as the slot manager. This job involved setting up slot marketing for the casino, initiating slot tournaments, and developing slot clubs. This developed into doing special events for the entire property. Ms. Cassese instituted the development of the specialty slot machines and promoted IGT's MegaBucks slots. About four years ago, she was in Las Vegas giving a lecture on slot clubs and slot marketing when IGT approached her and asked her to consider lecturing at different locations around the country about slot clubs. All of the slot clubs she has opened have been very successful. She left the Mirage and opened a company called T and T Enterprises, a slot marketing/management company. She traveled around the country and opened twelve casinos in two years. She laid out the casino floor, hired the employees, and set up the property.

Luxor's Gold Chamber slot club card. *Source:* Luxor Hotel and Casino.

The casinos were a mixture of Indian-run casinos and riverboats. She returned to Las Vegas and had the luxury of choosing between two casino jobs: one at MGM and the other at the Luxor Hotel/Casino in the Marketing Department. She chose to be the Director of Casino Marketing at the Luxor.

Ms. Cassese believes that in the past, slot machines have always been considered a second-class game; the pit and the floor were more important. However, that is not true today. Las Vegas casinos are the first to say that the floor and pit games are not their primary source of business—it is the slots that generate the most income. The industry as a whole is beginning to realize that the slot players pay the majority of the bills. At the Luxor, 60 to 65 percent of the revenue for the casino is produced by the slots. Ms. Cassese believes that is why slot clubs are so important.

Slot Clubs

Casino patrons have become more and more educated throughout the years and want more value for their money. Ms. Cassese has been involved in opening over twenty-six slot clubs in the past ten years. Slot clubs have become especially important in today's competitive marketplace because of all the new casinos opening up worldwide. The value of the slot club is that it allows casinos to pinpoint their slot market. Without this information, it is like taking handfuls of money and throwing them it the air, hoping to contact some potential players. A slot club provides the basic demographics of the slot players, allowing management to track players' names and addresses, social security numbers, and amount spent each hour, each day, and each visit. When customers receive a slot club card, they should be told how to use it and what its benefits are. Many casinos do not properly inform their customers how to use their cards; they assume that everyone already knows. Casinos can target their market more accurately through the information provided by the demographic data. For example, Ms. Cassese started an advertising campaign specifically targeted at $500-a-day slot players. Without the slot clubs she would not be able to identify or target this group.

The Luxor's slot club is called the Gold Chamber. The Luxor informs the players that to receive the benefits of a slot club membership, they must use their Gold Chamber card each time they play the slot machines or table games. The more they play, the more comp room, meals, and vacations they will be eligible for. This allows management to track those players that are most desirable.

A study done for casinos has shown that the average customer belongs to six to twelve slot clubs throughout the country. The slot clubs are marketing tools; they allow casinos to more effectively market to their best customers and provide them with the strokes they need so that they will continue to use the casino. Slot clubs today are like keeping up with the Joneses—you have to be able to offer all the usual benefits and advantages plus some unique ones in order to retain the customer base.

Slot clubs are extremely expensive, and some smaller operations have to use makeshift systems. When the Luxor sets up slot clubs, it trains its employees to use the technology and the results because the results are only as good as the ability of the marketers to use them. Some slot clubs are free, some you pay to join, and some you are asked to join.

High Limits slot club. *Source:* Harrah's Casino, Las Vegas.

The Luxor, in addition to comped rooms and meals, provides its guests with special services, including a guaranteed room at the Luxor or another property owned by Circus Circus, special events, discounts, line passes, special check-in windows, Gold Chamber floors (the top three floors of the Luxor hotel), and a lounge with a full-service bar and a staff of fifteen that waits on the customer's every need. Slot machine and pit and floor players are eligible to become members of the Gold Chamber club. Each one has a minimum number of playing hours or dollars that are needed to qualify for discounts. The ratio is approximately 64 percent slot players and 36 percent pit and floor game players.

Marketing

The majority of large casinos use an outside marketing agency whose primary mission is to get the names of the casinos known to the general public. At the Luxor, once a customer enters the building, the marketing staff takes over the operations and turns this person into a lifelong client. For special events, Ms. Cassese's marketing department comes up with the ideas and then hires an outside agency to design and set up the specifics of the theme or tournament play. Some of these events have been extremely elaborate and have been very successful in generating the desired revenue levels.

When gaming enters a new area of the country, slot machines are normally the most popular item within the casino. The slot machines build a following, which then enters into the video poker, keno, and VLT machines. This is a normal growth cycle within slot operations. One of the ways Ms. Cassese increases players' interest in new slot games is through instructional classes; that way she can ensure the continued development of the slot player. In many jurisdictions where gambling is in its infancy, groups of professionals band together to start their own casino, thinking that they are going to become wealthy or even another Steve Wynn. They cram their casinos full of slot machines and games but for some reason this doesn't work. That is when they hire Ms. Cassese. She evaluates the layout of the floor and changes the traffic flow and then eliminates half the games and slots. One of the first things she does is put the employees through extensive training programs, which include courses in casino psychology, slot psychology, and public relations/customer service. With all of the new casinos opening, Las Vegas has to distinguish itself. It has to be number one in service and entertainment, and it has to promise potential players that Las Vegas will meet or surpass their expectations. What makes the gambler come back are the employees who go that one extra step for the customer. That is what will stand out in the customers' minds when they make their next reservation.

The Luxor has a very aggressive direct-mail campaign. Everyone who becomes a member of the Gold Chamber receives a letter within three days of leaving the hotel explaining the benefits they will receive as a member. The Luxor employs **casino hosts,** who are each responsible for two hundred and fifty premium customers. They introduce themselves to these customers and contact them at least once every three months. If one of the players hits a jackpot, he or she receives an Egyptian good luck pin. It is the Luxor's primary function to make every customer feel wanted, needed, and special. The employees at the Luxor go through a one-month customer relations training program; this program then continues throughout their employment at the Luxor.

Many casinos make the mistake of giving the store away to their customers, and when the inevitable slowdown occurs, it is extremely difficult if not impossible to retract these fringe benefits from customers. So, at the Luxor, Ms. Cassese decided to limit the initial benefits to players until the Luxor had established a firm customer base. Like any other major property that has opened on the Strip, the feeling has been that for the first two years everybody will come to the casino. This might be true, Ms. Cassese realizes that she has only this time to make a positive impression and build a loyal clientele. She does this by giving the customers more than she promised them. She disagrees with the statement, "Build it and they will come." Just because a casino is opened doesn't mean it will make money. A casino needs a hook or a gimmick, something that makes it different. For the Luxor, it is its architectural style. There is not another hotel like it in the world. One of the things that people do not understand about casino operations and management is that it is a business, and a business only survives as long as it meets the customers' value needs. One of the things that will be occurring in the slot machine business is the institution of slot machines that can take money from credit cards and bank cards. She has a block of five hundred rooms to use for comps on the weekends and three hundred rooms during the week to use for comps.

Ms. Cassese believes in a hands-on approach. She does this through daily meetings with her personnel, and she expects them to do the same. Every day, everyone in the management team discusses where they are, what they are doing, and where they want to be, so that they can recognize their goal and how to achieve it. By keeping her hands on things, nothing gets so out of hand that Ms. Cassese can't fix it.

THE FUTURE OF SLOT MACHINES

Slot machines are ensured a positive future. Articles have been written about the end of casino gambling as we know it today. Predictions are that in forty years there will be no casino games, just slot machines (the third wave). In the world today, casino managers and gambling advocates are telling municipalities that vast numbers of the populace can be employed within the casino industry. But if the third wave is correct, employment will be meager at best. It is presently estimated that for every billion dollars in gambling revenue, sixty-seven thousand jobs are created (Niagara Survey, 1979). The question that municipalities must ask themselves is: Will these sixty-seven thousand jobs be there in the twenty-first century?

REVIEW TERMS

casino host	slot mix
slot club	slot psychology
slot machine	video lottery terminal (VLT)

REFERENCES

Allen, J. E. (1993). *The basics of winning video poker.* New York: Cardoza Publishing.

Cardoza, A. (1994). *Winning casino play.* New York: Cardoza Publishing, pp. 126–150.

Cassese, D. (1994). Interview by author. August. Las Vegas, Nevada.

Cook, J. (1992). Legalizing the slots. *Forbes,* 2 March, 78.

Friedman, B. (1982). *Casino management.* Secaucus, NJ: Lyle Stuart, pp. 271.

Grochowski, J. (1999). Making poker pay. *Slot Manager,* 14.

Moreland, R. F. (1994). *IGT SMART SYSTEM: Overview & Features Presentation.* Instructor's Manual developed by IGT.

Ortiz, D. (1982). *Casino gambling.* Secaucus, NJ: Lyle Stuart, p. 188.

Rzadzki, J. (1998). The hands-on approach. *International Gaming and Wagering Business* 19(11):44.

Chapter 4

Games of Chance

OBJECTIVES

- Discuss the various games of chance.
- Develop an understanding of the house advantage for each game.
- Discuss the new games of chance.
- Discuss career opportunities in the casino industry for prospective employees.

TRADITIONAL GAMES OF CHANCE

Blackjack

Twenty-one, which is commonly called **blackjack,** is the most popular table game in American, Canadian, and Caribbean casinos. In fact, it has become so popular that it has ushered out the previous high-money game of craps and become the number-one table casino game. Unlike many other casino games, blackjack can allow the player with skill to gain a slight advantage over the casino. Blackjack takes many forms, and the same game may be played differently in the same casino. Rule changes and variations are evident in Las Vegas, Atlantic City, Canada, and the Caribbean. In the majority of casinos, more than one deck of fifty-two cards is used, and the cards are dealt from a shoe (a **shoe** is a mechanical device with a spring that enables the dealer to remove one card and one card only at a time). Each player may be dealt two cards face up. Most casinos have from five to eight chairs at each table. Patrons sit on stools with back supports. On a green- or red-felt table in front of each of the players is a square outlined in white. There are no slots in the table to hold the player's chips, and each player has his or her own outlined card area. The dealer sits in the center of the table facing the players. In front of the dealer is the deck of cards, or to the left of him or her is the shoe containing the cards. The main advantage to the player is that once the dealer has shuffled the cards, he or she no longer handles them, making cheating far more dif-

Blackjack. *Source:* Harrah's Hotel and Casino, Las Vegas.

ficult. In some casinos, the cards are dealt one face down and one face up, or both face down. The dealer gets one down card and one face-up card.

The rules remain the same no matter how many decks are used. In blackjack the object is to get as close to twenty-one as possible without going over, which is called **busting.** A player who goes over twenty-one loses. Each player is dealt two cards. It is impossible for any player to lose on the first two cards. The face values of the card are the number of points you have—for example, a four is four; a seven is seven. All face cards and tens count as ten points. The ace counts as one or eleven points; this is an advantage to the player and is at his or her discretion. For example, a hand that contained an ace and a five could be counted as six or sixteen. Any combination of an ace with a picture card or ten is a blackjack and automatically wins. The normal payout, except in ties, is three-to-two. Every dollar bet would receive payout of $1.50. All ties between the player and the house are considered standoffs and neither side collects. The house must draw when it has a hand of sixteen or lower, and it may not draw (must stand) when it has a hand of seventeen or more. There is only one exception to this rule. In certain casinos, dealers must draw if they have a soft seventeen, that is, an ace and a six. If the dealer's open hand is a ten, he or she must peek at the bottom card; if it is an ace, the dealer must declare blackjack and collect all bets immediately except for ties. When dealers have an ace up, the players have the right to buy

BLACKJACK

Blackjack, sometimes called Twenty-One, is a popular and fun casino game favorite. Everyone plays against the dealer. The dealer gives each player two cards. The dealer also gets two cards; one face down, and the other face up. The object is to draw cards that total 21, or as close to 21 as possible without going over (busting).

Ten, Jack, Queen and King count ten. Aces count either one or eleven as you choose. Other cards play at their face value. If you receive an Ace and a Ten value card as your first two cards, you have "Blackjack," and win one and one-half times your bet unless the dealer also has Blackjack. If the dealer has Blackjack as well, it is a "standoff." If you "hit" and your total is more than 21, you have busted, and you lose. If you do not go over 21 and the dealer does, you win.

These simple key rules will help you play:

1. If your total is closer to 21 than the dealer's, you win.
2. If you "hit" and your total is more than 21, you lose.
3. If you and the dealer have the same total, it is a tie.

Don't hesitate to ask your friendly dealer if you have questions.

Blackjack Terms

Doubling Down — If on the first two cards, you feel you can win with only one more card, you may double your bet. Remember — you get only one more card.

Splitting Pairs — An option you have with two original cards of the same value (4's, 8's, etc.). You can split the two cards and play each hand individually. You must bet the same amount as your original wager on the split hand. If your next card is of equal value to the first pair, you may split again. This may be done to a total of four hands. Aces may be split only once. You may also "double down" on the first two cards of each hand after the split, except when splitting aces.

Insurance — If the dealer's "up card" is an Ace, you can take insurance. You're betting that the dealer has a ten-value card in the "hole," making Blackjack. You can bet one-half of your original wager, but a winning insurance bet pays 2 to 1.

Push — A standoff between you and the dealer. Neither hand wins.

Hand Signals — Non-verbal communication between you and the dealer to indicate "hit" or "stand." Ask your dealer for the proper signals.

Blackjack rules. *Source:* Casino Niagara, Niagara Falls, Ontario.

insurance, which pays off at two to one. In reality, the player is betting that the dealer has blackjack. Players who have blackjack immediately turn their hand over and collect three to two on their bet. Players who go over twenty-one by drawing too many cards must immediately notify the dealer and the dealer will collect their chips and cards. If dealers go over, they pay off the players who still remain in play; thus players who go bust before the dealer cannot collect. Players determine their bet before any cards are dealt. The bet can range within the table limits, for example, $1 to $500 or $5 to $1,000. All the players play against the house, and the dealer represents the house.

The house and the players each have advantages on their side. The house always deals, the house always takes bust winnings, the house can win even if it busts, the player must bet before he sees his cards whereas the house does not, and the house gets its cards last. However, the player gets three to two on black-jack; the player can draw or stay on sixteen; the player can split pairs; the player can double down, double the bet, and in some cases double down on two cards totaling ten or eleven; the player can count cards; and the player can insure bets. (To double the initial bet and receive exactly one more card is called doubling down. The option to double down is often allowed on the first two cards only, although some casinos allow doubling down after splitting any pair.) All of these privileges are to the player's advantage and are denied the casino.

Players often use a system to achieve an advantage over the house. In one system, called **card counting,** the player assigns a weighted average to each card face and sums up the card weights as each new card is turned face up. The count that the player accumulates indicates when the game is favorable for the player, so that the player can place larger bets or make changes in his or her playing strategy. The casinos would like the players to believe that card counting is ille-gal; however, the card counters are using a higher level of skill than the normal blackjack player, thereby improving their odds.

Nevada courts have ruled that blackjack players are free to use any infor-mation that is made available to them except for cheating between the player and the casino personnel. For example, if a dealer exposes his hole card to the play-ers, players can use this information to improve their odds. If a player has the ability to count four decks of cards and develop a strategy as a result of that strat-egy, then he or she has a right to that information. In New Jersey a skillful player cannot be barred from the casinos. However, in Nevada the casinos can refuse service to anyone, at any time, for any reason.

Poker

America has one great game, and that is poker. Poker began in the United States and spread around the world. It is popular in almost every country. Poker is played in private homes as well as in casinos. It is played for pennies as well as for hundreds of thousands of dollars. Whichever way it is played and for what-ever amount it is played, it is a fascinating and exciting game. It involves more than simple luck; it involves card skill and human psychology. A good poker player must take into consideration the mathematical probabilities and the psy-chological conditions present at the table, intermingling this with his or her own personal knowledge and courage.

There are many variations of poker, such as straight, stud, whiskey, and lowball. A look at draw poker will give you an idea of why the house always takes its rake and is not involved in the gamer, and why poker parlors have been an intricate part of casinos in the past.

The rules for poker vary from location to location. The generally accepted rules and the standard laws for draw poker follow. Draw poker, or simply poker, is played with an ordinary deck of fifty-two cards. From two to eight players can play the game; when eight players play the game, the dealer stays out of the game so that seven is really the maximum, with five or six being the ideal number of players. The dealer deals each player one card at a time, going clockwise from left to right and ending with the dealer, and continues this until each player has five cards. At this time an opportunity is given to open (place the first bet). The player has the opportunity to place the first bet or to drop out. Those individuals who stay in match the amount bet, and an individual may raise the amount that he or she is betting when it is his or her turn to put money into the pot. Players can raise up to whatever limits are set by the house. Those who stay in the hand can now discard any number of their cards and receive an equal number in exchange for those cards face down. Cards can be received only once, and after the cards have been received (the draw), the player who made the opening bet has the opportunity to bet. This player is betting that he or she can defeat the other hands. Then each player clockwise from the opener either drops out, places a bet, or raises. The action ends when there is no further raising. Then the player who makes the last bet or last raise is called by the last player. At this time the last player indicates his or her hand, and if it is the best hand, and only the best hand, he or she collects the pot. If it is not the best hand, the player who actually does hold the best hand will win. However, only the winner and the called hand need show their cards.

In poker the best hand wins. First, the cards are ranked from deuce to ace, with ace being the highest and deuce the lowest. The next possibility is that there will be a pair (any two cards that are the same); for example, a pair of sixes. Next are two pairs; for example, a pair of aces and a pair of eights. Following are three of a kind, which is any card of equal rank or the same denomination; for example, three sixes. There can be no ties with three of a kind; however, there can be with two pairs, a pair, and high cards. The next highest hand is a straight, which is any five cards in sequence, but not of the same suit, for example, a two of hearts, three of clubs, four of diamonds, five of clubs, and six of spades. In the case of two straights, the higher straight would win. Flushes are the next highest hand. In a flush the player has five cards of the same suit but not in sequence, such as an eight of hearts, nine of hearts, two of hearts, three of hearts, and six of hearts. Next is a full house. A full house is made up of three of a kind and two of a kind, such as three aces and two threes. The next highest hand is four of a kind—any four cards of equal value—for example, four kings. The next hand is a straight flush, which consists of five cards in the same suit and in a row; for example, five hearts from five to nine. The straight flush is the highest ranking of all hands. A straight flush is the ace to ten of a single suit. In most cases, if the hands are identical, the pot will be divided among the players with the same hand. Sometimes an individual is dealt a pat hand. This is a hand that requires no further cards; for example, a straight. Most games have a limit established, that is, the highest amount that can be bet, and an ante that is established before the game starts. Each player contributes this before each hand is played (Silberstang, 1972).

Stud poker is played with face-up and face-down cards. The basic rules are the same, but an individual is unable to draw cards and must play only with those cards that are dealt. Certain poker games require a minimum poker hand; for example, jacks or better, which means that the person who opens (makes the first bet) must have a minimum of a pair of jacks or a better hand to open. Another form of poker that is very popular is called lowball, or western poker. In this game the lowest hand wins; for example, ace, three, four, five, six (Dawson, 1991).

Poker continues to be one of the most popular games in the world. A number of states are opening poker parlors as an alternative to casino gambling. Fortunately for us, a number of people see poker as a venial sin rather than a mortal sin.

Baccarat

Anyone who has ever gone into a casino and wandered around has been fascinated by the pit. Years ago, the pit was located in the center of the casino. It was an area where high rollers played, and one of the biggest money games they played was baccarat. However, recently the high rollers and the pits have been moved to adjoining rooms or upper floors. In the past, other gamblers sat and watched spellbound as piles of hundred-dollar bills changed hands.

Baccarat is a card game that is usually dealt from the shoe. This unique shoe holds six to eight decks of cards, each deck containing fifty-two cards. A designated player acts as the bank. Two hands are dealt, the bank hand and the player hand. The bets are made before the hands are dealt. Players can bet on the player's hand, the bank's hand, or a tie. All bets are paid by the house at a one-to-one rate. However, a 5 percent commission is charged to any player who bets on the bank's side. Those individuals betting for a tie are paid at eight to one. Once a player makes a bet, there is no further opportunity for the player to make any decision, because both the player's hands and bank's hands are dealt according to a fixed set of rules.

The game of baccarat is started by dealing two cards, one to the player and one to the bank, followed by another card to both player and bank. The cards are dealt face down. The object of the game is to have the highest possible hand closest to nine. The cards rank in value according to their numbers (pips). Aces count as one, tens and face cards count as ten, and the rest of the cards are counted by their numerical value. The value of the hand is determined by totaling the value of each individual card. If a card is added that would give a total greater than nine, the hand is adjusted by subtracting ten from that hand. The bank now looks at his or her own two cards. If the sum of those two cards comes to eight or nine, the bank turns the cards over and declares a natural. This is an automatic win if the player's hand has a lower total. Then the player turns over his or her cards to see whether he or she has a natural. If the player's hand and the bank's hand are both either eights or nines, then a tie has occurred, and neither side wins unless

BACCARAT

Easy to learn and easy to play, Baccarat is a game to be enjoyed by everyone.

A total of four cards are initially dealt. The first and third are the Player's hand, and the second and fourth are the Banker's hand.

Once the initial cards are dealt and exposed, the dealer announces the totals for each hand and additional cards are then drawn in accordance with the rules. (A maximum of one additional card may be dealt to either hand.)

The object of Baccarat is to bet on which hand will have the highest value. The highest hand in Baccarat is 9 and the lowest is 0. Tens, Jacks, Queens and Kings are counted as zero, an Ace counts as one, and all the other cards count their face value. When totaling the cards on each hand, only the right-hand number of the total figure is used to determine the hand's value.

Example:

$$7 + 8 = 15 \qquad K + 5 + 6 = 11$$

The hand value is 5.   The hand value is 1.

You have three betting options in Baccarat. You can bet that the Player's hand will win, that the Banker's hand will win, or that both hands will tie. If you win with a bet on either the Banker's or the Player's hand, your bet will be paid at 1-to-1 odds (even money).

Baccarat rules. *Source:* Casino Niagara, Niagara Falls, Ontario.

an individual player has bet on the tie. If neither hand is natural, then additional cards might be drawn before the game has ended. If the player's hand totals five or less, then a third card is drawn for the player's hand, and the player must stand regardless of the point count. The bank stands when holding seven, eight, or nine and always draws one card when holding zero, one, or two. The drawing of cards is predetermined by the rules of baccarat. Players who do not understand the rules of the game merely ask the croupier what to do and they will be told correctly every time. When eight decks are used for baccarat, the probability of the bank winning is 45.86 percent, the probability of the player winning is 44.62 percent, and the probability of a tie 9.52 percent. The house's edge on a player's bet is about 1.24 percent; however, the winning bank bets are charged a 5 percent commission, resulting in a 1.06 percent edge for the house. In the case of a tie, the edge for the house is approximately 4.5 percent (Dawson, 1991).

Now that baccarat is played as a table game in a number of the casinos in Las Vegas and Atlantic City, the intimidation of being in the pit is absent and all players have an opportunity to try this previously elite game. This was a smart move on the part of the casinos because it gives the players one more game at which to try their luck and the casino one more chance to enhance its profitability. Table baccarat is played much the same as pit baccarat.

Roulette

The roulette table is a rectangular table divided into two parts—the wheel, or roulette, and the illustrated portion of the table. The table is covered in green felt. The roulette contains numbers from zero to thirty-six, and in the United States zero and double zero to thirty-six. The green felt is divided into three columns and marked with numbers from one to thirty-six. At the bottom of each of the columns are three spaces representing the numbers in each one of these columns. To the side are spaces filled with a red diamond, a black diamond, numbers one through eighteen on one side, numbers nineteen to thirty six on the other side, and even or odd. The wheel is made up of small slots. In the United States it contains seventy-four slots, zero to thirty-six and double zero to thirty-six. The circle within the wheel is spun and a small ball is rolled around the outside ring. Bets are made prior to the rolling and during the rolling. As the ball slows, all bets are stopped. The ball falls into one of the seventy-four slots. This number is the winner. The number will also indicate a color, which indicates that either red or black has won. It also indicates whether even or odd has won. Bets are made on individual numbers, on odd or even, on rows or columns, or combinations of numbers. If an individual bets on a single winning number, such as one, he or she is generally paid at the rate of thirty-five to one. The chances of winning are thirty-seven to one, so the house maintains a 2 percent advantage. The bets placed in the columns and rows win two to one. The red, black, even, and odd are paid one to one.

There are thousands of systems that are employed by players to beat the house at roulette; these systems are used throughout the world. However, mega casinos such as the MGM Grand in Las Vegas, Nevada, built at a cost of $1.25 billion, are not built on the winnings of these systems, but on the losses.

Craps

Craps, or dice, is one of the more popular table games played in the United States. Its popularity has spread to the Caribbean, South America, Europe, and Asia. Unlike poker and blackjack, **craps** is a game of pure chance, no skill, no reason; only luck is the determiner of the outcome. However, in any casino where

Roulette. *Source:* Windsor Casino, Windsor, Ontario.

Americans are playing, over the bells and the noise of the slot machines, you can hear the roar of the crowd. The majority of the interest and excitement is around the craps table. Craps is a fast, exciting, and high-stakes game in which fortunes are won in an instant in the roll of the dice. In casino craps games, the banker is the house. The house pays off the players and the house bets.

Craps is played on a rectangular table covered with green felt. Around the table is a wooden frame with slots into which each player's chips can be fit. Laid out on the green felt table is a diagram of all the possible bets that can be made. Normally the game is run by four people working at one table. Two dealers stand at each end of the table, placing bets for people who cannot reach them, as well as paying off and collecting losses. Between them is the boxman, who sits in the center. The boxman supervises, watches, and determines the correctness of pay-outs and is the one who initiates markers, extends credit, and raises or lowers the house limits (the amount that the players can bet). Standing at the other side of the table, across from the boxman, is the stickman. The stickman holds a wooden stick with which he or she retrieves and returns the dice to the players. On the table near the stickman are the dice. Each die has six sides, each side with a different number of spots ranging from one to six. A player called a shooter rolls these two dice at the same time. The shooter must place a bet on the pass,

Craps. *Source:* Circus Circus, Las Vegas.

meaning he or she expects to win, or the don't pass meaning he or she expects to lose in order to be eligible to roll the dice. Once the dice are rolled, the spots on the top of the dice represent the total, which is known as the roll or point.

A game consists of a series of rolls. A roll of two, three, or twelve is called craps. This means that the bettor on the pass line loses. The first roll by the shooter during a game is called the come-out roll. If the come-out roll is seven or eleven, the game is over. Bets on the pass line are paid one to one; bets on the don't pass line lose. If the come-out roll is craps, the game is over. Bets on the pass line lose, bets on the don't pass line win. Anytime a player makes a come-out role on four, five, six, eight, nine, or ten, it is their point; the object of the game is to make this point before making a seven. The player who makes the point wins; the player who rolls a seven loses if he or she has bet on the pass line. If the game is over on the come-out roll or because the player makes his or her point, the shooter may continue to shoot for another game, or the dice will pass clockwise to the next shooter at the table.

Casinos allow players to place odds or to take odds on different bets at the table. Most casinos advertise the maximum odds bets they allow as the maximum amount times the original bet the odds bet may be. Players are able to play a number of different areas on the craps table; they can bet on any crap or any seven at any time, any number coming up before the seven, and what the next roll will be in a field (the numbers two, three, four, nine, ten, eleven, and twelve). They can also bet the hard ways, meaning that a number will be made up of a combination of two of the same. For example, a pair of deuces being four the hard way, or a pair of fives being ten the hard way.

Many casinos offer classes for players in all the games they offer within their casino. In craps, the casinos advise players who are unfamiliar with the game to take their courses. The courses provide insight to the player as to the odds and the advantages or disadvantages of each bet.

NEW GAMES OF CHANCE

Keno

Keno is a form of lottery offered by most casinos in the Nevada region, although it is illegal in New Jersey. **Keno** is very similar to bingo in that there are eighty numbers on the card and players pick from one to fifteen of these numbers. Players are paid based on twenty numbers that are drawn by the house from a bin. Players have the opportunity to win from $25 to $100,000, depending on how many numbers they get correct. The tickets cost anywhere from 50¢ to $5. The house has approximately a 25¢ advantage, making it a true sucker bet. However, it is a game played by a number of gamblers who are not familiar with other games and wish to wager small amounts, or serious gamblers who have stopped for a bite of lunch or dinner and wish to continue gambling. Keno offers the casino one of the best advantages of any game played in Nevada.

Let-It-Ride Stud Poker

Let-it-ride stud poker is a relatively new game offered by a number of casinos in Las Vegas. It provides the players with the opportunity to control two of their three bets while wagering on an exciting poker game.

Let-it-ride stud poker is based on five-card stud poker and is relatively easy to learn. The players do not play against the dealer or any other player. The game is played by each player placing three equal bets on three circles in front of them labeled one, two, three. Each player is dealt three cards, and two cards are placed face down in front of the dealer. Players are not playing against any other players or the dealer; they are simply trying to get a good poker hand by using their three cards and the dealer's two down cards. Winners are paid according to a payout schedule. After looking at their first three cards, the players may choose to receive their first bet back or they may say let it ride. One of the dealer's cards is then turned up, and at this time players may ask for their second bet back or let it ride again. Next, the dealer's second down card is turned up and the players lay their cards down face up. The dealer then pays all winning hands according to the predetermined payout schedule.

STUD POKER

Payout Schedule

Royal............................. 1,000 to 1
Straight Flush.................. 200 to 1
4 of a Kind...................... 50 to 1
Full House........................ 11 to 1
Flush................................. 8 to 1
Straight........................... 5 to 1
3 of a kind....................... 3 to 1
Two Pair.......................... 2 to 1
Pair of 10's or better........... 1 to 1

MGM GRAND

"Let it Ride" Stud Poker

Let it Ride Stud Poker was designed to offer our casino guests an opportunity to control two of their three bets wagered on an exciting poker game. It's enjoyable and easy to learn. It is based on the five card stud poker game. The players do not play against the dealer or any other player.

How To Play

Bets
Each player places three (3) equal bets as indicated.
● ● ●

The Deal
Each player receives three (3) cards and two cards are placed face down in front of the dealer.

The Play
You are not playing against the dealer or the other players. You are simply trying to get a good poker hand by using your three cards and the dealer's two down cards.

The winners are paid according to the payout schedule (pair of 10's or better, two pair, etc.).

After looking at their first three (3) cards, the player may ask for their first bet back or they may "Let It Ride".

One of the dealer's down cards is then turned up. The player may then ask for their second bet back or "Let It Ride".

The dealer's second down card is turned up and the players lay their cards down, face up - the dealer then pays all winning hands according to the payout schedule.

Players cannot show their hands to other players.

MGM GRAND

Let-it-ride stud poker rules. *Source:* MGM Grand Hotel and Casino.

Let-it-ride stud poker is relatively uncomplicated and offers new casino players an opportunity to participate in poker without having the advanced knowledge of the skill involved in the game.

Caribbean Stud Poker

Another game that is becoming popular among the casinos around the world was invented in the beautiful Caribbean. The game's popularity can be traced to its excitement and universal acceptance of poker combined with the opportunity and thrill of winning a meagbucks-type jackpot. This jackpot can be won with an investment of as little as $1 (Levenson, 1994).

Caribbean stud poker is played on a twenty-one-type table and is based on the game of five-card stud poker. It was the first game to offer a progressive jackpot for its players. Each player makes his or her opening bet as in poker. In addition, players have an opportunity of participating in a progressive jackpot for $1. The winning hand determines the amount of the progressive jackpot that the player is eligible for. After looking at their hand, players who feel that their hand can beat the dealer's hand will make a bet. This bet cannot be more than twice the amount of the ante, and players who do not feel they have a strong enough hand may fold and invest no additional funds. The dealer must have an AK or higher for the game to continue. If the dealer cannot open, the hand is over; the dealer collects the cards and pays the antes bet only for players who stayed in the hand. If the dealer's hand is high enough to open and the player's hand is higher than the dealer's hand, the dealer may qualify for a bonus based on the chart below. Caribbean stud poker's progressive jackpots have ranged from $250 million to $10 thousand. It is the player's ability to win a 250 million times his or her bet that has made this game a popular pastime in modern casinos.

Pai Gow Poker

Pai gow poker is an offshoot of the ancient Chinese domino game. It has been played throughout Asia for centuries and is the predecessor for such modern games as baccarat, chemin de fer, and blackjack. **Pai gow poker** offers the player the unique opportunity to bank against all other players, including the dealer. It is played with a normal poker deck of fifty-two cards plus one joker. The joker can be used only as an A, or to complete a straight, flush, or straight flush. Each player at the table is dealt seven cards, which the player arranges into two hands, a five-card hand and a two-card hand. Ranking of the hand is the same as poker ranking; that is the highest two-card hand would be two aces and the highest five-card hand would be a royal straight flush. The only twist to the game is that the five-card hand must be higher than the two-card hand. For example, if the two-card hand is a pair of deuces, then the five-card hand must contain a pair of threes or higher.

The basic object of the game is for both of the player's two hands to rank higher than both of the bank's hands. If one of the hands should rank exactly the same as the player's, it is considered a tie and the bank wins all tied hands. If the player loses on both hands it is considered a push and no money is paid or lost. All winning hands are paid even money by the bank less a 5 percent commission that goes to the house. Losing hands pay no commission but lose their wager.

Pai gow poker is becoming popular in a number of casinos, but the Chinese version played with dominos is extremely difficult and complex; it takes years to fully understand. The game has been showing up in a number of casinos in Las Vegas and elsewhere because of the large number of Asian customers who have been frequenting these markets.

PAI-GOW POKER

A combination of elements from the ancient Chinese game of Pai Gow and the American game of poker. A traditional deck of 52 playing cards is used, plus one joker. The joker is used only as an ace or to complete a straight, a flush, or a straight flush.

The game begins with a random generated number, or a roll of the dice, the total of which determines which player receives the first set of cards. Each player receives seven cards and creates two hands. The high hand is made up of five cards, and the second high hand is made up of two cards. Both the high hands and the second high hand must be higher than the bank hands to win.

If only one hand is higher, it is a tie. If both hands are lower, the player loses.

Payoffs are even money, and the house collects a 5% commission on all winning wagers.

The house dealer may explain the rankings and assist you in arranging your hands, but is not responsible for wins or losses.

Pai gow poker rules. *Source:* Casino Niagara, Niagara Falls, Ontario.

THE FUTURE OF PIT AND FLOOR GAMES

The pit and floor games have always been the predominant revenue producers for casinos throughout the world. The mere presence of these games has practically guaranteed the success of casinos. This scene is changing and will continue to change into the twenty-first century. In the future, slot machines, video slots, and VLTs will become the mainstay of the gaming and casino industry. The rationale for this is simple: labor. Pit and floor games are labor intense. Slot and VLT games are technically oriented and not labor intense. In the future, even change attendants will be obsolete; they will be replaced by players' Visa, MasterCard, or bank cards. Money will never change hands. The blackened graphite hands of the typical slot player will no longer be recognizable. Winnings or losses will be posted directly to the account. Gambling will change forever.

REVIEW TERMS

baccarat	craps
blackjack	keno
busting	let-it-ride stud poker
card counting	pai gow poker
Caribbean stud poker	shoe

REFERENCES

Dawson, L. H. (1991). *Hoyles games.* New York: Gallery Books, pp. 116, 152.

Levenson, L. (1994). Caribbean stud poker. *Fun and games*, September, 22.

Silberstang, E. (1972). *The book of games.* Chicago: Playboy Press, p. 9.

Chapter 5

Gaming Regulations

OBJECTIVES

- Discuss the historic development of the casino regulatory bodies in Nevada and New Jersey.
- Identify and describe how regulations occur within the casino industry.
- Describe the structure of the regulatory gaming bodies in Nevada and New Jersey.
- List and describe the different types of casino licenses in Nevada and New Jersey.
- Identify the various types of gaming licenses granted in Nevada and New Jersey.

INTRODUCTION

All societies need to regulate and control gambling activities. The nature and history of gambling and casinos demand that effective regulations are in place to uphold the integrity of the industry. At the turn of the twentieth century, gambling was widespread and illegal, especially in the United States. One way to deter cheating, and also improve its image and integrity, was to design and implement controls that would regulate the industry. Successful casino jurisdictions have learned how to maintain a balance of controls and regulations. If regulations were too lax, crime and corruption might flourish; if regulations were too strict, it would be difficult to attract entrepreneurs to invest within a specific area.

In this chapter, we will take a close look at the regulatory agencies of Nevada. It is important to review the Nevada model because it was the first state in the United States to legalize casino gambling in this modern era. The Nevada model is also significant because many other states used it as a model to form their own regulatory bodies.

A review of Table 5-1 shows the historical events that shaped casino regulation in the state of Nevada. Prior to 1931, gambling within the United States, and especially in Nevada, was disorganized and had a reputation as an illicit, dishonest activity. Many legislators both in Nevada and in Washington, D.C., were concerned about this reputation. Some of the concerns were real, and others were stereotyped. There were immediate concerns that the state, or the government, had been cheated of an enormous amount of tax revenue.

Three catalysts caused the refinement of gaming in Nevada and elsewhere. The first concern of any jurisdiction is to make certain that all revenues from the casinos, or any other gambling activities, are taxed properly. Another force behind regulating gaming is to make sure that all the games are conducted honestly. A third force for the regulation of gaming was to sanitize the industry of relations with organized crime.

Nevada developed a three-tier system of control and regulation. The first body was the Gaming Control Board, which was created in 1959. Later during the same year, the Nevada Gaming Commission was formed to act on and

Table 5-1   Historical Events of Nevada Gaming Regulations

Date	Event
1931	Passage of Gambling Act
1931–1945	Licensing and taxing done by the sheriff
1945	Nevada Tax Commission responsible for the collection of casino tax
1950	U.S. Senate committee on Nevada concluded that numerous casino owners were associated with organized crime
1955	Full-time Gaming Control Division created within the Nevada Tax Commission
1959	Nevada Gaming Control Act
1959	Nevada Gaming Commission
1959	Gaming Control Board
1961	Gaming Policy Committee
1967	Corporate Licensing Law
1969	Modification of Corporate Licensing
1971	Gaming Policy Committee
1975	Employee labor organizations
1977	Permission for foreign gaming
1979	Supervision Chapter

endorse the recommendations of the Gaming Control Board. Two years later, the state created the Gaming Policy Committee to serve as an advisory body to the commission and the board.

When gambling is being considered for a region, officials must develop regulations for conducting the gaming operations. Serious considerations should be given to a variety of factors. The most important component of a regulatory structure is a reporting system. Most gaming jurisdictions create a gaming commission to facilitate this need. A system of checks and balances should be incorporated into such a commission. An effective regulatory strategy is to develop three separate agencies as members of the gaming commission. One of the agencies should have the final authority over all legal matters concerning gambling and provide final approval for gambling licenses. The second agency would advise the state on gambling policy and inform the industry of those policies. The third agency would enforce all of the regulations and policies.

Regulations usually occur in the following areas: quality, public space requirements, layout of facilities, accounting records, table and slot drop counts, credit procedures, and game rules. Quality is concerned with the extent to which the actual casino facility is maintained. The level and standard of maintenance should always be high. The public space requirements refers to the following of local zoning regulations.

The layout of facilities is another important regulatory consideration. This factor includes a determination, on a square-foot basis, of the number of games that can be placed in any room. It should also include a specific breakdown of types of games allowed. For example, for every five thousand square feet of space, there cannot be more than three craps tables, twenty slot machines, and so on.

The accounting procedures are a very important regulation in the casino industry. These procedures safeguard and maintain the integrity of the industry. These policies provide specific guidelines for cash flow and control of records, and also specify the use of prenumbered forms to be used.

The table and slot drop counts are another area of concern for regulations. All effective jurisdictions stipulate the specific number of times the table and slot count should be conducted daily or weekly. There should also be a stipulation of the number of personnel involved in the counting activity. Such rules as wearing only full length, pocketless garments with openings for only the arms, feet, and neck are also important. Also, those employees working on the count team should not be allowed to bring any food or drinks into the count room.

Regulations about credit procedures are thorough. The gaming commission must look at check-cashing procedures and the use of money orders, credit cards, and traveler's checks. Credit must be established by obtaining a bank report on the applicant from a credit reporting agency, another legal casino, or the applicant's bank. Persons issuing credit must also be examined. Credit should be authorized only by casino executives in the credit department under the direction of the credit manager. Many jurisdictions make sure the credit manager reports to the controller.

Another regulation that the casino industry is concerned with is the game rules. A full and complete listing of the rules for each casino game must be published. It should be consistent among casinos; therefore, it should be developed by the gaming commission. The published rules should be available to every customer upon request.

One of the last regulatory considerations in the casino industry is employee licensing. Each employee involved in the operation of a casino game or slot machine should obtain a license from the county, state, or province. To obtain such a license, the applicant must meet minimum standards for the job or position for which he or she wishes to be employed in. A personal history disclosure should be available to stockholders, directors, and necessary managers within the casino upon request and on file for the gaming control board, gaming committee, and gaming commission.

Photographs and fingerprints should be handled by a division of the gaming control board. They should conduct an investigation for each applicant. The investigation should include a review of criminal records and credit history at the federal and local levels. Based on the preliminary review, a field investigation may be required for further disclosure of key employee licenses or follow-up when incriminating evidence is found for any employee license.

Although this chapter focuses specifically on the regulatory process that occurred in Nevada and Atlantic City, the above concerns are important to the casino industry worldwide.

Casinos and gambling have always been associated with an image of dishonesty. Throughout the centuries, individuals involved in gambling have always been looked at awkwardly by either the religious right or those who toiled hard for a living. Numerous stories have been told about gamblers who spent endless amounts of time in smoke-filled saloons, drinking, gambling, and cheating their ways in and out of fortunes.

Gambling in the United States began amidst this background of drinking, smoking, carousing, and cheating. It has been on a roller coaster of respectability. At one time it was illegal to gamble in the United States, and later it was legal. It was popular on riverboats and in several of the southern states. After much flip-flopping, a few factors influenced its legalization. An important reason for the legalization of gambling was an opening for the states to obtain funds by taxing the gambling establishments. Nevada was the pioneer state for legalized casino gambling.

NEVADA

Prior to the 1930s, gambling within the United States was unregulated and disorganized. In 1931, Nevada legislators passed the Gambling Act, which legalized gambling in the states. Under this act, the sheriff was responsible for the licensing and taxing of the casinos. This period is regarded as the "modern era" of casino gambling in Nevada.

During the following years, gambling activities grew throughout the entire state. In the 1930s and 1940s, the majority of the gaming activities were in the north of Nevada, around Reno. Casino expansion began in Las Vegas in 1941 (Greenless, 1988). As the years passed, the revenue from casino gambling increased every year, with the state and various counties collecting millions of dollars. This increase of revenue brought about the need for a more systematic method of collecting the taxes.

In 1950, the United States Senate, in a committee report, concluded that numerous casino owners were associated with organized crime. During the following years, more efforts were made to regulate the industry. One effort in that direction was the formation of the Nevada Gaming Control Board as an autonomous body.

Gaming Control Board

The **Nevada Gaming Control Board** was formed in 1959. The primary purpose of this board was the enforcement of the regulations for licensing and operation of gaming establishments. The board consists of three full-time members who are appointed by the governor. All members serve a staggered four-year term. One of them serves as chair as well as executive director of the board. The chair must have at least five years of experience in the public or business sector. The second member must be a certified public accountant with five years of experience in accounting or finance. The last member must have a surveillance background and experience in investigation.

The Nevada Gaming Control Board fulfills its legal mandate by having a professional staff of more than three hundred employees servicing seven enforcement divisions. The divisions of the board are: Administration, Audit, Special Investigation and Intelligence, Investigations, Electronic Services, Tax and License Economic Research, and Enforcement. More than half of the staff are located in Las Vegas, with the remainder located in branch offices in Reno and Carson City.

The primary responsibility of the **Investigation Division** is to complete a thorough background check of all applicants to the commission. The division also scrutinizes the planned operational methods. Additionally, the agents travel extensively to verify references, with all the travel expenses paid for by the sponsoring casino.

The largest division of the board is the Audit Unit. One of its purposes is to audit the accounting records of all licensees to determine whether the licensees have complied with the gaming regulations. All of the agents in this division have accounting degrees, and several of them are also certified public accountants. With their specific backgrounds, the agents review the internal controls and also make surprise visits to observe the cash-counting procedures.

Another important division is the Enforcement Unit. This division has offices that are open twenty-four hours a day, seven days a week. Its main responsibility is to enforce the Gaming Control Act. The agents routinely pick up playing cards from games and inspect them. Their responsibilities include undercover observations, and they also have the power to arrest cheaters. Another role this unit serves is to oversee a hearing examiner for complaints.

The Special Investigation and Intelligence Division investigates postlicensing, nonroutine gambling problems. It is concerned with organized crime and hidden ownership interest. A large amount of the division's time is spent in gathering casino industry intelligence.

It is almost impossible to operate a modern casino without electronics. The Electronic Service Division is responsible for monitoring all electronic devices within the industry. The agents recommend approval or disapproval of newly designed machines. Also, they develop methods for detecting malfunctioning machines. Equally important, they develop standards for electronic and gaming devices, and they periodically check slot machines.

The Tax and License Economic Research section plays an important role for the Gaming Control Board. The function of this section is to collect, control, and provide accounting for the taxes and license fees. It also conducts a continuous study of the gaming industry and reports findings to the various gaming constituents. This section produces the Nevada Gaming Abstract.

The primary responsibility of the Administration Division is issuing and amending licenses for casino games as well as slot machines. This unit is also responsible for updating files, which contain additional information for corporate licenses.

Gaming Commission

The **Nevada Gaming Commission** was created in 1959. Its purpose was to act on the recommendations of the Gaming Control Board on licensing matters. It also rules on work permit appeal cases. It is the final authority on licensing matters. It has the authority to approve, restrict, limit, deny, revoke, condition, or suspend gaming licenses. If the Gaming Control Board recommends denial, the commission can exercise one of three options. These include granting the license, denying the license, or referring the matter back to the board for additional investigation (Greenless, 1988). A unanimous decision is needed to grant a license after it was denied by the Gaming Control Board.

The Nevada Gaming Commission has five part-time members, each appointed by the governor. The members are limited to plural representation by profession or major industry. Each member serves a four-year term. The commission has a full-time executive secretary as well as a complete office staff and is required to meet at least once a month.

Gaming Policy Committee

The third statutory gaming body in Nevada is the **Gaming Policy Committee.** This committee was created in 1961 to serve as an advisory body to both the commission and the board. The governor serves as its chair, and the other eight members include representatives from the legislative bodies, the gaming industry, the regulatory agencies, and the public. This group holds public hearings and makes recommendations, which need not be accepted, to the other two bodies.

Types of Gaming Licenses

The state of Nevada issues three categories of licenses: gaming, manufacturer's, and distributor's.

The **gaming licenses** are classified in three subgroups (Greenless, 1988). **Restricted licenses** are granted to operations with fifteen or fewer machines, and no other gaming. These licenses are granted to establishments whose primary business is not gaming. They are issued annually and must be renewed quarterly. **Nonrestricted licenses** are given to operations with sixteen or more slot machines, or one or more slot machines operated in synergy with table games. They also are issued annually and renewed quarterly. The third type of gaming license is called **nonrestricted slot machine licenses,** which are granted to large-scale slot operators. These licenses are issued and renewed annually.

The second category of licenses is called **manufacturer's licenses** and are issued to manufacturers of gaming devices, equipment, and related materials. The licenses are issued and renewed annually.

The final category of license granted is **distributor's licenses.** This license is issued to distributors of gaming devises, equipment, and related materials. These licenses are also issued and renewed annually.

Who Can Be Licensed in Nevada

All individuals who are engaged financially in the casino industry must obtain a license. In Nevada, there are four types of licenses in this category: individual, partnership, corporation, and key employees.

An individual license is required for those who have specific financial revenues or profits from gaming. This type of license is usually granted to casino owners.

The partnership license is given to both general and limited partners involved in the gaming industry. The only exceptions are partners who are passive investors (Greenless, 1988). If the partnership is a corporation, the corporation must be approved for a gaming license.

The third type of license is corporation. It is important to differentiate between publicly traded and closely held corporations. In Nevada, all owners and stockholders of publicly traded gaming corporations must be registered. The Gaming Control Board and the Gaming Commission will decide whether it is necessary for all of them to be formally licensed. On the other hand, all officers, directors, and shareholders of closely held corporations must be licensed.

All key employees of a casino must obtain a specific license to work within a casino. Generally, key employees are considered any employee in the supervisory level and above. However, Regulation 3.100 of the Gaming Commission specifically identifies a key employee as "Any executive, employee, or agent of a gaming license having the power to exercise a significant influence over decisions concerning any part of the operations of a gaming licensee or who is listed or should be listed in the annual employee report." Individuals with a key license are not permitted to gamble within their sponsored casino.

In Nevada, as in other places, the granting of a license to work within the casino industry is considered a privilege. It is also necessary for labor organizations and their leaders to be licensed. All individuals who desire to work within the gaming industry in the state of Nevada must be approved by the Nevada Gaming Commission. This process can easily be completed by submitting one's fingerprints and background information to the local police or sheriff department.

Hotel Room Requirements

Any operator who applies for a nonrestricted casino license is required to build a minimum of two hundred hotel rooms within the casino structure. This requirement is essential throughout Nevada, except in Reno. In Reno, all casino properties must have a minimum of three hundred rooms. These room requirements became effective in July 1992. Casinos built prior to 1992 are not required to adhere to this regulation.

NEW JERSEY

The licensing procedure in New Jersey is different from that of Nevada in many ways. Table 5-2 shows a brief history of some of the important gaming events in New Jersey. After the referendum to legalize gambling was passed in 1976, the Casino Control Act authorized the New Jersey Casino Control Commission to monitor gambling activities. Gambling is permitted only in Control Commission–approved hotels; approved hotels must have at least five hundred guest rooms and must meet certain minimum meeting and exhibition space.

Table 5-2   Historical Events of New Jersey Gaming Regulations

Date	Event
1976	Referendum permitting casino gambling
1977	Casino Control Act
1977	Casino Control Commission
1978	First casino, resorts, opened in New Jersey
1980	Members of the Casino Control Commission made full-time

They must provide dining facilities, live entertainment, and indoor sports. Credit practices and the collection of winnings are also stringently controlled by the act.

In New Jersey, the Division of Gaming Enforcement and the Casino Control Commission are responsible for all of the gambling regulations and enforcement within the casino industry. Their procedures are considered stricter, and their workforce is larger than their counterparts in Nevada.

Division of Gaming Enforcement

The **Division of Gaming Enforcement** is under the jurisdiction of the Attorney General. Its purpose is to thoroughly investigate the backgrounds of all applicants wishing to engage in any type of activities within the casino industry and to report nonbinding recommendations of their findings to the Casino Control Commission. They are also responsible for enforcing all of the criminal provisions of the Casino Control Act (Friedman, 1982). The activities of the Division of Gaming Enforcement must be endorsed by the Casino Control Commission. The Division of Gaming Enforcement has four main departments: Investigations, Intelligence and Research, Legal, and Administration.

Within the Investigations Department there are four units. The Enforcement Unit investigates cheating and complaints from players and ensures that the casinos conduct their operations properly. The Compliance Unit is responsible for the supervision and security of each casino. Both the Casino License Team Unit and the Individual Background and Gaming School Unit conduct background investigations on individuals and companies involved in the casino industry.

Casino Control Commission

In 1977, the Casino Control Act was passed, which created the **Casino Control Commission** (CCC) and the Division of Gaming Enforcement. The CCC, as it is commonly called, is an independent unit of the New Jersey Department of the Treasury. Its primary responsibility is to "ensure the integrity and vitality of the gaming industry," as well as help revitalize the economy of Atlantic City (Friedman, 1982). It fulfills this mandate by evaluating the financial performance and reviewing the internal controls of each casino. Included in its responsibilities is the licensing of individuals and companies, as well as the collection of licensing fees and taxes. This board also holds administrative hearings and has subpoena powers within the state of New Jersey.

The Casino Control Commission has five full-time members who are appointed by the governor. In contrast to Nevada, there are no specific membership requirements other than that no more than three of its members can be from the same political party. One member is appointed chair. None of the members can have an active involvement in any casino interest. Each commissioner serves a five-year term, which overlaps. Commissioners can only be removed from office "with cause."

There are four divisions within the Casino Control Commission: Financial Evaluation and Control, Legal, Administration, and Licensing. The chief responsibility of the Licensing Division is to provide licenses to casinos, casino employees, and casino service industries. In contrast to Nevada, the licensing process in Atlantic City is more selective and time consuming. As in Nevada, applicants must pay for their initial license.

Types of Gaming Licenses

Any individual who wishes to engage in employment in the casino industry in Atlantic City must be licensed. There are four categories of licenses: casino service employee (CSE) nongaming license, 2-1 casino gaming license, key license, and junket license.

The **casino service employee nongaming license** is required of most employees who work in a hotel-casino. These licenses are required for people who work within the room division, food and beverage, and front office departments. A one-time registration fee is required, and no renewal is necessary. Applicants must complete a Personal History Disclosure Form 4A for this license (Davis, 1994).

Another type of license is the **2-1 casino gaming license;** it is required of all persons, such as dealers and floor persons, who work directly on the casino floor. Security personnel and persons involved in the accounting and financial departments of a casino also are required to have this license. The initial license is valid for three years, and there is a renewal cost every three years. All gaming personnel must complete a Personal History Disclosure Form 2A (Davis, 1994).

A specific type of 2-1 casino license is a **key license.** These licenses are granted to managerial personnel. There is an initial license fee, which is invariably paid by the casino. This license is granted after a thorough background check by the Division of Gaming Enforcement. Key licenses must be renewed every three years.

Individuals who operate junkets also need a special kind of 2-1 casino license called a **junket license.** These licenses are only granted to junket operators after they have completed a comprehensive disclosure form and have been investigated by the Casino Control Committee. An average cost for these investigations is at least $3,000 (Raymond, 1992). These licenses must be renewed every three years.

Hotel Room Requirements

Another difference between casino gambling in Nevada and Atlantic City is the room requirement for granting a casino license in New Jersey. All of the casinos in Atlantic City must have a minimum of five hundred rooms to be eligible to receive a license (Friedman, 1982).

CONCLUSION

This chapter briefly describes the background of the regulations of the two major gaming regulatory agencies in the United States. Most of the states that have introduced gaming after 1978 have used one or both of these documents to write their own documents. The main purpose of licensing and regulation is to maintain integrity within the gaming industry. Atlantic City is still regarded as the most difficult jurisdiction in which to obtain a casino license.

REVIEW TERMS

Casino Control Commission

casino service employee nongaming license

distributor's license

Division of Gaming Enforcement

gaming license

Gaming Policy Committee

Investigation Division

junket license

key license

Nevada Gaming Commission

Nevada Gaming Control Board

nonrestricted license

nonrestricted slot machine license

restricted licenses

manufacturer's license

2-1 casino gaming license

REFERENCES

American Institute of Certified Public Accountants. (1984). *Audits of casinos*. Prepared by the Gaming Industry Special Committee. New York: American Institute of Certified Public Accountants.

Davis, Warren. (1994). Personal interview, Atlantic City.

Greenless, E.M. (1988). *Casino accounting and financial management*. Reno: University of Nevada Press.

Friedman, B. (1982). *Casino management*. Secaucus, NJ: Lyle Stuart.

Nevada Gaming Commission & State Gaming Control Board. (1990). *Gaming Nevada style*. Carson City, NV: SPO.

Chapter 6

Economic Impact
of Casinos

OBJECTIVES

- Describe the economic factors that lead to legalizing casino gambling in certain communities within the United States.
- List and describe economic factors in the casino industry.
- List and describe the direct and indirect employment of the casino industry.
- Describe the various multiplier effects of a casino within a community.
- Discuss the social costs of a casino.
- Discuss career opportunities in the casino industry.

INTRODUCTION

Casino revenues have more than doubled in the last four years (Harrah's Survey, 1996). In 1991 the revenue was estimated at approximately $9 billion. In 1996, the casino industry estimated an increase in its revenue between $22 and $25 billion. Approximately $16.3 billion was a direct result of activities within the casino industry (Arthur Andersen, 1996). In 1997 the casino industry's revenue increased to approximately $51 billion (Christiansen, 1998). This increase in revenue occurred in both the new casino destinations, such as riverboats casinos, Native American reservation casinos, slot machine gaming at pari-mutuels, and limited-stakes casinos, and the traditional casino destinations, such as Nevada and New Jersey.

Some of the factors that have contributed to this economic growth within the casino industry are the increase in disposable income of the population at large and the increasing number of households participating in casino activities.

The Harrah's Survey (1996) indicates that the median household income of casino players is $41,000 compared with the median income for the U.S. population, which is $32,000. This study also shows that there are slightly more male casino players than female, that casino players are slightly more educated, and that they are more likely to be white-collar workers.

Casinos are an important economic engine to communities for a number of reasons. Perhaps an important attraction of casinos to depressed communities is that they are labor intensive. The Andersen (1996) study revealed that "for every $1 million in revenues, the casino gaming industry creates 13 direct jobs." This number dwarfs the number of jobs created by other industries, such as

Casino Niagara, Niagara Falls, Ontario, one of the most successful casinos in the world. *Source:* Casino Niagara.

cable services, video cassette sales, or even the soft drink industry. In 1995, the national average wage paid to a casino employee was approximately $26,000. In contrast, the national average wage for the amusement and recreational industry, hotel/motel, and motion picture was $20,000, $16,000, and $22,000, respectively (Andersen, 1996). All of the above factors encourage casino operators and communities to become involve in a partnership.

Economically depressed communities are attracted to casinos for other reasons as well. In most instances, casinos pay at least a 12 percent tax on the total revenue generated within a casino. Besides local taxes, casinos are also taxed by the state. Casinos, in particular the mega-casinos, have also been spending millions of dollars for construction of new and magnificent edifices. These large constructions provide jobs for the communities prior to the opening of the casino, as well as after the casinos have been opened. Casinos afterwards become a generator for creating jobs both directly and indirectly within the industry. Some of the jobs created indirectly from casinos are seen in Table 6-1.

During the past sixty years, one of the main reasons for the development of the casino industry has been to revive an economically deprived area. These new gambling venues provided employment opportunities for the immediate population, increased municipal and state revenues, and also attracted a number of people to the surrounding shopping areas. The end result of these activities was the circulation of more money within the economy, thus producing more revenue to the local and state treasuries.

Previously, when casino gambling was illegal in Nevada and other states, these states lost millions of dollars in tax revenues to illicit gambling activities. Therefore, after weighing the pros and cons of legalized casino gambling, the ultimate decision to legalize casinos is an economic one. Thus, the movement

Table 6-1   Industries and Jobs Created Indirectly from the Casino Industry

• Construction	• Change machines
• Transportation	• Accounting professionals
• Dealer's schools	• Legal professionals
• Slot machines	• Surveillance equipment
• Playing cards and card shufflers	• Cameras
• Dice	• Video games
• Tokens	• Uniforms
• Entertainment	• Change machines
• Hotels	• Housing
• Casino furniture and carpets	• Computer software
• Gaming tables	• Food and beverage

toward legalizing gambling in a variety of locations was primarily an economic decision. In retrospect, all jurisdictions that have introduced any form of casino gambling during the past twenty years have been economically hard pressed. They viewed casinos as the economic catalyst for revitalization.

The legalization of casino gambling in Atlantic City, New Jersey, was definitely an economic decision. Atlantic City was an economically depressed city. Businesses on the Boardwalk had shrunk, and the city was a mere skeleton of what it used to be. After fervent lobbying and two referenda, the legislation was finally passed. It appears that this venture paid off: Atlantic City's twelve casinos now pay almost one-third of the property tax of the city and Atlantic County's total budget (Harrison, 1992).

Economic depression has been the basis for casino gambling in South Dakota, Colorado, Iowa, Illinois, Indiana, Louisiana, and Mississippi. With the introduction of casino gambling, many legislators envisage a rejuvenation of their cities similar to that of Atlantic City.

Currently within the United States, the casino industry is a multi-billion-dollar enterprise. Billions of dollars are spent for the construction of large edifices such as the MGM Grand, the Mirage, and the Luxor. Thousands of jobs are created during the construction phase. Afterwards, about half of that number obtain permanent employment in the casino industry.

A FEW ECONOMIC CONCERNS FOR THE CASINO INDUSTRY

Before looking at the economic benefits of the casino industry, it is important to define several economic concepts. **Economics** may be described as the study of scarcity resources and their allocation to meet society's needs. An important branch of economics is macroeconomics, the study of aggregate elements such as overall employment, output, or prices within an economy. A key test for explaining how aggregate employment and income are determined is the **income multiplier.** This theory is important because it tries to determine the degree to which money spent by consumers is recycled throughout the local region (Fridgen, 1991). The multiplier can be expressed quantitatively: the higher the multiplier, the more the money remains and circulates within the community. Conversely, a small multiplier indicates that large sums of money are leaving the community.

Money leaving a community is known as **leakage.** This occurs when a community has to pay for goods and services not produced there. Additionally, a leakage occurs when the owners of an enterprise do not reside in that community and eventually take the company's profits outside the community or state. Unfortunately, unless certain legislated guidelines are imposed, the leakage would be high in many of the new casino communities. Ironically, the main purpose of introducing casino gambling in a community is to inject as much revenue as possible into it.

One of the negative economic impacts of casinos is that they cause land speculation. This speculation can be considered negative, because property values increase so much that many local residents get displaced. This is ironic because the original purpose for casinos was to benefit as much of the local community as possible. What invariably happens is that property values become inflated because of the demand for property for the actual casino and for parking and housing. These demands cause higher taxes and increased competition for the scarce resource. Inevitably the competition displaces the local elderly and minority population, because they cannot afford the increased cost of real estate.

ECONOMIC BENEFITS OF TOURISM

There are several benefits from the casino industry. The three main local benefits are tax revenues, employment, and income. Each of these benefits will be discussed in the following paragraphs.

The casino industry, which is part of the tourism industry, is labor intensive. Relative to other industries of a comparable size, casinos require more employees. These industries have a greater impact on reducing level of unemployment. Communities with casinos benefit from both direct and indirect employment. Jobs created from direct employment within the casino industry include individuals who actually work in the casinos. Included within this category are dealers, cocktail waitresses, casino managers, and regulatory agents. Table 6-1 shows a listing of jobs created indirectly from the casino industry.

Although the casino industry creates many jobs directly (Table 6-2), local residents are not the principal beneficiaries. Management positions, which pay

Table 6-2   Job Categories in the Casino Industry

Job Category	Average Percentage of Employees within Casinos
Officials and managers	17.2
Professionals	20.3
Technicians	2.0
Sales workers	3.0
Office and clerical	13.6
Craft workers	3.1
Operatives	0.4
Service workers	37.0
Laborer	2.6

the most, are typically filled by outsiders. The local residents are left with the majority of the other lower-paying jobs, many of which pay the minimum wage. A large number of employees in these low-paying jobs are dependent on tips, which vary depending on the type and volume of clientele.

Table 6-2 gives an overview of the **job categories** created by the casino industry. A review of reports from the New Jersey Casino Control Commission (CCC) reveals that the majority of the jobs paying more than $35,000 are held by non–Atlantic City residents. Additionally, these reports consistently indicate that minority group members are underrepresented in job categories having salaries of more than $35,000.

As a result of this imbalance of job opportunities, the CCC, through its Division of Compliance, has mandated that at least 46 percent of casino employees should be women and at least 25 percent should be minorities. To this end, a quarterly report is prepared by all of the casinos in Atlantic city to monitor their efforts to comply.

As a precaution, before a job with a salary of more than $35,000 can be given to a nonminority, an extensive search must be completed. If no suitable candidate can be found, the Affirmative Action Department must certify that no suitable minority was available for the job. All individuals involved in the casino industry help to generate millions of dollars, initially by their salaries and then by their other spending. Some of the earnings will inevitably be spent in the local community. When employees spend their salaries within a local community, this practice boosts the multiplier effect. The higher the multiplier, the better the economic impact for the community.

So far, we have described only how individual citizens have benefited economically from the casino industry. Taxes are the most important revenue collected by a community with casinos. There are five states within the United States that do not charge a sales tax. None of these states have casino gambling. The sales tax is one of the most rewarding tax imposed by states. Table 6-3 shows the major casino gambling states and the amount of the sales tax they charge. The greater the amount of money spent specifically within the casino industry, the more money the state will be able to collect via sales tax.

A close review of Table 6-3 shows that most of the states have a sales tax of at least 6 percent. Mississippi and Washington charge the largest amount of sales tax with 7.0 percent and 6.5 percent, respectively. In Atlantic City, there is an extra $2, levied per day for all visitors who use any of the hotel's parking lots. The charge is known as a tourism fee, which should go directly to the city for the construction of a throughway into the city. Many of the thirty million visitors to Atlantic City use these parking lots. At the end of the year, this fee accumulates into a handsome purse for the city.

Table 6-4 displays the variety of taxes that are directly associated with the casino industry. It is important to note that the property tax in casino areas is normally much higher than the tax in other commercial and residential areas.

Table 6-3 States and Amount of Sales Tax

State	Sales Tax
Nevada	5.75%
New Jersey	12.00% plus $2.00 tourism fee
South Dakota	4.00%
Colorado	3.00%
Iowa	5.00%
Illinois	5.00%
Connecticut	6.00%
Arizona	5.00%
Louisiana	3.00%
Minnesota	6.00%
Mississippi	6.00%
Oklahoma	4.50%
Washington	6.50%
Wisconsin	5.00%

Actually, one of the complaints by many of the citizens is that immediately after a casino is established within an area, the cost of real estate and property taxes increase tremendously.

The state or the local communities are responsible for determining the amount of the gaming tax to be levied. Some authorities impose a straight 10 percent of the gross revenue, whereas others levy a specific amount for each slot

Table 6-4 Types of Taxes Associated with the Casino Industry

• Gaming privilege and casino entertainment	• Insurance
• Cigarette	• Property
• Alcohol	• Corporate
• Gasoline	• Personal income
• Sales	• Gaming

Table 6-5 Gaming Tax of Selected States

State	Percentage Gaming Tax
Nevada	6.5
New Jersey	8.0
Mississippi	8.0
Louisiana	18.5
Illinois	20.0
Indiana	20.0

machine. In addition, some riverboat states charge an admission fee. All of these methods of taxation help to increase a city's budget. In 1990, it was estimated that more than $286 billion was legally wagered in the United States. It was also calculated that over $9.4 billion was transferred to the local governments and states in taxes (Connecticut Task Force, 1993). These taxes, if used properly, can help many depressed communities significantly.

An inspection of Table 6-5 reveals that the gaming tax can vary from 6.5 percent in Nevada to 20 percent on the riverboats in Illinois and Indiana. In 1992, in Atlantic City, with only twelve casinos, the gaming tax collected was over $255 million (Epifanion, 1993). In 1997 the gross revenue was close to $5 billion, resulting in a gaming tax collection that was over $395 million (Christiansen, 1998).

INFRASTRUCTURAL COSTS AND LIABILITIES OF CASINOS

For any casino to be successful, it should be able to attract large numbers of people. Accessibility by land or air is paramount. In many cases, the lack of adequate highways restricts the profitability of the casino. Also, narrow, unkept roads can cause localized congestion within the community. Apart from inadequate roads, there is an additional problem of parking within the town. This parking issue can also increase the traffic problem. Without exception, large sums of money must be expended for the construction or upgrading of roads and the construction of parking lots within a casino community.

Casinos cause an increase on the demands of other pieces of a city's infrastructure. Signs will be needed to direct casino patrons to the casinos. The demand for water, sewage, and trash collection increases. Moreover, because of the large number of visitors, there will be a need for increased law enforcement officers. These services place extra expenses on the host casino community.

SOCIAL COSTS OF CASINOS

It is difficult to quantify the social cost of a casino on a community. Some of the **social costs** include traffic congestion, air pollution, increased criminal activities, water pollution, and problem gambling. Although many of the infrastructural costs are noticeable and can be quantified, the social costs of problem gambling and the impact on the family cannot be easily accomplished. Some of the invisible social costs of gambling include suicide, bankruptcy, lost of jobs, and domestic violence. Several studies completed in Michigan, Minnesota, and Iowa consistently show that the number of problem gamblers increase at least threefold after the introduction of casino gambling. These figures are higher among adolescent gamblers (Westphal and Rush, 1996).

Invariably, when a casino is built, there is a need for specialized workers who cannot be found within the host community. Large numbers of individuals from other communities and states flock to the new casino destination for employment. These individuals bring different cultures, values, and lifestyles to the host community. Almost by accident, these casino workers make the host community more cosmopolitan. The local community must then make efforts to accommodate these new residents as well as the transient gamblers. Energies must be exerted to balance the social needs of the new residents with the economic costs of providing them with adequate social services.

CAREER OPPORTUNITIES

A casino operation is a labor-intensive enterprise. A small casino would require individuals working within at least seven departments. The essential departments within a casino include human resource management, security, surveillance, accounts, marketing, slots, table games, and food and beverage. Experience is the name of the game within a casino. College education is helpful, but the longer individuals stay within the casino industry, the greater their chance to develop their career. Many of the current casino executives in Atlantic City started as unskilled line staff who worked their way up the ladder.

CONCLUSION

During the past decade there has been a phenomenal growth in the casino industry within the United States. The growth is economically beneficial to both casinos and their host communities. During the next millennium, this increase will continue to grow with the greater accessibility of casinos within the United States. Although there will continue to be opposition from certain groups and communities about the introduction of casinos, the increased employment and taxes will always be a driving force for the legalization of casinos within economically depressed communities.

REVIEW TERMS

economics   job categories

leakage   social costs

income multiplier

REFERENCES

Arthur Andersen. (1996). "Economic Impacts of Casino Industry in the United States." Available at: http://www.americangaming.org/Media/Impact/compare.html

Casino Control Commission. (1994). *Affirmative Action Compliance Quarterly Report, 2nd Quarter.*

Christiansen, Eugene Martin. (1998, August). "A New Entitlement." *International Gaming & Wagering Business*, 19, no. 4, p. 8.

Connecticut Task Force on Casino Gambling. (1993). *Final report—Casino gambling.* Hartford, CT: The Task Force.

Economic Research Associates. (1982). The role of gaming in the Nevada economy. In W. R. Eadington, *The gaming papers: Proceedings of the Fifth National Conference on Gambling and Risk Taking* (vol 8, pp. 223–249). Reno: University of Nevada.

Epifanion, M. (1993, Summer) Where does all of the money go? *Casino Player*, Special Souvenir Edition, 36–37, 52.

Fridgen, J. D. (1991). *Dimensions of tourism.* East Lansing, MI: The Educational Institute of the America Hotel & Motel Association.

Harrah's Survey, "U.S. Casino Industry Revenue." (1996). Available at: http://www.harrahs.com/survey/ce97/ce97_revenue.html

Harrison, K. (1992). Economic effects of commercial gaming in New Jersey. In W. Eadington and J. Cornelius (eds.), *Gambling and commercial gaming essays in business, economic, philosophy and science* (pp. 105–119). Reno.

Raymond, Leslie. (1992). Personal interview, Indiana University of Pennsylvania.

Westphal, J. R., and Rush, J. (1996). Pathological gambling in Louisiana: An epidemiological perspective. *Journal of Louisiana State Medical Society*, 148.

Chapter 7

The Sociological Impact of Casino Gambling

OBJECTIVES

- Discuss factors that promote casino gambling.
- Describe three different types of gamblers.
- List and describe the reasons people gamble.
- Identify some of the social problems associated with casino gambling.
- Name and discuss reactive agencies for gambling addiction.
- Identify and discuss at least four social costs of casino gambling.
- Review at least four factors that contribute to underage gambling.
- Discuss future social trends of gambling.

INTRODUCTION

Gambling has been a part of most cultures throughout civilization. Gambling artifacts have been found in Egyptian tombs as well as in archaeological discoveries in Nevada. Many Native Americans were involved in various forms of gambling thousands of years ago (Nevada Gaming Commission, 1990). There is some speculation that games and gambling were invented as a form of pastime or recreation. It was discovered, however, that invariably some of the participants cheated. The cheating aspect of gambling has haunted its reputation up to the present time.

When the European colonists arrived on the North American continent, the Native Americans were already playing many games of chance. The Europeans also brought with them some of their own games. Many of the gambling games that are played today in the United States came with the colonists during the late sixteenth century. Several of these games originated from games of chance and tournaments held in Europe (American Institute, 1984). When the games changed to gambling, puritan England, the church, and other moralists did not support it. To an extent, the Puritans' rejection of "something for nothing" has continued to the present; gambling is still not accepted in many sectors of society.

One of the objections of legalizing casino gambling is the whole concept of work. The Puritans believed that if you worked hard, you would obtain your reward. The casino industry does not subscribe to that philosophy. Casinos encourage a mentality of "something for nothing," or "easy come, easy go," or "gambling is just entertainment." The problem with this type of entertainment is that it is expensive and can become addictive. Communities should seriously look at the social costs of a casino before approving it within their neighborhood.

A classical example of the unacceptability of gambling is captured in 1866, in Fyodor Dostoyevsky's novel *The Gambler*. In this classic, the society at that time condemns the gambler because he failed to make a positive contribution to society and more directly to his wife's financial need. Dostoyevsky was himself a gambler and was able to empathize with the novel's character. He confessed the "main point is the game itself." The pressures of compulsive gambling were present even at that time with Dostoyevsky's neglect of his wife's financial need.

It is important to highlight some social and historical events to completely appreciate the social impact of casino gambling. During the past fifteen years, there has been a tremendous proliferation of casino gaming within the world. Within the United States, after the legalization of casinos in Atlantic City, casinos have spread on the riverboats and on the Indian reservations. The opening of the gambling frontier has meant that a greater number of Americans and other nationals have increased access to gambling.

The purpose of this chapter is to enlighten its readers about the social impact of the casino industry. This chapter will focus on several social impacts of gambling and casinos on individuals specifically and communities at large.

SOCIAL CONCERNS OF GAMBLING

Puritan values support the viewpoint that a person should work hard and that hard work is good. The whole concept of gambling undermines this philosophy. Historically, we notice that people not only gambled to win, but they became so obsessed with winning that they cheated. This observation also tarnishes the practice of gambling. A typical gambling generalization leads one to imagine that all persons who gamble are cheaters and, hence, dishonest.

One of the concerns about gambling has always been the environment in which it occurs. Historically, in the United States of America, gambling usually occurred in saloons, bars, back rooms, or smoke-filled chambers. There were drinking, music, and women. Cheating in the games was also present. Although the times have changed, there is still the drinking, smoking, and women. Presently, the back rooms have been replaced with glitzy, brightly lit rooms. Women are still there, either as cocktail waitresses or scantily dressed cabaret dancers, and in some cases as gamblers. Included in the above environment, gambling can bring addiction, prostitution, substance abuse, and crime.

The argument for casino gambling in a community usually boils down to economic and social concerns. Many communities that are economically depressed usually present the argument that a casino would provide jobs and help with taxes. On the other hand, those who are against casino gambling usually cite the social costs incurred by communities because of casinos. The situation is a double-edged sword. Can the economic benefits overcome the large social costs?

The increase in the number of casinos caused an increase in the number of people who engage in casino gambling. Interestingly, this increase was also observed in the amount being wagered (Better Government Association, 1993). The pattern will become a vicious circle; as the government makes casino gambling more accessible, more people will gamble, and they will gamble more money.

WHY PEOPLE GAMBLE

Before further discussing the social activities about casinos, it is important to try to understand why people actually gamble. Many theories have been postulated to explain the motivation for gambling. People gamble for many reasons. Brenner (1988) states quite simply that many people gamble to get rich. However, as seen in the following list, the reasons range from boredom to improving one's financial lot.

Reasons People Gamble

1. Greed
2. Snobbery
3. Sexual compensation
4. Boredom
5. Masochism
6. Intellectual exercise
7. Desire to prove one's superiority to the forces of chance

8. Inexplicable excitement
9. Help in attaining unfulfilled goals

Freud, on the other hand, equates some gambling acts as a sublimation for copulation or masturbation. He interprets the acts of blowing the breath of life on dice or cards as sexual in origin. Similarly, Dostoyevsky compares winning with a sexual orgasm (Walker, 1992). Regardless of the reason, some people gamble so much to fulfill one of the above desires that they become addicted.

COMPULSIVE GAMBLING

Between five and ten million people in the United States are considered compulsive gamblers. Additionally, another 3 percent may be considered problem gamblers (Abbott et al., 1995). Lorenz (1995) estimated that as much of 7 percent of teenagers may be addicted to some form of gambling. No type of addiction occurs in a vacuum; it produces several social issues. Three issues we will review are (1) compulsive and problem gambling, (2) underage gambling, and (3) gambling among minorities and low-income individuals.

In 1980, the American Psychiatric Association (APA) officially recognized pathological gambling as a diagnosable mental disorder. This was a landmark in the medical and psychological communities.

Most people view gambling as recreational entertainment, but a number of studies indicate the serious consequences of gambling for specific segments of the population. Compulsive, problem, or pathological gamblers experience adverse reactions to gaming. The 1994 APA *Diagnostic and Statistical Manual (DSM-IV)* notes that the prevalence of pathological gaming may be between 1 and 3 percent, stating that the vagueness of the statistic is due to the limited availability of data (Shaffer, 1997). The *DSM-IV* has enabled practitioners to diagnose and treat patients using specific criteria.

There are several typologies for gamblers. A **problem gambler** is defined as "a person who suffers loss of control over his or her gambling behavior, leading to negative consequences" (Hashimoto, 1995). The Council on Compulsive Gambling of New Jersey gives a problem gambler the following profile:

- 96 percent began gambling before the age of 14 years
- 91 percent had their gambling losses paid off to continue gambling
- 90 percent are men; the remaining 10 percent are women from different ethnic backgrounds
- 17 percent attempted suicide

A **pathological gambler,** also known as a compulsive gambler has a chronic and progressive disorder characterized by emotional dependence, loss of control, and accompanying negative consequences in the gambler's school, social or family life. They have a psychologically uncontrollable preoccupation and urge to gamble. They exhibit similar withdrawal symptoms and tolerance similar to other addictions.

The third type of gambler, **probable pathological gambler,** is an individual who has not been clinically diagnosed but has the behavior and potential to be a pathological gambler.

There are two other types of gamblers worth mentioning. A social gambler is a person who gambles with a predetermined amount of money. This individual is able to curtail his or her gambling activities at any time. Another typology of a gambler is a professional gambler. Professional gamblers choose gambling as a livelihood. They are not addicted to gambling per se; they just prefer gambling to a more conventional way of earning a living. They have a keen knowledge of the games they play and are able to stop and analyze their losses.

Compulsive gamblers can be a serious financial concern for casinos. One of the main problems with compulsive gamblers is that they incur large credits, and when they are required to pay, they declare bankruptcy. Another problem is they sometimes commit white-collar crimes such as fraud, forgery, and embezzlement to support their gambling activities. In some cases, they do not consider themselves to be stealing, but merely borrowing funds they will replace after they win. Unfortunately, these individuals do not always win, and they cause great financial hardship to themselves and their families.

As a result of the increase in compulsive gaming, many casinos, Harrah's being the first, started preventive programs. All of the casinos in Atlantic City now place *"Bet with your head, not over it"* on all of their advertisements. Additionally, these casinos sponsor a gambler hotline for persons who need help with their gambling habits.

The National Council on Compulsive Gambling believes this is a good start, but it is not enough. The council believes that a more effective way to control the disease should be through the following four strategies: (1) Education programs should be conducted in the schools and churches; (2) the media should focus on the negative sides of gambling and the prevalence of addiction; (3) casinos should make a contribution to a fund for gambling education and treatment programs; and (4) casino employees should be trained to recognize signs of compulsive gambling.

One of the problems with gambling addicts is that they are easily accepted in the mainstream of society. Moreover, because these individuals do not have any physical characteristics, they are not helped as much as other addicts. There are only four states, New Jersey, New York, Maryland, and Connecticut, that fund treatment centers for compulsive gamblers. Altogether, there are twelve centers nationwide, which contrasts with two thousand and four thousand centers for drug and alcohol addiction, respectively. The philosophy behind the centers is, "total abstention from further gambling and full payment of debts" (National Council, 1998).

There are two other important self-help groups available for gambling addicts. In 1959, **Gamblers Anonymous** was founded to help compulsive gamblers control their gambling problems. Its membership consists of compulsive gamblers who attend regular meetings. There are no dues. Three conventions are held annually, and a monthly bulletin is published.

In 1960, **Gam-Anon** was sponsored. The members of this group are the spouses of compulsive gamblers. Its purpose is to counsel and aid its members. This group holds informal meetings, which are usually held in churches or halls. No fees are charged, and there are no membership requirements. The members help each other by exchanging telephone numbers and calling each other during crises.

Studies have shown between eight and ten million people in the United States are compulsive gamblers. Claims have been made that legalized gambling particularly victimizes women, youth, and minorities. Although over 90 percent of the members of Gamblers Anonymous are men forty years of age or older, a New York State study found that 36 percent of problem gamblers are women, 32 percent are non-white, and 33 percent are under 30 years of age.

SOCIAL PROBLEMS ACCOMPANYING GAMBLING

We have previously mentioned the need for regulations in the casino industry. Even if all regulations are implemented, the locality must still consider the social problems that have accompanied gambling in cities such as Las Vegas and Atlantic City as well as small towns such as Deadwood, South Dakota. Accepting the fact that gambling brings some social troubles into an area, proactive measures should be taken to minimize these problems.

Deadwood, South Dakota

Undoubtedly, when casino gambling arrives, it brings jobs and more money to an area. However, along with increasing employment and swelling local economies, gambling can be followed by increased crime rates, addiction, misuse of allocated gambling revenue, and possible adverse effects on children.

Deadwood, South Dakota, suffered some of the above effects after gambling was legalized in 1990. Gambling brought more money into the town of Deadwood, but in other ways it has changed the lives of these small-town residents forever.

The population of Deadwood plummeted between the years 1960 and 1980. Because of this, the tax base declined and various city services, including highway maintenance, deteriorated. Summer tourists on their way to Mount Rushmore simply did not spend enough money in Deadwood to compensate for the decreasing tax base.

Deadwood was listed as one of America's eleven most endangered historic places in 1991. After gambling was legalized, many small businesses were sold to real estate developers, causing the community to go without services. More specifically, a drug store, a couple of hardware stores, and a department store were among those that became casinos and souvenir shops. Arrests increased 250 percent, reports of child abuse and neglect increased, and a local chapter of Gamblers Anonymous was founded.

Many families chose to move away rather than subject their children to the many changes occurring in Deadwood. Parents were particularly disturbed by the fact that a drugstore 100 feet from the town's middle and elementary schools was converted into a casino. Parents worried about their children witnessing gambling first hand, but they were also concerned that winners, in their elation, and losers, in their despair, may not be conscious of the children's safety when entering or leaving the casino. The debt and addiction that gambling has brought to the area are also a concern (Brenner, 1988).

Atlantic City, New Jersey

Atlantic City, New Jersey, has also experienced social problems related to gambling. This seaside resort is visited by approximately thirty-three million people annually. The local population has declined by 20 percent, and residents continue to migrate to the suburbs as a result of gambling. Atlantic City has 7,472 casino hotel rooms, but its housing stock is down by at least 15 percent. There are roughly 18,100 slot machines in the city, but one is hard-pressed to locate a car wash or movie theater, and there is only one grocery store.

The police department's budget has more than tripled at $24 million, but Atlantic City's crime rate is the highest in the state (Boardwalk, 1992).

The casinos have created 41,000 new jobs; however, the welfare rolls have also increased and the number of overnight guests at the rescue mission has risen from an average of 25 in 1976 to around 220 today. The revenues from the casinos do assist the local taxpayer by contributing to the funding of public education (Boardwalk, 1992).

Some people contend that gambling contributes to broken homes, depression, and suicide as well as prostitution, drunkenness, and organized crime. Americans placed legal bets worth more than $286 billion in 1990, which was about 5 percent of our gross national product. This is well over the $213 billion that was spent on elementary and secondary education.

UNDERAGE GAMBLERS

There is a growing population of **underage gamblers.** In 1991, it was estimated that there were at least one million compulsive teenage gamblers in the United States (Chavira, 1991). Currently, the legal age for gambling and alcohol consumption in

Atlantic City and Nevada is twenty-one years. Many teenagers enter the casinos illegally and receive all of the benefits such as drinks, food, and complimentary (comps) items. It is the casino's responsibility to prevent these minors from entering.

The issue of underage gamblers is a concern because teens are creative in obtaining money to gamble. Although they have limited budgets, they sometimes resort to dishonest means, such as selling drugs, stealing money from someone they live with, or committing other types of stealing to acquire funds. Another concern about teens in casinos is that they will have access to alcohol, which is also illegal. The problem of underage gambling has caused even the casinos in Atlantic City to be concerned. In the twelve casinos, more than 200,000 underage persons were stopped and escorted off the casino floors and premises in 1992. As a result of this increasing problem, Harrah's Casino initialed a program called **Project 21**, which discourages teenage gamblers (Bennett, 1993).

Adolescence is a time of rapid growth and change emotionally, socially, and physically. It also represents a time of experimentation. During this period many adolescents begin drinking, smoking, engaging in sex, and engaging in gambling. Excessive risk taking and the use of various substances decreases with maturity, and the excitement brought about by gambling will be replaced by alternate activities. For adolescents at risk of developing gambling disorders, this is a critical period (Gupta, 1998). The 1994 meta-analysis by Harvard Medical School found that adolescents and college students have higher rates of gambling than adults in the general population, and females have lower gambling rates than males (Shaffer, 1997).

The number of underage pathological gamblers is expected to increase even more in the future because of the video machines that are used in the casinos. These machines determine winners quickly and are very similar to other video games underage gamblers have used legally. As more casinos open up with these video games, it will be interesting to see how this affects the number of underage gamblers being stopped or barred from entering casinos. Interestingly, just as there is an increase in the number of adult problem gamblers, there has also been an increase of underage gamblers. This should not be surprising because teenagers now have more models and accessibility to casino gambling. Unfortunately, a significant number of the underage gamblers also have a gambling problem.

CASINOS AND CRIMINAL ACTIVITIES

Historically, casinos have always been associated with crime. At the turn of the century, casinos were looked upon as places for unsavory personalities. Sometimes these characters were the operators; at other times, they were the gamblers themselves. Sometimes gamblers became victims of criminals. Although casinos in the main have been regulated, there is still some dishonesty associated with gambling outside of the operation of the casino.

Many criminals try to launder money inside a casino; that is, they try to use illegitimate money inside casinos to make it become legal. To combat this activity, the Internal Revenue Service (IRS) has mandated that any individual who wins more than $10,000 must complete a **Currency Transaction Report (CTR).** This form is then reported to the IRS to record legal gambling earnings (Rucsher, 1993).

Inevitably, there is an increase in the number of persons in an area wherever there is a casino. Casinos have been shown to be a catalyst for a variety of crimes. Some of the crimes associated with casinos include street crimes, prostitution, drugs, and embezzlement. Occasionally, casino patrons are drugged, robbed, or pickpocketed (Connecticut Task Force, 1993).

Although this topic is not openly discussed in public, there is a high incidence of prostitution in casino locations. Many prostitutes are attracted to places with casinos. Gambling is a perfect environment for prostitution. Sometimes, a person who wins money wants a companion with which to share it. Conversely, people who lose money may want someone to comfort them and make them forget about it. Prostitutes fit the bill in both occasions. In Nevada, prostitution is legal in certain areas. In contrast, in New Jersey, it is illegal and not tolerated (Pritchard, 1991). Some casinos also provide prostitutes for their high rollers (Connecticut Task Force, 1993). It seems that prostitutes are a factor that must be calculated into some casino environments.

The casino industry, especially in Atlantic City, is very concerned about drug and alcohol abuse. During the past decade, serious efforts have been exerted to rid the industry of employees who use illegal drugs or abuse alcohol. Many companies subscribe to a drug-free environment, which includes a preemployment drug-testing program. Afterward, employers can send employees for random drug tests during their tenure with the company (Davis, 1993). Employers also provide drug rehabilitation programs for employees who voluntarily seek help.

Loan sharking is another social phenomenon that is common in the casino industry. This activity is a concern to the image of the casino industry for several reasons. First, it is illegal. Second, patrons who participate in loan sharking may be forced to participate in illegal activities to repay their debts. These illegal activities may include forgery, fraud, and extortion.

NEGATIVE IMPACTS OF CASINO GAMBLING

Two factors that contribute to compulsive gambling are legalization and accessibility. Thus, with the increase of casino venues, accessibility is also increased. The same two factors also contribute to pathological gambling. Therefore, as more casinos open, there is also a greater probability of increasing the number of pathological gamblers.

Compulsive or pathological gamblers are a concern to a casino community for many reasons. Some research indicates treatment cost may vary from $3,000

When does gambling become "compulsive"?

INTRODUCTION

Gambling in one form or another has been with us since the dawn of time. Certainly, today, gambling is widespread throughout North American society.

For most people, gambling is a pleasurable pursuit, providing relaxation for some, a release from tension to others.

To a certain percentage of the adult population, however, gambling is much more than that. It is a way of life, one which is bound to cause growing problems in many areas.

While exact statistics are not readily available, estimates point to some three percent of the adult population being pathological (compulsive) gamblers.

It may seem like rather a small statistic but it translates into hundreds of thousands of Canadians!

This pamphlet is aimed at those people, their families, friends and employers. Unfortunately, many of them are probably not even aware of the problem and have an urgent need to be informed.

WHAT IS COMPULSIVE GAMBLING?

Compulsive gambling may be most easily described as a progressive behavioural disorder in which an individual has a psychologically uncontrollable preoccupation and urge to gamble. This results in excessive gambling, the outcome of which is the loss of time, money and self-esteem.

The gambling reaches a point at which it compromises, disrupts and ultimately destroys the gambler's personal life, family relationships and vocational pursuits.

These problems in turn lead to intensification of the gambling behaviour. The cardinal features are emotional dependence on gambling, loss of control and interference with normal functioning.

Compulsive gamblers develop a need to gamble, just as an alcoholic has a need to drink or a heroin addict has the need to "shoot up." What he or she is looking for is the "high" that comes from being involved in gambling activities.

This feeling of elation is more important to the compulsive gambler than winning or losing. It's the action that counts!

THE EARLY SIGNS OF COMPULSIVE GAMBLING

The American Psychiatric Association has officially labeled compulsive gambling as a disorder of impulse control. In other words, a person may be diagnosed as a compulsive gambler if he or she has been unable to control chronic gambling and if the gambling has continued despite causing harm to family, friends or employers.

Unfortunately, many compulsive gamblers are not diagnosed as such until the late chronic stages of the disorder. In most cases, family members, friends, co-workers and employers simply are not able to recognize the symptoms.

But this does not have to be the case!

Definite patterns of compulsive gambling manifest themselves early in a person's life and can be readily observed by anyone familiar with the telltale signs. These early signs are invaluable in recognizing the need for intervention.

WHAT TO LOOK FOR SPECIFICALLY

How much time is spent gambling? This is a key element in judging a person's addiction to gambling. He or she may have a real problem if the amount of time spent gambling is excessive as perceived by general standards or, if the time spent gambling is out of proportion with the person's other activities. Listening to, or watching several sports events at the same time, could spell trouble even if the person does not admit to having wagered on a number of events.

Increasing the size and frequency of wagers. This is often the telltale sign of a person chasing lost money and trying to get even. The tendency to bet larger amounts more frequently often characterizes the real onset of compulsive gambling.

Absenteeism: Frequent, unexplained absences from work or home are common signs of a gambling problem, particularly if the person is secretive about how the time is spent. A compulsive gambler will often spend an inordinate amount of time making telephone calls which he tries to conceal. Absence from work or normal home activities to attend the races or play cards may also indicate a gambling problem.

Bravado: A social gambler may talk jokingly of a bet he won but he never belabors the point. Boasting about winning and minimizing losses are signs of compulsive gambling. The need for recognition of power, the big shot image, is a vital ingredient to a compulsive gambler.

Mercurial Mood Changes: Compulsive gamblers experience highs when they win and lows when they lose. Severe mood swings are common characteristics of all addictive behaviour but compulsive gambling is at the head of the class. Often, a compulsive gambler will be able to shake the blues merely by the thought of going into action again soon. The problem gambler is under constant pressure for action. If he is unable to get it, he takes out his hostility on those close to him - his family, friends and co-workers.

Financial Resources: A compulsive gambler always is in need of money. He will do anything, often of an anti-social nature, to acquire it to feed his habit. Secret loans, withdrawals from family bank accounts and hidden deals are surefire signs of compulsive gambling. While a social gambler will work to make up for money lost gambling, an addicted gambler will come up with a variety of schemes to acquire funds. When he has exhausted legal means, he will invariably turn to criminal actions. Embezzling money from an employer is common. The compulsive gambler, however, never considers his action as stealing. He rationalizes it by claiming he is merely borrowing the money and will return it as soon as he makes a big score. Unfortunately, of course, this rarely happens. Sooner or later the compulsive gambler's actions are discovered and he, as well as his family and friends, have to pay the consequences.

Special Occasions: A person may be diagnosed as having a gambling problem if he or she insists on spending free or vacation time where some form of gambling is available. Compulsive gamblers have been known even to plan their honeymoons to coincide with the availability of a casino or race track.

Good Time to Gamble. A compulsive gambler doesn't need much of an excuse to gamble. He will do it under almost any circumstances, good or bad. He will gamble to feel better when facing a crisis. He will gamble when facing a disappointment. But he will also gamble to celebrate good fortune such as a birth, a promotion, a pay raise.

The Compulsive Trait: Compulsive gamblers often are people with high energy levels who are intolerant of boredom. They are usually charming and attractive personalities but have low self-esteem. They are often overachievers.

The Big Score: A common characteristic of a compulsive gambler is his quest for the "big score." It is this faith in his or her future ability to hit it big that keeps them going, often enduring countless heartaches. There is no evidence that any compulsive gambler ever hit it big. On the contrary, compulsive gamblers often wind up at the extreme other end of the social scale, - destitute, bereft of family and friends and alone!

Signs of compulsive gambling. Source: Canadian Foundation on Compulsive Gambling (Ontario) and Casino Niagara, Niagara Falls, Ontario.

to $10,000 per gambler. Another concern for these gamblers is the gambling debts they incur. A report by Dr. Rachel Volberg indicates patients in treatment may have gambling debts ranging from $35,000 to $92,000. Invariably, many of the gamblers declare bankruptcy.

All of the social costs listed below are inevitably paid by the casino community. Psychologists speculate that one pathological gambler will affect ten to seventeen persons. The gambling problem can manifest itself in the form of physical and psychological abuse of spouses and children. In severe cases of compulsive gambling, divorce and suicides are contemplated and pursued (Better Government Association, 1992).

Social Costs of Casino Gambling

- Rehabilitation costs
- Gambling debts
- Insurance company costs
- Loss of productivity at work
- Bankruptcy declaration
- White-collar crime costs
- Family problems
- Borrowed money
- Abusive relations
- Police costs

Casino gambling causes work-related problems that are normally overlooked within a casino environment. Many employers fail to recognize certain actions of compulsive gamblers. Several signs of problems with gambling revealing itself on the job are borrowing money from other employees, asking for salary advances, gambling on the job, stealing company property, and being late for and absent from work (Better Government Association, 1992).

SOCIAL CONCERNS OF CASINO EMPLOYEES

The lives of casino employees are not as picture perfect as many people believe. Yes, jobs are created, but at what price? For many employees, working in a casino can be very stressful. Many casinos are open twenty-four hours, which requires at least three shifts. During these shifts, casino employees are sometimes victims of sexual harassment and racial discrimination by patrons. They are also subjected to working within a smoke-filled room. Moreover, casinos are not ordinarily quiet. Players yell at employees because they are losing, winners scream because they're winning, and constantly there are the ringing noises of slot machines in the background. This is a stressful atmosphere.

Working within an "excited" environment without exposure to the outside, or an awareness of time, can affect an employee's health. Reports have indicated that there is a high incidence of substance abuse among casino employees. Casino employees also have other stress-related problems such as anorexia, panic attacks, and back problems.

Many casino employees also have gambling problems. After their shifts, they go to other casinos and gamble. Some casinos encourage this practice by providing check-cashing facilities for employees who wish to gamble. This practice can be the foundation for other serious social pathological problems.

MINORITIES AND LOW-INCOME INDIVIDUALS

When looking at the sociological impact of casino gambling on a community, it is essential to look at the repercussions of gambling on minorities and low-income individuals. Research has shown that there is an overrepresentation of minorities and low-income individuals as compulsive gamblers (Better Government Association, 1992). Studies have also revealed that these individuals are less likely to receive treatment for their gambling problems. If compulsive gambling continues to grow among minorities and low-income individuals, it is quite likely that gambling will be a significant contributing factor to homelessness.

FUTURE SOCIAL TRENDS

There will be an increase in the number of casinos both in the United States and the rest of the world. Communities will have to implement strict policies to counteract the social challenges of having a casino. The issues of drug abuse, prostitution, loan sharking, and underage gambling will not be washed away. These social problems that plague the casino industry must be attacked head on. Future casino developers must try to find solutions for these problems in their specific communities. Although there are many economic benefits from a casino, it must be carefully weighed to determine whether the economic benefits really outweigh the social cost.

In 1993 President Bill Clinton signed the National Gambling and Policy Commission Act. This act provided for a commission to study the social, economic, legal, and illegal aspects of gambling within the United States of America. In 1998 hearings were held with several individuals actively involved in the gambling industry. The hearings revealed that gaming is being marketed specifically to both seniors and young people, with strong emphasis on the seniors (Weed, 1998).

Ronald Karpin indicated there was an increase in the number of calls at the 1-800-GAMBLER hotline. He similarly agreed with Ed Weed that seniors were being targeted as good potential future clients (Karpin, 1998). During the same hearing before the Commission, Kevin O'Neill indicated there was an increase in the number of adolescents gambling. He emphasized the results of the study by

Dr. Henry Lesieur and Dr. Durand Jacobs that indicated at least 50 percent of high school students had gambled for money during the past twelve months (O'Neill, 1998).

The testimony at the National Gambling Impact Study Commission revealed there are many opportunities for legalized gambling within the United States of America. The study also indicated there was a rise in the number of pathological gamblers in the population at large. One way to combat the ever-increasing spread of gambling is to have mandated education programs for grades K–12. It has also been suggested that the advertising of gambling be placed in a category similar to tobacco promotion in light of the research indicating that gambling is addictive (Looney, 1998).

CONCLUSION

Marketing promotion describes casino gambling as adult entertainment. Some religious organizations, such as the Mormons and the Methodists, have voiced their objections to the expansion of casino gambling on moral grounds. This chapter highlights some of the social consequences of casino gambling. Some of these challenges can be overcome by consistent enforcement of the law and the education of the public at large about gambling. Additionally, there is a need by both casinos and regulatory agencies to help with the ongoing concern of compulsive and underage gamblers. The model used by the U.S. Surgeon General and the cigarette industry may be helpful.

REVIEW TERMS

compulsive gambler

Currency Transaction Report (CTR)

Gam-Anon

Gamblers Anonymous

pathological gambler

probable pathological gambler

problem gambler

Project 21

underage gamblers

REFERENCES

Abbott, D. A., Sheran, L., Cramer, J., and Sherrets, S. D. (1995). Pathological gambling and the family: Practice implications. *Families in Society* 76 (4):213–217.

American Institute of Certified Public Accountants. (1984). Audits of casinos: Prepared by the Gaming Industry Special Committee. New York: American Institute of Certified Public Accountants.

Bennett, H. (1993). Affirmative Action Representative, lecture presentation.

Better Government Association. (1993). Staff White Paper: Casino gambling in Chicago.

Boardwalk. (1992). Newspaper pamphlet from Atlantic City.

Brenner, G. R. (1988). Why people gamble? Reno: The gambling research. Proceedings of the Seventh International Conference on Gambling and Risk Taking, p. 95.

Chavira, R. (1991). The rise of teenage gambling: A distressing number of youths are bitten early by the betting bug. *Time*, 25 February, 78.

Connecticut Task Force on Casino Gambling (1993). Final report: Casino gambling. Hartford, Connecticut: The Task Force.

Davis, W. (1993). Human Resource Associate, Resort Casino, lecture presentation.

Frank, M. L. (1990). Underage gambling in Atlantic City casinos. *Psychological Reports* 67:907–912.

Gupta, R. (1998). An empirical examination of Jakobs' general theory of addiction. *Journal of Gambling Studies* 14(1):17–46.

Hashimoto, C. (1995). Gambling addiction: Casinos and the actual act of gambling, the cause of gambling addiction, or other people with personalities who are predisposed to addictive gambling. Paper presented for the Association for Casino Gambling at CHRIE.

Karpin, R. J. (1998). Testimony to the National Gambling Impact Study Commission. Available at: http://www.800gambler.org/testimony_ron.htm

Looney, E. (1998). Testimony to the National Gambling Impact Study Commission. Available at: http://www.800gambler.org/testimony_elooney.htm

Lorenz, V. (1995). *The national impact of casino gambling proliferation.* Hearing before the Committee on Small Business, House of Representatives, 103rd Congress, 2nd sess. Washington D.C., September 21, 1994.

National Council on Compulsive Gambling Pamphlet.

Nevada Gaming Commission & State Gaming Control Board. (1990). *Gaming Nevada style.* Carson City, Nevada: SPO.

O'Neill, K. (1998). Testimony to the National Gambling Impact Study Commission. Available at: http://www.800gambler.org/Testimony_koneill.htm

Pritchard, M. (1991). A.C. tries to put the squeeze on prostitution. *Atlantic City, New Jersey, The Press* 18 August.

Rucsher, P. (1993). Casino Controller, Harrah's Casino, lecture presentation.

Shaffer, Howard, Hall, M., and Bilt, J. (1997). Estimating the prevalence of disorder gambling behavior in the United States and Canada: A meta-analysis. *Harvard Medical School*, 1–87.

Walker, M. B. (1992). *The psychology of gambling.* New York: Pergamon Press.

Chapter 8

Native American Gambling

OBJECTIVES

- Identify at least five events that facilitate Native American gaming in the United States.
- Describe the three different classes of Indian gaming.
- Identify the steps needed for a tribal-state compact.
- Describe the role of the National Indian Gaming Commission.
- Discuss the arguments of the Tenth and Eleventh Amendments that states present to prevent Indian Class III gaming.
- Identify the states with thriving Indian gaming.

INTRODUCTION

This chapter examines the evolution of Indian gambling and reviews the role of the National Indian Gaming Commission. Next, it describes the rationale and function of the Indian Gaming Regulatory Act. Later, it looks specifically at the structure and challenges faced by Native Americans in their quest to obtain legalized gambling within their reservations. A review also is made of some of the economic and social challenges Native American tribes face. Afterward, we review the various classifications of Indian gambling. Finally, we will scrutinize the states and sites that currently have legalized Indian gambling and look at the function of the National Indian Gaming Association.

EVOLUTION OF INDIAN GAMING

In the United States, Native American (Indian) reservations are sovereign, self-ruling nations. Sovereignty should mean that the Native American nations can establish their own laws and regulate their citizens on their own land (reservations). Native Americans should be free from the control of state and local governments. This provision is one of the bases for widespread gambling on Native American reservations within the United States.

Throughout this chapter, the term *Native American* will be used interchangeably with *Indian*. The term *Indian* is being used specifically to conform to the wording of the legislature. The authors fully accept and respect that the first inhabitants on the continent of North America should be called generically Native Americans. We also recognize that there are many Native American nations or tribes.

Currently, there are 557 federally recognized Native American reservations. Although only approximately one-third of them engage in some form of commercial gaming activities, many non-Indian gaming companies are jubilant about their presence and their ability to participate in the casino industry with almost no interference from the state or federal government. How did this anomaly happen?

Table 8-1 shows a historical time line of significant events that shaped Native American gaming in the United States.

Prior to the arrival of the Europeans, the first inhabitants on the North American continent controlled power, culture, and gaming activities. After the Europeans arrived, many things changed. The original residents were abused physically and culturally and were deprived of their possessions of land, minerals, and livestock. Following this initial period of abuse, they were then physically removed from their green luscious environment and misplaced into all areas of the torrid southwestern part of the continent.

In 1824 the Bureau of Indian Affairs (BIA) was created to oversee all affairs of the Native American Indians (Schlesinger, 1988). Its primary duty was to provide economic assistance to all of the Native Americans living on reservations. This act was, however, challenged in the Supreme Court in 1831. In the *Cherokee Nation v. Georgia*, the Court ruled that the Indian Nation had complete legal rights to manage their own affairs. Later, when the Native Americans were placed on reservations (1840–1910) by the Bureau of Indian Affairs, the white settlers were given their land. In 1887, the General Allotment Act, also known as the Dawes Severalty Act, gave small parcels of reservation land to individual families. This act broke up the Indian land claims and destroyed tribal government.

This period was followed by the Indian Reorganization Act (1935–1950). During this time, Indian tribes were further broken up, and purposeful efforts were made to make Native Americans become "brown farmers." The 1950s and 1960s was a time wherein Native American tribes tried to bring some closure in their relationship with the U.S. government. Concerted efforts were made to

Table 8–1   Historical Highlights of Native American and Gaming Activities

Time Period	Significant Events
B.C.	Before Columbus—Native American tribes held the balance of power
1824	Formation of the Bureau of Indian Affairs
1825–1840	Removal of Native American nations
1831	*Cherokee Nation v. Georgia*
1840–1910	Reservation
1885–1910	Allotment
1887	General Allotment Act
1935–1950	Indian Reorganization Act
1950–1968	Termination
1970–1990	Self-determination
1976	*Bryant v. Itasca County*
1979	*Seminole Tribe v. Butterworth*
1985	Native Indian Gaming Association
1987	*Cabazon Band of Mission Indians v. California*
1988	Indian Gaming Regulatory Act
1993	Native Indian Gaming Commission
1993	Opening of Foxwood Casino, Ledyard, Connecticut, with slot machines

obtain recognition and reclaim some of the land that was taken away fraudulently. The late 1970s and 1980s were a time of legal action.

Attempts to develop Indian gaming started in 1976 (Connor, 1993). During that year, a U.S. Supreme Court ruling, *Bryan v. Itasca County,* declared that states did not have regulatory jurisdiction over Indian tribes. This was a landmark case for Indian gaming. In 1979, *Seminole Tribe v. Butterworth* was a case in Florida in which the Court decided that the state could not "prohibit Indian bingo because it does not have the regulatory power over the tribe" (Connor, 1993). In *Cabazon Band of Mission Indians v. California,* 1987, the Court further ruled that it did not have jurisdiction to prohibit Indians from engaging in gaming.

On October 17, 1988, Congress passed the Indian Gaming Regulatory Act (IGRA). This act permitted legalized gambling by Native American tribes on their home state (Connor, 1993). During the years that followed, several suits were entered by Indian tribes against various states. Eventually, in 1993, the National Indian Gaming Commission (NIGC) issued its final rules, which defined the terms for the Indian Gaming Regulatory Act.

A question of paramount importance needs to be asked. Why has there been such a push by the Native American Indian tribes to have gaming? First, it is important to understand that as a sovereign nation, the tribal leaders and governments have the same responsibilities as other governments to provide a certain quality of life for their people. Many of the tribal governments have tried different means of raising finance. So far the most successful method of raising finance has been through gaming profits.

Before the introduction of the IGRA, several Indian nations were operating small bingo parlors. This movement evolved into high-stakes games, which attracted people from many miles away. Now, Indians are involved in all types of casinos with electronic bingo, video gaming devices, and regular casinos. The 115 Native American Indian tribes who are now engaged in gaming are responsible for 5 percent of the entire gaming industry. This accounts for approximately $5 billion.

NATIONAL INDIAN GAMING ASSOCIATION

In 1985 the **National Indian Gaming Association (NIGA)** was established as a nonprofit organization to represent Indian tribes and organizations involved in tribal gaming throughout the United States. Its main objective is to "protect and preserve the general welfare of tribes striving for self-sufficiency through gaming enterprises in Indian Country (NIGA, 1993)." This association serves as a clearinghouse and public policy resource for decision makers on Indian gaming and liaises with the federal government on Indian gaming matters. Currently, the NIGA represents more than one hundred Native American Indian organizations; it acts as their lobbying group and is a strong advocate for their sovereignty.

Two cases heralded the Indian Gaming Regulatory Act (IGRA). The first case occurred in Florida. In 1979, *Seminole Tribe v. Butterworth* was tried. In this landmark case, the Seminole tribe had opened a high-stakes bingo operation that exceeded the normal Florida state prize limit. Sheriff Butterworth wanted to close the operation. The matter was taken to the courts of Florida, which ruled that the state could not regulate a statute for Native Americans that was not prohibited within the state. In 1987, the United States Supreme Court ruled on the case of *Cabazon Band of Mission Indians v. California*. The Court affirmed that the Cabazons had the rights to conduct gambling operations on reservation soil without the interference of state laws.

INDIAN GAMING REGULATORY ACT

The **Indian Gaming Regulatory Act (IGRA)** was passed in 1988 because many Indian tribes had become involved in gaming activities. The purpose of the act was "to establish a regulatory structure that balances the rights of states and tribes-states' rights to maintain public health and safety and tribes' rights to promote economic development, self-sufficiency and strong tribal governments" (Greenberg and Zelio, 1992). The act gave Native Americans exclusive rights to regulate all gaming activities on their land. This document is important because it established the National Indian Gaming Commission (NIGC) and stated the responsibilities of the chair and the powers of the commission. In addition, the act created three classes of Native American Indian gaming.

TYPES OF INDIAN GAMING

Class I gaming includes social games solely for prizes of minimal values or traditional forms of Indian gaming. Games in this class were played by individuals as part of, or in connection with, tribal ceremonies or celebrations. All gaming in this class is under the exclusive jurisdiction of the tribe.

Class II gaming is "subject to tribal regulatory jurisdiction with an extensive oversight by the National Indian Gaming Commission" (Alexander, 1993). This class includes games of general chance, such as bingo, instant bingo, lotto, pull tabs, punch boards, and tip jars. This class does not include any electronic or electromechanical facsimiles, or any slot machines of any kind. A tribe is allowed to license and regulate gaming in this category when practiced on Native American land or reservations.

Class III gaming includes all other forms of gaming not included in the other two classes. Included in this class are casino games, slots, banking card games, jai alai, pari-mutuel wagering, and horse and dog racing (Connor, 1993). "Class III gaming is lawful on Indian land only if the gaming has been authorized by a tribal ordinance and approved by the chairperson of the NIGC" (Alexander, 1993). For Indians to participate in class III gaming, the specific type of gaming must be practiced by other organizations within the state. The Indian tribe must then enter a tribal-state compact between itself and the state to make class III gaming legal (Alexander, 1993).

A tribal-state compact is an agreement between a tribe and a state. It outlines the procedures for licensing, terms of the contracts, taxation by the tribes, gaming regulations, and the cost for the administration of the gaming. The chair of the NGIC must first approve the ordinances for class III gaming. The document must be approved by the Secretary of the Interior, and later submitted to the state.

The term **good faith** is defined as an attempt by the state "to assume that the interest of both sovereign entities are met . . . [through] a viable mechanism for setting various matters between two equal sovereignties" (NIGA, 1993). Several tribes have claimed that their states have not acted in good faith.

This is an important concern because all tribes wishing to engage in class III gaming must make a declaration to the state. The state may negotiate in good faith. If the state does not negotiate in good faith, the tribe may file action against the state to the Secretary of the Interior. The burden of proof is then on the state to determine the contrary. The court may appoint a mediator to assist with the negotiation. The mediator makes recommendations to the Secretary of the Interior who establishes procedures for the implementation of class III gaming consistent with the state's laws and practices. For example, if bingo, dog racing, and casino nights currently take place within the state, it is possible for a tribe to petition for a compact to conduct the same gaming events.

THE NATIONAL INDIAN GAMING COMMISSION

The Bureau of Indian Affairs was responsible for all matters that related to Indians. In 1988, the Indian Gaming Regulation Act (IGRA) was passed, and the National Indian Gaming Commission (NIGC) was established as a part of the Department of the Interior. Its full-time membership consists of a chair and two associate members. The chair is appointed by the President of the United States to serve three years. The associate members are appointed by the Secretary of the Interior. One of them serves a three-year term, and the other serves an initiate term of one year. Two of the members of the commission must be members of an Indian tribe, and no more than two members can be from the same political party. The commission meets at least once every four months, and at least two members, one being the chair or vice chair, are required for a quorum. The commission also employs a general consul who is appointed by the chair.

The commission's powers include the ability to charge fees, issue civil fines, distribute permanent orders, and require subpoenas for individuals or documents for an investigation over class III gaming. Its powers also consist of scrutinizing the conditions of the contracts and the backgrounds of individuals involved in gaming, as well as determining management contracts. Other responsibilities of the commission include monitoring, inspection of premises, hearings, oaths, regulations, and investigations.

The NIGC is responsible for reviewing the regulations adopted by the leadership of the Indian tribe. Once the regulations have been submitted, they must be approved by the chair of the NIGC. An important concern of the chair is that the Indian tribes "have the sole proprietary interest and responsibility" for conducting the gaming activities. The chair also tries to verify that the net revenues from Indian gaming are channeled toward promoting tribal economic activity, donated to charitable organizations, as well as used to fund tribal government operations and programs. Each registered member of the tribe receives a per capita payment if the tribe originally submitted a plan to the commission.

The NIGC is funded by each establishment that operates a class II gaming activity. The members of the commission vote on the fee, which is allocated in two scales. The first scale is a fee of "no less than 0.5 percent nor more than 2.5 percent of the first $1,500,000," and the second fee is "no more than 5 percent of amounts in excess of the first $1,500,000" of the gross revenue. The regulations indicate that the maximum amount of fee cannot exceed $1,500,000 (Mikelberg, 1992).

In 1995 at least 115 tribes were involved in class III gaming activities. There were also at least 131 tribal-state compacts in twenty-three states. Table 8-2 shows that there are Native American class I and class II gaming activities in

Table 8-2   Native American States with Compacts and Casinos, 1998

Number of States	Compact States	Number of Casinos
1	Arizona	17
2	California	12
3	Colorado	2
4	Connecticut	2
5	Idaho	3
6	Iowa	3
7	Kansas	4
8	Louisiana	3
9	Michigan	7
10	Minnesota	11
11	Mississippi	1
12	Montana	6
13	Nebraska	1
14	Nevada	6
15	New Mexico	16
16	New York	2
17	North Carolina	1
18	North Dakota	5
19	Oklahoma	7
20	Oregon	9
21	Rhode Island	1
22	South Dakota	9
23	Washington	18
24	Wisconsin	11

twenty-nine states; the states with the majority of Native American gaming activities are California, Oklahoma, Washington, Arizona, and Wisconsin, respectively. These states participate in both class I and II gaming activities. These games of chance vary from pari-mutuel wagering to full-fledged casinos with entertainment and slot machines.

PENDING LEGISLATION AND INDIAN LITIGATION

Although at least twenty-nine states currently permit tribes to engage in gambling, the following eleven states have litigation pending against them by Indian tribes:

- Alabama
- Florida
- Michigan
- Mississippi
- Montana
- New Mexico
- New York
- North Dakota
- Oklahoma
- South Dakota
- Washington

The grounds for most of the litigation have been the states' claim of sovereign immunity as provided in the Eleventh Amendment of the U.S. Constitution. States claim that gaming is challenging some of the powers given to them in the Tenth Amendment. In most cases, the two aforementioned challenges have been articulated as defenses after tribes have claimed that the states have not negotiated in good faith to allow them to engage in class III gaming (Monteau, 1993).

Two of the current defenses used against the tribes by states have been the Tenth and Eleventh Amendments. The **Tenth Amendment** asserts that Congress cannot tell a state, which has its own sovereignty and freedom, what it must do. As a defense, some states, in their defiance of IGRA, are saying that the U.S. federal government cannot force a state to do something that is not written in the state's constitution. In addition, some of these states are claiming that they do not wish to be involved in any type of gaming, and the terms of the IGRA force them to become involved because it is necessary to obtain the state's approval to engage in class III gaming.

On the other hand, the **Eleventh Amendment** protects states from being sued. In this case, when a Native American tribe attempts to sue a state because the state refused to bargain in good faith, the states are saying it is illegal. The defense here is that "Congress lacks the power to subject states to suits by tribes, even in the exercise of the plenary federal power provided by the Indian Commerce Clause of the U.S. Constitution." Some states further argue that without a state's consent to suit, "federal courts have no jurisdiction over them" (Crowell and Strauss, 1993).

ECONOMIC IMPACT OF GAMBLING ON SELECTED NATIVE AMERICAN INDIAN TRIBES

Undeniably, the opening of a casino on an Indian reservation has improved the economic climate of the area. Many of the reservations are located in rural, undeveloped areas of the states. These areas do not have the infrastructure to accommodate any type of industry. With the arrival of a casino, the economic climate improves. Large sums of money are spent to construct casino buildings. Local construction increases, and more jobs are available in the communities.

A study of three states—Wisconsin, Minnesota, and Michigan—revealed that many residents on Indian reservations in the states were unemployed or on welfare (Marks, 1993). With the arrival of the casinos, the level of both welfare and unemployment decreased considerably. Table 8-3 illustrates several aspects of the economic impact of Indian gambling within these states.

Some of the revenues generated from the casinos become payroll. This payroll is spent on the Indian reservation not only by Indians, but also by non-Indians who create an economic multiplier effect to the local area within a one- to two-hundred-mile radius. The end result is that both the Native American reservation and the local area and the state benefit from the casinos. Within the above states, the level of unemployment and welfare dropped considerably. In some communities, the number of felony crimes on the reservations also decreased.

Table 8-3   Economic Impact of Indian Gambling in Three States

	Wisconsin	**Minnesota**	**Michigan**
Number of class III facilities	15	17	8
Total number of employees	4,500	9,975	1,931
Percentage of non-Indian employees	44.4	75.0	38.0
Estimated payroll	$68 million	$116 million	$13.5 million
State income taxes	$18 million	$37 million	$700,000*

*State and federal tax

EXTERNAL CONCERNS

Nevada and New Jersey are extremely concerned about all of the casinos spring-ing up on Indian reservations for several reasons. Initially, the main reason for objection may have been a fear of loss of market share of casino profit. On the other hand, they may really have some legitimate concerns. America at large is just becoming accustomed to widespread gambling. One of the main stereotypes about gambling is that it has been controlled or influenced by the mob. Although many Americans are still not convinced this is false, there is a fear that criminal elements may become involved in gambling on the Native American reservations because of their lack of experience in this area of business (Rum-bolz, 1988).

Another concern about gaming on Indian reservations is the licensing process. Vigilant observers have indicated that there is a need for a more com-prehensive and strict system of regulation and background investigation. The same zealousness that is seen in Nevada or New Jersey is not seen within the licensing process on Indian reservations. The immediate problem here is that the integrity and public confidence of the industry come under question. Other crit-ics also indicate that the original reason for gambling on Indian reservations was to improve the local economy. However, several of the contracts for class III gam-ing are now contracted to non-Indian corporations and the Indians are not the greatest beneficiaries. Furthermore, only a small percentage of Native Americans actually work in the casinos. Without exception, when Native Americans are working within the casinos, they are not in any supervisory or management posi-tions (Rumbolz, 1988).

There are several other very important concerns about Indian gaming. Because these casinos are located on reservations, it is impossible, or at least extremely difficult, to enforce state laws because of their tribal sovereignty. This restriction makes it difficult to oversee criminal activities. Some activities of great concern are money laundering, fraud, and skimming, which may be problems in well-established casinos.

SOCIAL CONCERNS

The NIGC should also be concerned with an effective affirmative action program for Native Americans within the casinos on the reservations. Another social con-sideration would be the building and development of adequate schools and counseling facilities for the Indians. On a long-term basis, large amounts of the revenue generated should be directly channeled toward tertiary-level education and scholarships.

The NIGC should insist on apprentice or training programs for all compa-nies who subcontract casinos from Native Americans. This practice would develop the Indian's potential, as well as avoid the economic leakage that currently occurs on the reservation. Additionally, this practice would encourage those who have left the reservation to return and make a contribution to their reservation communities.

One of the main reasons for the proliferation of gaming on Indian reservations was to improve the economic conditions on the reservation. Statistics for 1993 indicate that the accidental death rate for Native Americans was 295 percent higher than the rate of the average American population (Rice, 1995). Surveys also indicate that the suicide rate is 95 percent higher, and the alcoholism rate is 663 percent higher than that of the American population (Rice, 1995). Another concern would be how the various Native American tribes will provide proactive services to prevent these occurrences. The question is, how can all of these gaming enterprises help to alleviate some of these problems?

RECENT DEVELOPMENTS

Previously, the Indian reservations in Minnesota have been a model for reservations elsewhere. In 1992 it was reported that tribal gambling was directly responsible for increasing employment by more than five thousand workers. Furthermore, approximately $900 million was wagered in thirteen casinos and bingo halls on eleven reservations (Tribal State Compact Lists, 1998).

Presently, the Minnesota casinos are out of the picture. At this time, the most revered Native American Indian casino in the United States is the Foxwood Resort and Casino operated by the **Mahantucket-Pequots'** tribe in Ledyard, Connecticut. This facility was the first Native American casino on an Indian reservation to duplicate the glamour and glitz of Atlantic City or Nevada. Currently, it has more than 2,300 employees and operates twenty-four hours a day (Mikelberg, 1992). In 1993, the Mahantucket-Pequot agreed to pay the state of Connecticut 25 percent of the slot revenue, or $100 million in return for exclusive rights to install slot machines (Connor, 1993). The Mahantucket's presence has now provided another venue for large-scale gambling for high rollers in a site other than Atlantic City for northeast coast gamblers.

In 1994, the governor of Connecticut signed a compact with another Native American tribe. The **Mohegans,** through an agreement with the Pequots, now have permission to operate slot machines in Connecticut (Connor, 1994). This agreement is significant because both groups will now pay 25 percent of the revenue from their slot machines, or $80 million, to the state of Connecticut. The Foxwood is now building more hotel rooms and a convention center.

The Foxwood Resort and Casino has 592 hotel rooms, 5 gourmet restaurants, 4,000 slot machines, a 1,500-seat showroom, and two hotels with spas, 24-hour room service, and indoor pools. Foxwood is by any standard a world-class casino. It has more than eight thousand people on its payroll, making it one of the largest employers in southeastern Connecticut. The profit from the casino has been injected in the originally small community to build child-development centers and community centers and also to provide health insurance and tuition for its tribal members. Additionally, the Pequot tribe has been extremely philanthropic with donations to the Smithsonian to highlight the Native American culture.

FUTURE TRENDS IN INDIAN GAMBLING

What does the future hold for Native American (Indian) gambling? Many states will initiate laws that will legalize gambling throughout the United States. The main reason for this change will be an attempt to try to capitalize on the millions of dollars that they are losing in taxes they cannot collect on the reservations. The outcome will result in more competition for casino market shares, and the more experienced financiers and business people will be more successful.

For Indian gaming to remain competitive, there must be an additional attraction. For instance, Native Americans should consider coupling gambling with cultural tourism. It is not sufficient to have persons drive, in some cases, hundreds of miles, just to gamble. The casinos in Las Vegas, Atlantic City, and the Caribbean are making the gambling trip an entertaining experience. Indian casinos should try to accentuate culture and hospitality that would make them different.

Most Native American tribes support casinos and the environment it produces. The Onedia tribe, which operates **Turning Stone,** is an interesting example of a cultural paradigm. They are renowned as the only "alcohol-free" casino. This casino employs more than 2,000 employees and attracts more than three million patrons annually, yet maintains a sanitized adult environment. In the future, there may be a trend for specific theme casinos.

In the future, the National Indian Gaming Commission must play a more forceful role by creating more stringent requirements and regulations for licensing Indian casinos, as well as by conducting more frequent audits. Currently, several tribes are being "victimized" by contractors. These problems occur because of mismanagement, conflict of interest, and business naivety. The NIGC should become a more vigilant watchdog.

The power that transforms communities is money—money is power. Money brings business leaders and tribal members to the negotiating table and empowers them to act in the best interests of the tribal members. Gaming revenue provides the tribe with funds for education, health care, scholarships, law enforcement, housing, and infrastructure. "Tribal governments [through gaming ventures] are building capacity to more effectively fulfill their government's responsibilities, not so much because they want to become more powerful governments but because they want to become more responsive governments," says Jacob Coin, executive director of the National Indian Gaming Association (Fortunato, 1999).

CONCLUSION

Within Native American religion, there is a belief that a white buffalo is a sign of good luck. Currently, many Native Americans believe that the introduction of gaming in both class II and class III is their contemporary white buffalo. The wealth generated by casinos is seen as a means to retrieve the past, rebuild the nation, and provide for its childrens' future. For the most part, it brings revenue to reservations that by most standards exist in third-world poverty (Rudd, 1996). Caution should, however, be applied to this current-day Indian situation. Native Americans should be reminded that many buffalos that roamed the Western prairies about a century ago were killed almost to the point of extinction. If preservation and planning are not cultivated in the casino industry, the casinos on Indian reservations may meet the same fate as the buffalo.

There is a need for a closer vigilance on the regulations of Indian gaming. Indian tribes should be more cautious about the corporations and individuals who desire to manage their casinos. Equally important, the NIGC should look at ways to first, increase its funding, and second, obtain the necessary human resources needed to screen and investigate the personnel employed in Indian gaming. A closer look at Nevada and Atlantic City illustrate that top-notch employees are needed to maintain an impeccable image and integrity for the casino industry.

REVIEW TERMS

Indian Gaming Regulatory Act (IGRA)	Mahantucket-Pequot
National Indian Gaming Association (NIGA)	Mohegans
	good faith
class I gaming	Tenth Amendment
class II gaming	Eleventh Amendment
class III gaming	Turning Stone

REFERENCES

Alexander, P. (1993). The development and context of the Indian Gaming Regulatory Act. In *Speaking the truth about Indian gaming.* (Doc. 1, pp. 1–12). National Indian Gaming Association.

Bunting, G. F. (1992). Absences mar hearing on Indian casinos. *Los Angeles Times,* 10 January.

Connor, M. (1993). Indian gaming: Prosperity, controversy. *Gaming and Wagering Business* 14(3):1–14.

Connor, M. (1994). Weicker signs agreement with Mohegans. *Gaming and Wagering Business* 15(6):56.

Crowell, S., and J. Strauss. (1993). States wrongly assert that the Indian Gaming Regulatory Act violates the Tenth and Eleventh Amendments to avoid fair dealing with tribes. In *Speaking the truth about Indian gaming.* (Doc. 5, pp. 1–11). National Indian Gaming Association.

Fortunato, L. (1999). Native Americans hit the jackpot. *Region Focus,* Fifth Federal Reserve District Economy.

Greenberg, P., and J. Zelio. (1992). States and the Indian Gaming Regulatory Act. Denver, Colorado: National Conference of State Legislatures.

Kachel, D. (1994). A ray of hope on the Indian Reservation. *Business and Society Review,* 36–39.

Leonard, S. (1992). Let's make peace with the Indians again. *Gaming and Wagering Business.*

Marks, P. A. (1993). Three studies of the positive economic impact on Indian tribal gaming industries. In *Speaking the truth about Indian gaming.* (Doc. 3, pp. 1–12). National Indian Gaming Association.

Mikelberg, F. (1992). Tribal gaming generates $0.5B for Minnesota. *Gaming and Wagering Business* 13(4):10.

Monteau, H. A. (1993). Tribal-state gambling compacts under the provisions of the Class III gaming in the Federal Gaming Act. In *Speaking the truth about Indian gaming.* (Doc. 3, pp. 1–8). National Indian Gaming Association.

National Indian Gaming Association. (1993). *Speaking the truth about Indian gaming.*

North American Gaming Report. (1994) *International Gaming and Wagering Business* (Suppl.).

Rice, G. W. (1995). Professor at Cornell University. Personal interview.

Rudd, D. (1996). Native American Gaming Symposium. Second Annual Gaming Educators Conference, May. University of Nevada Gaming Institute.

Rumbolz, M. (1988). Indian gaming gambling research. Proceedings of the Seventh International Conference on Gambling and Risk Taking. Volume I: Public Policy and Commercial Gaming Industries Through the World, pp. 18–25.

Tribal State Compact Lists. (1998). Available at: http://www.doi.gov/bia/foia/compact.htm

Worsnop, R. L. (1994). Gambling Boom. *CQ Researcher,* 18 March, 244, 255.

Chapter 9

Riverboat and Cruise ship Gambling

OBJECTIVES

- Identify the factors that encouraged riverboat gambling.
- Name the states with riverboat gambling.
- Identify and discuss the legal requirements for riverboat gambling in each state.
- Discuss the future of riverboat gambling.
- Identify important historical events that influenced the introduction of casinos on cruise ships.
- List the differences between land-based and ship casinos.
- Describe the different types of cruise ship casino gambling.
- List the types of casino games played on cruise ships.
- List and describe the cruise companies with casinos.
- Explain the types of credit on a cruise ship.
- Discuss the different types of management of casinos on a cruise ship.

INTRODUCTION

This chapter discusses the development of casinos both on riverboats and cruise ships. A historical review will be made of states within the United States that have legalized riverboat gambling. During the last part of the chapter, a brief review will be made of the historical and current casino activities on cruise ships. Finally, speculations will be made about the future of riverboat gambling.

RIVERBOAT GAMBLING

Riverboat gambling was first prevalent in the United States in the 1800s. The gambling occurred mainly on the Mississippi River on paddleboats and steamships that traveled up and down the river carrying cargo and transporting passengers. During these trips, the most popular game played was poker. Many of the participants in these games cheated. Some of the cheaters operated in pairs. While one partner played at the table, the other confederate would be watching the game giving signals that ranged from blowing smoke to scratching various parts of the body (Sifakis, 1990).

Riverboat gamblers built reputations as both gamblers and cheaters. The games were tolerated on the riverboats because during a poker game, large quantities of alcohol were consumed, and this was revenue for the boat's captain. Eventually, when the standard of players changed, dishonest players were thrown overboard or were left stranded on a sand bar.

During the nineteenth century, another popular riverboat gambling game was three-card monte. Most of the time this game was played with an accomplice or shill. The objective of the game was to move around three cards, two queens and an ace. A bettor would then try to locate the ace. Invariably, the winning card was palmed, making it impossible for the bettor to win.

One of the contributing factors to the decline of riverboat gambling was the start of the Civil War. At the end of the 1800s, other modes of transportation became more efficient, which caused a decline in the use of riverboats. Riverboat gambling was dormant until 1990.

Many things have changed with the modern-day riverboats. They vary in size, shape, and design. Some of these boats can carry from six hundred to fifteen hundred passengers. In Louisiana, the riverboats must be paddle wheel in design. They must duplicate the historic steamboats of the past. Other states have modern ships that are as comfortable and luxurious as cruise liners. Fast-moving

Table 9-1 History of Modern Riverboat Gambling in the United States

Year	Event
1989	Iowa legalized riverboat casinos
1990	Illinois legalized riverboat casinos
1990	Mississippi legalized riverboat casinos
1991	Louisiana legalized riverboat casinos
1992	Missouri legalized riverboat casinos
1993	Indiana legalized riverboat casinos

catamarans are also used after being redesigned to accommodate a variety of casino games.

Today, there are more than sixty riverboats sailing in the six states within the United States listed in Table 9-1. At one time during the past eight years there were almost seventy boats sailing. Although the number of ships may have decreased since the industry's inception, the revenue generated has increased tremendously. In 1998, riverboat casinos generated almost $4 billion for the casino industry.

Iowa

Iowa was the first state to revitalize riverboat gambling since its dormancy in the late nineteenth century. In 1989, legislation was passed that permitted gambling to occur on riverboats that sailed on the Mississippi River in Iowa. The first ship did not actually sail until April 1991. Within six months after the passing of riverboat legislation to allow gambling, there were five boats sailing from cities within Iowa (Doocey, 1994b).

All of these ships had to comply with many regulations (Table 9-2). The main reason for introducing legalized riverboat gambling in Iowa was to revive

Table 9-2   Riverboat Activities in Iowa

Activity	Specification
Date of legislation	July 1989
Riverboat launched	April 1991
Governing body	Iowa Racing and Gaming Commission
Application fee	N/A
Tax levied	• Adjusted graduated scale • 5% for the first $1 million • 10% for the next $2 million
Regulations	• Twenty slot machines for every table game • Two-hour cruise • Cruise for 100 different days
Games	Slot machines, roulette, blackjack, big six, craps, video game of chance, red dog, Caribbean stud, and 21 super bucks
Type of vessel	Modern or historic
Competition	Illinois and Missouri
Number of boats sailing in the state	9

economically depressed communities. Proponents of riverboat gambling say that this type of investment would be good for the local community and the state. The community would benefit in several ways. First, there was the payroll that would be generated from the new jobs created. These individuals would in turn spend portions of their salaries within the community. Next, the residents would also pay local tax. Third, the infrastructure of a community would be tremendously improved by the introduction of riverboat gambling. In addition, the state would benefit from state income tax and other licensing fees.

Legislators felt that, with proper regulations, it would be possible to generate a crime-free gambling environment that would attract respectable gamblers. Table 9-2 highlights and summarizes several of the important factors about riverboat gambling in Iowa. In Iowa, the riverboats are required to make cruises, which may last from ninety to one hundred and two minutes. Initially, passengers were allowed to gamble a maximum of $200 per cruise. The legislation also required there should be at least twenty slot machines for every table game.

In June 1994, only two of the original six riverboats were sailing in Iowa. One of the main reasons cited for their leaving Iowa was the restriction of both the maximum amount for each bet as well as the maximum possible loss.

After much pressure, legislators repealed the above restrictions during the later part of 1994 (Johnson, 1994). Presently, Iowa does not have any restrictions on the space limitation and wagering. In 1998, there were nine riverboats operating in Iowa. In August 1998, their gross gaming revenue was $41.6 million (National Gaming Summary, 1998).

Illinois

The second state to legalize riverboat gambling in the United States was Illinois. The legislation was passed in February 1990, and boats actually started sailing in Illinois on the Mississippi River in September 1991. Riverboat gambling in Illinois was very different from that of its neighbors in Iowa. One of the main differences in the legislation was that there was no maximum loss per cruise. Also Illinois decided to have Las Vegas–style entertainment to make the gambling experience more exciting. Table 9-3 gives an overview of the specifics of Illinois gambling. Illinois also levies a 20 percent tax on the gross gaming receipt. Additionally, the riverboats charge a boarding fee, which is given to the city.

Riverboat gambling in Illinois occurs on the Mississippi, Des Plaines, Ohio, and Illinois rivers. The ten licenses are in nine cities. The boats make several cruises for approximately four hours. On the cruises the games listed in Table 9-3 are played.

Mississippi

Riverboat gambling was legislated in Mississippi in 1990. Actual gambling, however, did not begin until the last part of 1992. One of the legislative conditions for riverboat gambling was that each county must first approve it. Currently, four

Table 9-3 Riverboat Activities in Illinois

Activity	Specification
Date of legislation	February 1990
Riverboat launched	September 1991
Governing body	Illinois Gaming Board
Application fee	N/A
Tax levied	• 20% of adjusted gross receipts • $2 boarding fee
Regulations	• Boat must cruise a limit of four hours when the weather is permitting • Thirty-minute board and disembarking periods • Boats cannot dock along the Lake Michigan shoreline
Games	Slot machines, big six, blackjack, roulette, craps, red dog, sic boc, and baccarat
Type of vessel	Modern or historic
Competition	Iowa and Missouri
Number of boats sailing in the state	10

counties—Tunica, Claiborne, Adams, and Hancock—have voted and approved riverboat gambling. Interestingly, these are four of the poorest counties in the state.

One of the main differences between gambling in Mississippi and the other states is that the boats must be **permanently moored** to the dock at all times. These casinos are built on stationary barges joined to the land by a gangplank. The boats utilize as much of the space as possible to accommodate the casino games and slot machines. There are several attractions for both operators and gamblers. Operators in this state are levied 8 percent of their gross winnings (Table 9-4).

Louisiana

Each state sets its own regulations for riverboat gambling. In Louisiana, when riverboat gambling was legislated in 1991, the legislation passed indicated that there must be a mandatory admission fee (Plume, 1994). In 1993, when the boats actually started sailing, many of the operators realized that this admission fee was causing them to lose business to competing neighboring states. As a result, many boat owners decided to pay the fee themselves in an attempt to attract more players (Plume, 1994).

Table 9-4 Riverboat Activities in Mississippi

Activity	Specification
Date of legislation	April 1990
Riverboat launched	August 1992
Governing body	Mississippi Gaming Commission
Application fee	• Initially $5,000–$50,000 • Renewal fee $5,000–$25,000
Tax levied	Capped at 8% with a sliding scale of the gross revenue
Regulations	• Boats must be permanently moored to a dock • Minimum length of 150 feet • Must be certified by the United States Coast Guard to carry at least two hundred passengers
Games	Slot machines, big six, blackjack, roulette, craps, red dog, sic boc, faro, monte, fan-tan, seven and a half, big injun, klondike, chuk-a-luck, wheel of fortune, chemin de fer, pai gow, beat the banker, panguingui, and baccarat
Type of vessel	Modern or historic
Competition	Louisiana and Missouri
Number of boats sailing in the state	29

Riverboat gambling in Louisiana differs in many ways from that in other states (Table 9-5). One of the main differences is the requirement that the boats must be of a nineteenth-century model. Another requirement is that at least 60 percent of the total square footage must be devoted to the passengers. For those vessels that cruise, no gambling is permitted when they are at dockside. Also, there is a requirement to encourage minority employment. Additionally, at least 25 percent of all of the high-alcohol-content beer or rum used on the boats must be bottled within Louisiana. The average length of the voyages is ninety minutes. During the cruises, there is no maximum loss. Gambling is permissible at dockside only during inclement weather.

Missouri

Missouri legalized riverboat gambling in 1992. Some of the regulations are similar, whereas others are different from that of its neighboring states (Table 9-6). There are no regulations for the maximum loss of a player. However, the most

Table 9-5   Riverboat Activities in Louisiana

Activity	Specification
Date of legislation	June 1991
Riverboat launched	October 1993
Governing body	Louisiana State Police, Riverboat Gaming Division
Application fee	$5,000 due at the time of application $5,000 due when the license is issued, and annually thereafter
Tax levied	• 18.5% weekly deposits plus monthly reconciliation return • Admission fee
Regulations	• 60% of total square footage devoted to passengers • 25% of all high-alcohol-content beer or rum must be bottled in the state • Boats have to cruise weather permitting, except in Shreveport • Encourages minority employment
Games	Slot machines, big six, blackjack, roulette, craps, poker and mini-baccarat
Type of vessel	Nineteenth-century vessel
Competition	Mississippi and New Orleans
Number of boats sailing in the state	12

significant difference about Missouri riverboat gambling is a State Supreme Court ruling that stated it is unconstitutional for slot machines to be used. The rationale behind this ruling was that only games of chance, which include poker and blackjack, can be played on the riverboats (Doocey, 1994d). However, these regulations have changed, and slot machines are now available on riverboats in Missouri.

Indiana

Riverboat gambling began in Indiana in 1994. State legislators had an opportunity to review many of the other riverboat laws before finalizing one for their state. In many ways, the regulations were similar to those of Illinois. There were, however, some differences (Table 9-7).

In Indiana, the riverboats are required to cruise for approximately four hours. Passengers may not gamble thirty minutes before or after the actual cruise.

Table 9-6 Riverboat Activities in Missouri

Activity	Specification
Date of legislation	November 1992
Riverboat launched	May 1994
Governing body	Missouri Gaming Commission
Application fee	N/A
Tax levied	• 20% gross adjusted receipts • $2 admission fee
Regulations	Boats must cruise when weather is permitting
Games	Slot machines, blackjack, poker, Caribbean stud poker, pai gow, Texas Hold'em, double down stud, and video games
Type of vessel	Modern or historic
Competition	Louisiana, Illinois, and Indiana
Number of boats sailing in the state	10

Table 9-7 Riverboat Activities in Indiana

Activity	Specification
Date of legislation	July 1993
Riverboat launched	1994
Governing body	Indiana Gaming Commission
Application fee	• $50,000 initially • $25,000 additional after receiving a certification of suitability
Tax levied	• 20% adjusted gross receipts • $3 entry fee
Regulations	• Excursion schedule approximately four hours • No playing thirty minutes before and after departure • Owner of one boat not allowed to have more than 10% stock of another boat • Owner of one boat not allowed to operate within ten miles of another boat • Maximum of eleven riverboat licenses in the state
Games	Slot machines, big six, blackjack, roulette, craps, and baccarat
Type of vessel	Modern or historic
Competition	Illinois and Iowa
Number of boats sailing in the state	9

There is an admission fee, and there is no loss limit. A 20 percent tax is levied on the gross earnings. Another requirement in Indiana is that an owner with one boat is not allowed to operate within ten miles of another boat.

CAREER OPPORTUNITIES

Riverboat casinos are floating casinos. All of the tasks and responsibilities normally done on a land-based casino must also be completed on the riverboat. There is also a need for additional staff to operate the boat and maintain its safety. Riverboats are therefore more labor intensive than their land-based counterparts. On the average, most riverboats employ at least one thousand employees, or approximately thirty-six employees per one thousand square feet.

One of the main reasons for legalizing riverboat casinos was to increase the economic base of the community. Riverboat casinos provide a large number of jobs and careers for the local residents. Careers in allied hospitality industries such as hotels, transportation, and laundering can also develop. Some of the career opportunities readily available on a riverboat casino include:

- Accounting clerk
- Barback
- Cage cashier
- Deckhand
- Food receiver
- Human resource clerk
- Money runner
- Prep cook
- PBX operator
- Surveillance operator
- Ticketing clerk
- Valet attendant

Some of the positions require no previous casino experience. This requirement enables the residents from the immediate area to enter the casino industry and work their way up the career ladder.

RIVERBOAT CONCLUSION

Currently, six states have legalized riverboat gambling. The regulations vary from state to state. Competition has caused the discontinuation of maximum loss. When new riverboat jurisdictions open, the communities invariably try to learn from the oversights of the older markets. Many communities are also requiring the riverboat operators to develop the infrastructures within the immediate docking areas. In some states, especially Mississippi, many of the table games are not normally played in land-based casinos.

Several states, including Ohio, Pennsylvania, and South Carolina, are working feverishly to pass riverboat legislation. Wisconsin, Kentucky, and Alabama have had legislation defeated and will almost certainly reintroduce it. Currently, communities that host riverboat casinos impose a 6 to 20 percent tax on the **adjusted gross receipts (AGR)** of the casino's operations. An AGR is the total revenue taken form the operations of the casino.

Riverboat gambling comes on the heels of a larger gambling issue in the United States. Many states are now in a quandary with regards to riverboat and other types of gambling. Gambling is present within the United States in some form or another in all but two states. Many legislators are asking the question, Why should we allow our residents to spend large sums of money in other states instead of our own? With this question in mind, many states with navigable rivers are seriously considering and will continue to introduce riverboat gambling legislation.

All in all, riverboat gambling must be properly planned to be successful in specific communities. Some states are already feeling the affects of oversaturation. It is essential to limit the number of riverboat casinos within a specific area. When effectively planned and regulated, riverboat casinos can benefit and improve the local communities by increasing the number of jobs, increasing the standard of living of the residents, and equally important, increasing the tax base of the communities.

CASINOS ON CRUISE SHIPS

There are many similarities and differences between riverboat and cruise ship gambling. In the preceding section, it was evident that the riverboat casino industry has been expanding from 1989 to the present. This expansion has occurred with the size and conveniences of the riverboats. Some riverboats can almost be regarded as cruise ships. Herein lies the competition.

Some riverboat casinos go from point A up the river and return to point A. Now we are observing the same thing with some cruise ships. The sole purpose of a "cruises to nowhere" is to gamble. Fortunately, these types of cruises only occur in a few states and do not present a large threat to the riverboat casino industry. Traditional cruises are now increasing in popularity and are attempting to obtain a part of the market share of casinos on the water. All of the major cruise lines have a casino on the boat as part of the cruise experience.

Cruise ships began to become popular in the late 1930s. The Queen Mary and the Queen Elizabeth popularized cruises, with the latter being the only transatlantic ship today. These ships were regarded as "floating hotels." They provided full accommodations, meals, entertainment, and activities. Casinos did not become popular on cruise ships until decades later.

In 1972, Ted Arison purchased a cruise ship named the Empress of Canada. He later changed the name to the Mardi Gras (Levin, 1993b). Arison formed a company called Carnival Cruise Lines. After a rocky start, Arison developed a "fun ship" theme and tried to increase Carnival's market shares by purchasing two more ships. In 1978, the Mardi Gras was the first cruise ship to operate a full casino with 140 slot machines, 6 blackjack tables, 2 roulette tables, 2 craps tables, and 1 big six wheel (Pagan, 1994).

The sizes of cruise ships have changed over the years. Previously, the average passenger load was between five hundred and one thousand passengers. Now, Carnival and several other companies have built "superliners," each of which carries almost three thousand passengers (Bain, 1994).

As the size of the cruise ships has increased, so has the size of the casinos. Previously, casinos were located in obscure, hard-to-find places. They had a few old slot machines, and the atmosphere was not conducive to having a good time. The modern-day cruise ship casinos now have all of the fancy new technology found in Las Vegas and Atlantic City. Actually, there are a few games that are played on cruises that are not played at these land-based venues because of stringent regulations.

Carnival Cruise Lines has also changed its size, from a fleet of one to its current complement of ten ships. After the Mardi Gras' success, many other cruise companies also introduced more sophisticated casinos on their ships. Currently, there are at least forty cruise ship companies operating approximately one hundred and twenty-seven casinos. The casinos on these cruise ships vary in size, operating from four to almost three hundred slot machines along with tables (Bain, 1994).

Carnival Cruise Line, Norwegian Cruise Line, Royal Caribbean International Cruise Line, Celebrity Cruises, and Princess Cruise Line are considered the industry leaders in both the cruise line industry and on-board casinos. Carnival's Destiny has the largest floating casino with nine thousand square feet dedicated specifically for casino entertainment.

Types of Cruises and Casino Gambling

Formerly, many of the cruises that originated from the United States were three, four, or seven days in duration. These cruises traveled to Caribbean or Mexican destinations. One of the competing activities on the ships was casino gambling. As the cruise ship industry grew, new ideas were developed to capitalize on casinos on the cruise ship. Instead of traveling to specific destinations, **"cruises to nowhere"** were introduced (Connor, 1993). These cruises give passengers an opportunity to gamble. The passengers pay an entrance fee, which sometimes includes food and entertainment. After the ship is 3 miles away from the shoreline into international water, the casino is opened. The cruise ships usually travel the ocean for about four to eight hours (Bain, 1994). Currently, the cruise ships operate from Florida, Georgia, and Texas. Previously, similar cruises operated from Connecticut, Mississippi, Maine, Louisiana, Washington, and California (Doocey, 1994b).

The ships that operate the "cruises to nowhere" are registered under the flag of a foreign country such as the Bahamas, Panama, or Liberia. Because they are foreign ships, they do not have to comply with the state laws that prohibit gambling (Connor, 1993). This provision is quite disconcerting to the American flag carriers, which represent only about 2 percent of the one hundred cruise ships that visit American ports (Connor, 1993).

Comparison of Land-Based and Ship Casinos

There are several differences between ship and land-based casinos. The primary purpose of a cruise is to give the passengers a complete vacation. Casino gaming is merely one of the competing activities offered on the ship. Conversely, the objective of land-based casinos is to attract individuals who wish to gamble. Land-based casinos are heavily regulated by a state regulatory agency. There is a noticeable absence of rigorous regulations on cruise ships. Many of the ship casinos follow some of the guidelines used by land-based casinos; however, without statutory regulations, casino operators are not obliged to adhere to any rules.

The table game limits on cruises are purposely kept low, usually from $100 to $200 (Stanley, 1990). The rationale for this policy is to prevent passengers from losing large sums of money, which would ruin their vacation and the cruise. On land, some players often encourage casino managers to raise the table limits much higher than $200.

Another big difference between the two venues is the practice of advertising. Cruise ship casino advertisement is permitted only on board the ship. Efforts are made to downplay gambling because there are still some negative connotations associated with gambling, and cruises are often touted as opportunities for families to spend time together.

In land-based casinos, it is customary to give complimentary rooms (comps) to players who spend a specific amount of money at a casino. Prior to 1992, this practice of comping was unheard of on cruise ships. Carnival Cruise Lines was the first company to break this tradition by giving away complimentary cabins (Roberts, 1992). Carnival initiated a **Comp-A-Cruise program** originally for $100 players. Afterwards, $25 players were allowed to earn complimentary trips if they played eight or twelve hours for a four- or seven-day cruise, respectively (Roberts, 1992).

Nongaming Cruise Ship Activities

On a cruise ship, the casino is not the only place where individuals can have fun. There are an assortment of other activities competing for the time and money of the passengers. Perhaps the greatest competition for money and time is shipboard bingo. This game appeals to all passengers: it is easy to play, it passes the time, and it is fun for groups.

Games Played on Cruise Ships

The reason Arison introduced casinos on a cruise was to make more money. When the Mardi Gras initiated casino gambling, the games it offered were slot machines, blackjack, roulette, craps, and big six. Twenty years later, all of the original games are still played, and there are some new ones, including progressive slots, video poker, Caribbean stud poker, mini-baccarat, wheel of fortune, bingo, let it ride, table baccarat, poker, and baccarat. The most popular table games on cruise ships are blackjack, roulette, and craps (Pagan, 1994).

Management of Casinos on Cruise Ships

Not all of the casinos on cruise ships are managed by the parent cruise line. Some of the larger cruise line companies, such as Carnival, Princess, and Royal Caribbean, have their own in-house management for their casinos. On the other hand, many of the smaller companies, such as Bajamar, Celebrity, and Commodore, use **concessionaires** to operate their casinos. Interestingly, some cruise line companies, such as Chandris Fantasy and Europa Cruise, use different concessionaires to manage the assorted ships within their fleet.

There are a few schools of thought about managing cruise ship casinos. Some cruise lines prefer to specialize and leave the gambling activities alone. They opt to leave the headaches of equipment, staffing, and insurance to someone else. The remuneration of the concessions are usually based on gross win. On the average, the split for table is 60–40 for the cruise line and concessionaire, respectively. The restitution for the slot machines is usually 70 percent of the gross win to the cruise company and the remaining 30 percent for the concessionaire (Pagan, 1994). The concessionaire is responsible for acquiring the slot equipment and paying the employees.

The six leading concessionaires who manage casinos on cruise ships include:

- Atlantic Association
- Casino Leisure
- Casino Austria
- Kloster Cruise Limited
- Oceanic Leisure
- Tiber Entertainment Group

Atlantic Association and Casinos Austria have the largest number of contracts to manage on-board casinos.

When a cruise line operates its casino, all of the casino staff are under the command of the ship's captain. However, if there is a concessionaire, the casino manager is responsible for the management and disciplining of casino staff.

Notwithstanding the management option, all ship employees must participate in safety drills and exercises (Pagan, 1994).

Establishing Credit on a Ship

Establishing credit on a ship is different from establishing it in a land-based casino. On land it is possible to run a credit check, which can be completed within a short time. On ships, the process is not as simple. Passengers may establish a credit line before boarding the cruise ship. To initiate a credit line, it is necessary to complete a credit application. This application will verify an individual's credit through a central credit bureau. If the application is approved, the credit line will be available when the passenger begins the cruise. At the end of the cruise, all debts must be settled (Norwegian, 1994).

There are several other ways of obtaining credit for gambling while on a cruise. One way is by depositing a specific amount of money with the cashier's department of the cruise line. This must be done prior to the ship's departure. This money will be forwarded to the ship's purser. The purser will then facilitate the credit line while the passenger is on board (Cunard, 1994).

Credit can also be established through personal check cashing. Usually, the ship will place a limit on the number of checks it will cash during a cruise. Another means of obtaining credit while on a cruise would be by using one's credit card. The only credit some cruise ships allow is a predetermined cash advance to be debited to a passenger's cabin or stateroom account (Levin, 1993b).

CRUISE SHIP CONCLUSION

In 1992, the Cruise Lines International Association indicated that only 4 percent of Americans had ever taken a cruise (Levin, 1992). This statistic signifies the cruise industry growth potential in the United States. Already, we see larger and more majestic ships being built. Carnival has just recently built Sensation, Fantasy, and Ecstasy, each carrying 2,600 passengers (Levin, 1992). Norwegian Cruise Lines and Princess Cruises are also constructing several superliners. The increase in passenger load has also brought about an increase in the number of slot and video poker machines. As people become more accustomed to land-based casinos, they will be less intimidated by the cruise ship casinos when they take a cruise. It is estimated that at least 33 percent of the passengers who take cruises also visit the casino.

As casino gambling becomes more popular, there will be a need for a regulatory agency to insure the integrity of the industry. Regulations will standardize games and practices on all cruises. Furthermore, the regulations will be beneficial to both the casinos and customers in preventing cheating and embezzlement.

In the future, without exception, there will be more progressive-linked slot machines on the ships. These links will be between cruise ships within a cruise line company. Companies with many ships and many slot machines will have a competitive edge.

CONCLUSION

There are great opportunities for gaming expansion in both the riverboat and cruise ship industry. Legislators must be diligent about the laws and the restrictions as they provide licenses to gamble at these venues. Diligent regulations must be applied to the licensing of gambling both on the river and on the high seas.

REVIEW TERMS

adjusted gross receipts (AGR)

Comp-A-Cruise program

concessionaires

cruises to nowhere

establishing credit

permanently moored

REFERENCES

Bain, J. H. (1994). *Casinos: The international casino guide.* Port Washington, New York: B.D.I.T., Inc.

Connor, M. (1993). The ripple effect of cruise-ship gaming. *Gaming and Wagering Business* 14 (5):1, 59–60.

Cunard. (1994). Personal interview with company representative.

Doocey, P. (1994a). Will the proliferation of land-based casinos sink cruise-ship gaming? *Gaming and Wagering Business* 15 (10).

Doocey, P. (1994b). An overview of riverboat gaming: Full steam ahead. *Gaming and Wagering Business* 14(11):1, 38–40.

Doocey, P. (1994c). Did Iowa miss the boat? *Gaming and Wagering Business* 15(4):1, 39–44.

Doocey, P. (1994d). Missouri voters say "no" to slots. *Gaming and Wagering Business* 15(5):1, 65–66.

Johnson, C. R. (1994). Riverboat gaming: The first 1,000 days. *Gaming and Wagering Business* 15(10):1, 67–70.

Levin, M. (1992). One from column A. *Casino Player* IV (4):38–39.

Levin, M. (1993a). A 20-year Carnival. *Casino Player* IV (5):44–45.

Levin, M. (1993b). Five stars on the seven seas. *Casino Player* V (1):34–35.

National Gaming Summary (1998). Available at:
http://www.casinocenter.com/summary/sample/html/iowa.html

Norwegian Cruise Lines. (1994). Personal interview with company representative.

Pagan, B. (1994). Personal interview, June.

Plume, J. (1994). The star comes out. *Casino Player* V(7):16–17.

Roberts, P. (1992). Carnival comp cruises. *Casino Player* IV (3):42.

Sifakis, C. (1990). *The encyclopedia of gambling*. New York: Facts on File, Inc.

Stanley, D. (1990). Cruise ship gaming. *Gaming and Wagering Business* 11 (5):41–43.

Chapter 10

Casino Marketing and Marketing Promotions

OBJECTIVES

- Identify the challenges of marketing within the casino industry.
- Define and discuss market strategy for the casino industry.
- Discuss the rules for various tournaments.
- Examine the requirements and objectives of casino junkets.
- Identify the four types of casino entertainment.

MARKETING

Database marketing is described as a comprehensive marketing strategy based on a memory of business transactions with its customers (Oppermann, 1999). Database marketing is essential to the growth and survival of the gaming industry, because it allows the industry to gain an advantage over competitors.

If the casinos accept the premise of service 1, where the customer is the most important aspect of their business and everything must be done to satisfy customers' needs the first time, then marketing becomes one of casinos' most important tools. **Marketing** is defined as all of those activities and procedures necessary to bring the buyer and seller together to consummate a sale. Casino marketing is unique because before one can sell the product one has to know the NWDs (needs, wants, and desires) of the customer (Rudd, 1980). Casinos need to provide the customer with a product that meets these NWDs. And last, casinos need to advertise and promote these services or product mixes to the customer. All basic marketing starts with the traditional four Ps of marketing set forth by E. J. McCarthy in his book *Basic Marketing*. They are product, price, place, and promotion.

Product

The product in the casino industry is seen as a combination of service and entertainment. By providing the customers with unique entertainment experiences and reinforcing these experiences through marketing incentives, the casino ensures its own survival. From the customers' point of view, the product or service that casinos offer is the mixture of the benefits that they will receive from the product. It is not the room, meals, flight, entertainment, or the gambling itself, but the combination of experiences and memories that are generated. This determines the true value of the product. For example, in a tour to Las Vegas, everything may be included. But are the customers buying the plane? Are they buying the room? Are they buying the slot machines or tables? No, they are satisfying their desire for excitement and adventure. Should casinos really be selling them the plane and the room? Or should the product be excitement and adventure? It is easy to fall into a production-orientation trap rather than a marketing orientation. The casinos that do make the mistake of selling their rooms rather than the adventure and experiences that they can give their customers lose their customers. Therefore, when a casino considers its product, it should take into consideration all of those things that meet the NWDs of their customers: the experiences, adventure, facilities, and services that are necessary to sell and maintain a customer's loyalty. Once the casinos start to take a look at their products, they realize that their customers' NWDs may be beyond their control. NWDs normally outside the casino's control, such as the weather, the surroundings, and the congestion, are called demand generators. Casino customers, therefore, may tend to view the casino's support elements as a means to an end rather than an end itself.

Price

The price is the amount that customers are willing to pay for the product or service that casinos offer. One of the most important aspects of price is that the customers must view the price that they are paying as value for their money. This isn't always easy because people see value in different lights. Value is normally based on the subjective experiences and thoughts of the customer. Price also has an objective factor. The customer normally sees the price in big red letters, and in most cases it is beyond the customer's control to determine what the price will be. By creating a value-added product, casinos can increase the value of their product and allow the price to remain relatively stable.

Place

The place is where the customer procures or uses the product. For a walk-in, the casino sells directly to the customer. For a travel agency or tour group, the casino's products are sold through different channels of distribution. Tour operators, wholesalers, and travel agents are the main channels of distribution for the casino industry.

Promotion

Promotion is the process by which one makes customers aware of one's products. It utilizes a wide range of activities, including personal selling, sales promotion, advertising, public relations, and publicity.

Personal selling is one of the most effective means of procuring business. It allows an immediate response to a potential customer's NWDs. It also allows one to deal with any question that may arise and to personally expand on the benefits of one's product or service. A number of casinos have used this approach, specifically with the senior market, and have found that it works quite well. A representative of a casino organization made a presentation at a local senior citizens center where he overcame any resistance or objections that a specific group had toward casino gambling. Personal selling is very expensive and time consuming and is generally done only with large organizations, clubs, or corporations. However, it can be very effective.

Sales promotion covers any promotional activity other than personal selling or advertising. It includes such things as the development of brochures, giveaway programs, discounts, contests, special offers, gifts, exhibits, trade show operations, signage, special events, and training programs and seminars. The purpose of sales promotion is to increase casino sales. In a number of cases, the sales promotion is not directed at the customer but at the intermediaries who provide the casino's information to the customer. Examples of this are the tour operators and travel agencies. The casinos might provide them with a familiarization trip and in return they promote the casino's product. Or on a lesser scale, travel agents might be encouraged to sell more of the casino's trips through attractive display posters or through contests (e.g., the travel agent who sells the most bookings receives a free trip to the establishment). In some cases when casinos are offering new products, they offer discount coupons, contests, specials, and incentive packages. Sales promotion is not meant to be a substitute for personal selling or advertising, but it can be an effective way of reinforcing these activities.

One of the main reasons for advertising is to create an awareness of a product before other sales approaches are initiated. Why should a casino advertise? First, no casino is an island unto itself. Broadcast and printed material reach thousands of potential customers. Even advertising that is not specifically targeted to a group is effective, such as brochure advertising. This may be seen by thousands of people, some of whom are interested and some of whom are not. Second, advertising is relatively inexpensive when compared to other promotional activities. Third, advertising itself can create customer demand. And fourth, advertising demonstrates a casino's competitiveness within the casino market. A casino that meets the consumers' NWDs will be the casino that the customer chooses.

Public relations is a process by which the casinos become involved with the affairs of the community, presenting a positive image of their business. Public relations is but one part of the promotional mix and should be combined with other promotional activities. Public relations covers more than just the community; it covers all the different publics: the customer, community, local media, travel/trade journals, and employees. Every employee of the casino should be a public relations specialist. Employees represent the casinos they work for whether they are at the casino or at home. Most of the larger casinos have public relations companies that handle their public relations for them.

Publicity is the way casinos keep themselves in the public eye. Some casinos see publicity as free and consider it highly cost effective. However, there are intrinsic costs in maintaining a casino's image. Publicity works because it has more credibility than a paid message. It does not just happen; it should be carefully planned and orchestrated. It is how the city, state, and country view the casino.

CASINOS' ADDITIONAL MARKETING NEEDS

The four Ps are not enough to adequately develop a marketing concept for casinos. Five additional Ps are needed to satisfactorily meet the needs of casino and gaming operations.

People

People are a casino's most important asset; they are and should be one of a casino's principal marketing forces. A casino's employees provide the direct link between the casino and the customer base. Therefore, properly trained and motivated employees will result in increased profits and a better bottom line. There is an old saying: It takes money to make money. If a casino does not take care of its employees, the employees will not take care of the casino's customers.

Positioning

Casinos must position (market niche) so that they cater to a specific market. In doing so, they will differentiate themselves from the competition. The position that a casino chooses must be consistent throughout the casino and its advertising mix. An example of poor positioning follows: A casino located in a downtown area of Las Vegas, catering entirely to the grind customers (low-end customers, whose money the casinos have to "grind" out), planned on opening a new restaurant. A restaurant theme was chosen because management wanted to upgrade its facilities. It opened a gourmet French dining room in which the prices for food were more than the prices for the casino's rooms. Unfortunately, those customers who were gambling in the casino were not interested in French cuisine, and those individuals who were looking for French cuisine did not consider the casino and hotel appropriate for this type of dining. All sources within the hotel, casino, and restaurant were affected by this inappropriate marketing strategy.

Packaging

Casinos have been using packaging since the 1960s. Packaging is actually a form of cooperative ventures whereby the casino includes a combination of facilities and services and offers these to potential customers. Within packages, all facilities and services are included in one price. This provides the customer with advanced knowledge of the total cost of a trip, and in most cases provides a reduction in the cost of the whole over the cost of all its parts. Packages often develop around one major component with other supporting components being added to enhance the total customer appeal. By doing this, a casino is able to create and develop a product that is more consumer oriented. This process allows the casino to meet the NWDs of its consumers. The major component within the package could be the casino operation, with the surrounding packages being a trip to the lake or ocean, helicopter ride, hot air balloon ride, and so on. A casino might build a package around an event happening within town, such as the rodeo or circus.

Partnership

The casino's customer base usually wants or is looking for an overall experience from a specific destination; it is logical that within that destination two, three, or four businesses might offer a cooperative package, pooling not only their products but their marketing. An example of this might be Las Vegas's attempt to relocate the National Restaurant Association's annual meeting from Chicago to Las Vegas. This enterprise would require the establishment of a partnership among hotels, restaurants, convention and visitor's bureaus, convention centers, transportation, and civic leaders. The NRA show attracts over 150,000 visitors per year and thousands of participants. No one mega-resort casino would be able to handle a show this size by itself. To convince them to abandon their present venue, all participating partners would have to be actively involved in an intensive recruitment campaign.

Programming

Programming is used extensively in the casino and gaming industry. It refers to any special event or activity that a casino might organize that expands on the product lines it is offering. Examples of this are soap opera weekends, murder mystery weekends, and theme tournaments. All of these activities expand on the product line that the casinos offer and provide the customer with an additional reason to stay at participating casinos and resorts. One of the more successful theme weekends revolved around a day-time soap opera in which patrons were invited to participate in the continuing soap opera. During this programming event, the casino invited patrons to participate in a slot tournament with the theme of a baby's birth, followed by its christening, birthdays throughout the years, school and college experience, marriage, and family. Each one of these events represented an invitation for slot players to return to the casino time and time again following this theme. In this way, the theme acts to draw potential customers and provides an incentive for the return of these customers.

REALIZING MARKET POTENTIAL

For the casino and gaming industry to develop its marketing potential, each of these nine P's must be developed into a marketing plan that provides the overall basic strategy for the marketing effort of the casino. Strategic planning and corporate and company efforts must be directed toward achieving the maximum potential of the target market. The hospitality industry is the fastest-growing industry in the world. It is growing because consumers now have more leisure time and discretionary income. They are, however, at a loss to decide what to do with their time and money. An effective marketing program can stir them into the specific direction of casino gambling.

Good management is essential for a successful business. Casino managers must have a high volume of people on the casino floor, as well as a high room occupancy. The approach to meet these standards requires specific marketing strategies. Therefore, the main function of a casino's marketing department is to attract the clients to a specific casino by highlighting its promotion, price, and location.

CUSTOMER SERVICE

Ms. Sandy MacInnes, casino shift manager for the Windsor Casino, in Windsor, Ontario, Canada, emphasizes customer service and insists that her employees undergo customer service training to ensure cooperative interaction between customers and employees. She feels that management's commitment to the customer and upper management's commitment to community relations, not public relations, are a necessity for successful casino operations in Canada. Windsor has a safe environment for its tourists, and it is the responsibility of management to develop within its personnel a concern for the overall welfare of the community.

MARKETING PROMOTIONS

Tournaments

Tournaments were first played in the eleventh and twelfth centuries in France. At that time, they brought together large numbers of people to watch competitions and enjoy themselves. The winner of the tournament usually won the armor and horse of the loser. Although times have changed, the basic philosophy of bringing large numbers of people together to spend money has not changed. Today's casino tournaments are created for the same reason. They are now being used as a means of promotion within a casino's marketing strategy.

Casino tournaments became popular in the late 1970s. Today, land-based, riverboat, cruise ship, and Indian casinos have gambling tournaments. Types of tournaments include

- Slot machine
- Blackjack
- Caribbean stud poker
- Seven-card stud poker
- Texas hold-'em poker
- Video poker
- Baccarat
- Keno
- Craps

As a promotional marketing tool, **tournaments** are held at different times of the year, usually with a theme. Normally, they last between two and three days. During this period, all of the participants play three or four twenty- to thirty-minute sessions. The time duration may vary depending on the game being played and the casino.

Tournaments usually have entry fees, which may range from $125 to $2,000. The fees typically include room, welcome gift, cocktail party, complimentary beverages, snacks throughout the tournament, and an awards banquet. The prizes can vary from cash amounts of $5,000 to $1 million. Some casinos also give automobiles. Profitable tournaments usually have as little as one hundred to as many as four hundred players. These participants normally register by using an 800 number.

Slot tournaments are both profitable and popular. During a slot tournament, each player is randomly selected to play a slot machine. The player must then participate in three twenty-five minute sessions. The entry fee includes three **buy-ins** (amount of chips or times you can play the slot machine) of a specific amount of credits. No cash is used during the tournament play. Each machine in the tournament is preset to twenty-five minutes by a timer. Players can bet by hitting the coin button up to three times. Each machine will keep a running total of a player's winnings or losses. Winners of each session are determined by the player who has accumulated the most credits from each session.

Tournament winners are determined by the most accumulated credits after a specific number of rounds. Ties are resolved by an additional twenty-five minutes of slot playing. The rules of the tournaments are at the discretion of the host casino.

A cursory review of Tournament Listings shows that the first prize for tournaments in Nevada ranges from $25,000 to $100,000. In Atlantic City, although tournaments are not as frequent, the prizes are equally attractive, ranging from $50,000 to $100,000. In the Caribbean, first prizes range from $15,000 to $75,000. There is also a difference with the grand prizes at Indian casinos. Their prizes range from $500 to $10,000. First prizes on the riverboats are the least attractive, ranging from $2,000 to $5,000 (Tournament Listings, 1994). As a rule, the more players participating in a tournament, the larger the possible grand prize and other prizes.

A typical slot tournament could have any or all of several features. An entry fee of $400 is always required. The entry fee provides the players with a buy-in, or competition money, a welcome party, a cocktail party, an awards dinner, and an opportunity to compete for a grand prize. In a tournament with at least 185 players, the grand prize could be at least $25,000, with consolation prizes of $150 (Corea, 1994). Some casinos give all of the entry fees back to the tournament players as prizes.

The rules for blackjack, baccarat, or poker tournaments are slightly different from those of a slot tournament. The objective in these tournaments is to win more money than anyone else, usually within an hour or less (Roberts, 1992). Initially, there are three elimination rounds. After the elimination, there are semifinal and final rounds to determine the winner (Corea, 1994). The buy-in, or nonredeemable tournament chips, vary from hundreds to thousands of dollars. There is always a minimum and maximum bet for these games (Corea, 1994). Minimum bets can start as low as $5 to $10, and the maximum can be as high as $500.

As was previously mentioned, there are several reasons tournaments exist. Casinos use them as part of their marketing strategies to attract more clients. On the other hand, many casino patrons participate in them to win large sums of money or prizes. Individuals also enter tournaments just for fun.

Slot Clubs

Tracking systems developed for slot machines were initially designed to monitor the play of the customer. The evolutionary change that has taken place in slot-tracking systems allows the casino to monitor every aspect of the customers' playing habits. It provides demographic, sociological, and economic data at a glance. Promotional material is designed specifically for these groups and the events that draw them to the casino. Casinos all over the world are developing slot clubs to increase consumer response in revenue production. "The purpose of the slot club is specifically to identify and reward loyal customers," said Marc Conella, Vice President of Sales and Marketing and Customer Support at Bally's Gambling based in Las Vegas (Rzadzki, 1995). International Gaming Technology (IGT) has gone one step further with its SMART system. The IGT SMART system is a slot-marketing and revenue-tracking system. SMART is an online real-time

Slot club. *Source:* Windsor Casino, Windsor, Ontario.

data-collection and reporting system that uses computer technology to monitor machine functions and to track the play of customers. The system consists of two major components, the player tracking system (PTS) and the slot information system (SIS). PTS and SIS provide casino management information in six important areas: accounting, maintenance, management, marketing, operation, and security. The SMART player tracking system helps management identify valuable customers, build player loyalty, and gather timely and accurate marketing information by

1. Identifying unknown players using the Hot Player feature.
2. Offering players membership in a players' club that offers real benefits.
3. Monitoring plays as they occur for club members.
4. Providing communication with individual players at their machine.
5. Qualifying players based on current and historical play levels and quality of play.
6. Building a detailed database of players from which to market over time.

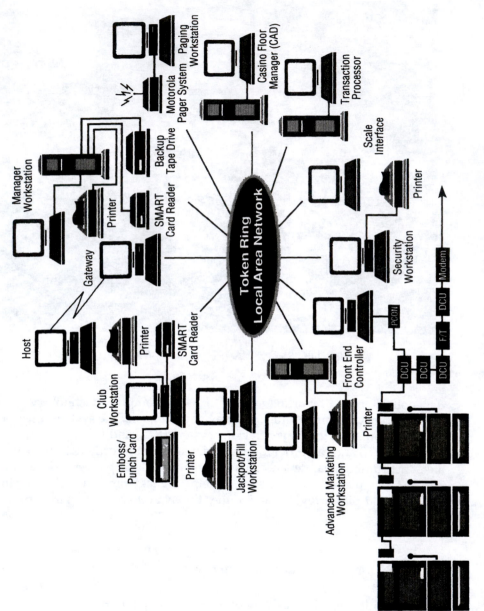

Manager Workstation

Backup Tape Drive

Motorola Pager System

Paging Workstation

Casino Floor Manager (CAD)

Transaction Processor

SMART Card Reader

Printer

Gateway

Token Ring Local Area Network

Scale Interface

Printer

Host

Printer

SMART Card Reader

Security Workstation

Club Workstation

Emboss/ Punch Card

Printer

Jackpot/Fill Workstation

Front End Controller

PCON

DCU

DCU

DCU

F/T

DCU

Modem

Advanced Marketing Workstation

Printer

IGT Smart System. *Source: International Gaming Technology, Las Vegas.*

7. providing several possible reward systems for good and loyal players

8. tracking groups of players and group providers to determine their worth.

9. providing a tournament function.

10. providing a marketing program that produces a list and mailing labels based on a variety of selection criteria to support direct-mail campaigns.

11. offering multiproperty recognition of corporate players.

12. providing a relational database of player information for use in marketing and analysis (Moreland, 1995).

Junkets

Junkets are another marketing strategy used in the casino industry. **Junkets** were developed in 1961 to increase the number of players inside a casino. Originally, junkets brought people to casino destinations packed in airplanes. The sole purpose of the junket passengers was to gamble for a specific period of time. The more an individual played, the more complimentary items he or she would receive.

The duration of a junket can vary. Some trips are three, four, or five nights. Junket clients are required to play a specific number of hours, usually four, each day. The junket players are observed, their average bet calculated, and the players rated. At the end of the trip, certain items such as airfare, room or suite, food, and beverage are comped, depending on a player's rate of play.

Many casinos hire **junket representatives (reps)** to solicit business for them on specified junkets. These reps arrange for and entice players to travel on their junkets. Some reps work specifically for one casino. These individuals are salaried. There are also independent reps who try to attract players to a number of casinos. Independent reps usually receive a commission of as much as 10 percent of the losses of the junket players.

All junket representatives must be registered to operate a junket. If they have a large volume of business, they must obtain a junket license, which requires an extensive background check. The reason these individuals are required to be licensed is to try to prevent criminal elements from entering the casino industry.

Entertainment

People go to casino destinations for a variety of reasons. Star-filled **casino entertainment** is a promotional technique used to attract customers to a casino. Casinos attract patrons by using five types of acts or entertainment. The types of entertainment are headline acts, reviews and musicals, boxing, comics, and lounge acts.

Headline acts are big name personalities. Many gamblers and nongamblers would like to see headlines perform, and therefore, they visit the casino. The marketing strategy is to use these individuals as lost-leaders to attract customers. Some of the renown headline acts include such performers as

- Barbra Streisand
- Frank Sinatra
- Johnny Mathis
- Englebert Humperdinck
- Wayne Newton
- Liza Minnelli
- Tom Jones
- Ray Charles
- Siegfried and Roy Circus & Magic Act

MGM Entertainment. *Source:* MGM Hotel and Casino.

Reviews and musicals are another type of entertainment enjoyed by casino patrons. Some of the mega-casinos have been able to hire outstanding Broadway reviews to perform in both Las Vegas and Atlantic City. Many individuals who would not have ordinarily been able to attend the review would have a chance within a casino environment. Casino management once again uses these attractions to obtain new gambling clients when they come to the review.

Another huge entertainment in many large casinos is **boxing.** The very nature of boxing is gambling. Casino entrepreneurs have capitalized on this desire and now hold large boxing matches, especially championship matches, in casino convention centers and parking lots. Huge crowds attend these matches. They usually visit the casinos before and after the boxing matches.

Comics such as Bill Cosby, Buddy Hackett, George Burns, David Brenner, and George Carlin are excellent casino entertainment. Some comics are headlines, whereas others are young talents waiting to be discovered. Notwithstanding their popularity, comics provide an invaluable portion of entertainment in the casino industry.

The last type of entertainment used as a promotional activity in casinos are **lounge acts.** Usually, these acts are local talent. The acts may include singers, pianists, and comedians. Lounge acts keep the casino alive into the wee hours of the mornings. Sometimes these acts are discovered and become stars.

Many of the aforementioned types of entertainment have to be booked at least five months in advance. The faces and names of the entertainment are usually advertised on billboards on the highways before you reach the casinos. Also, the casinos use in-house advertisement. The acts serve as an effective method of promoting the casino.

Interestingly, most of the entertainment provided in casinos is given free to high rollers. Ticket prices can vary from $20 for a review to $1,000 for a ring-side seat at a world championship boxing match. Casino entertainment is show business. People will pay for it one way or another.

One of the most successful marketing techniques used in Las Vegas is the opulence of casinos' exterior and interior design. One casino offers $633,000 rooms for $99 to $200 per night. The Bellagio, a 3,000-room resort, cost $1.9 billion to build; it is considered the most expensive hotel in the world. One of the main attractions of the resort is the $300 million Gallery of Art. The Gallery of Art contains original works by Cézanne, Gauguin, Matisse, Monet, Picasso, and Van Gogh. The shops at the Bellagio are marketed as a place where you can fantasize and spend your winnings from the megabucks jackpots (Casteman, 1999; Lister, 1998). This is the first attempt at using art to attract potential patrons to a casino resort (Lister, 1998).

Another form of entertainment that draws potential customers to the casino is sports betting. During the Super bowl, tens of thousands of fans descend on the Nevada casinos to place their bets on the Super bowl winners and losers. In 1999, over $80 million was wagered in the Nevada sports books during the Super bowl weekend. Although this is a tremendous amount of money, most casinos

Circus act. *Source:* Circus Circus, Las Vegas.

are not in sports booking for the profits, but use it as a means of marketing to potential high-margin game players. Most casinos view sports booking as a marketing tool. The first hotel to offer sports booking was the Stardust Hotel; "a typical sports bettor may put twenty dollars on a football game that is broadcast that weekend then spend several hundred dollars on slots or table games" (Mullen, 1999).

FOREIGN MARKET

A resource that has been tapped by the Las Vegas market is the foreign traveler. In 1990, 40 million visitors came to the United States. By the year 2000, the figure is expected to pass the 67-million mark, and in 2020 it is anticipated that it will reach 102.4 million. Projections call for the United States to rank second in international arrivals. International travelers come to the United States for numerous reasons: favorable exchange rates, shopping bargains, entertainment, business, vacations, and sight-seeing. Being aware of this, the casino marketing department should tap into this lucrative market by promoting its products and services in the countries that have the greatest number of potential travelers with disposable income (Weld, 1998).

Most large casinos market to the high-end, international baccarat or craps players, but there is another market, the international not-so-high end. This market is somewhere between the travel-budget-tour and the million-dollar-bankrolled groups from South America, the Middle East, and Asia. There is a defined segment of international tourist gamblers in those parts of the world who see American gaming experiences as a way to enhance a family or business trip. This group is more varied and has a more sharply defined profile than the normal international traveler; it also has a great deal of disposable income. "While they don't even approach the bankroll levels of the whale population around the world, many of them, uprooted from some research I did some time back, had gaming budgets in the $15,000 to $35,000 range. These were real budgets, not empty credit lines never used" (Klein, 1999).

SENIOR MARKET

Today, 65 million Americans over the age of fifty have the time and money to travel and to visit casinos. However, this segment of the population is still given little attention by casinos, which continue to focus on younger and middle-aged clientele. The growth in number and the relative affluence of this population implies an expanding potential market for the casino industry. Research on the senior market identified the needs of the senior population and established a behavioral profile of this market segment. The senior market can be segmented into smaller homogenous groups based on their needs, wants, and desires. The casinos that include appropriate services and structural enhancements of facilities will dominate the senior marketplace if they consider the biological, psychological, and sociological aspects of aging. For example, from the psychological and physical standpoint, many seniors are concerned with their physical safety and security. They often make decisions about where to stay based on their personal safety concerns. Before visiting a casino, they will ask their friends, relatives, and associates if they have visited a specific casino or casino resort to determine what level of physical safety they may encounter. Seniors need to be able to feel comfortable while traveling. To accomplish this, casino marketers must promote their faculty as being a secure and safe environment. "Respect was another factor that seniors considered important. The senior population expects courtesy and old-fashioned service. Although good service is very important to them they do not want to be treated like children. They do not want their limitations emphasized and prefer to make accommodations in advance. The senior traveler will not hesitate to make casino or hotel personnel, tour guides, or other members of the hospitality industry aware of their limitations" (Rudd, 1993).

Seniors are attracted to facilities that provide promotional material that highlights and addresses their concerns, such as brochures depicting large rooms, well-lit hallways, and a good price-value relationship. If a casino marketer can successfully address these concerns and provide the senior market with its needs, wants, and desires, its facility will become a forerunner within this emerging market segment (Rudd, 1993).

CONCLUSION

The casino industry has changed its customer focus from high rollers and grind customers to family and family entertainment. Recent contracts worth millions of dollars have been paid to headlines in order to attract this new customer base. The Mirage recently guaranteed Siegfried and Roy $57.5 million for its magic act (Buckley, 1992). This enormous sum of money was the highest amount ever paid in the history of Las Vegas entertainment. Surprisingly, the Mirage feels it will net at least three times that amount from the show for the duration of the contract.

Entertainment is now being used as a catalyst to bring people into the world of gambling and fantasy. The Las Vegas Hilton became the first hotel to launch a television campaign showing actual gambling in the ad. The spot featured upscale players crowding around and shooting dice. The depiction of

Luxor's laser show. *Source:* Luxor Hotel and Casino.

actual gaming in a television ad breaks new ground in a country where the Federal Communications Commission has prohibited such activities on the screen. The convention and visitors bureau still prefers advertising that establishes the city as an entertainment mecca and not a casino destination (Plume, 1999).

As gaming continues to mature and growth rates head for single digits, casino marketing is the most important tool of casino management. "Growth for individual operators will increasingly be a function of what they do to build repeat business through visitor loyalty. The most responsive properties will be the most successful. Efficient companies will emerge as the winners in this environment, and the strategic use of technology will play a key role in their success" (Amderer, 1998).

REVIEW TERMS

boxing	junkets
buy-in	lounge acts
casino entertainment	marketing
comics	reviews and musicals
headline acts	tournaments
junket representatives (reps)	

REFERENCES

Anderer, C. (1998). Strategies for a new age. *International Gaming and Wagering Business*, June.

Buckley, J. T. (1992). Rewriting the Las Vegas record book. *USA Today*, 1 December.

Casteman, D. (1999). The new new wave. *Nevada Magazine* 59(1):15.

Corea, L. (1994). Interview by author, July.

Felsenstein, D. (1998). Simulating impact of gaming on a tourism location. *Journal of Travel Research* 37(2):145.

Klein, H. J. (1999). Crowd control at the high end. *Casino Journal* 12(4).

Lister, H. (1998). Perry Como meets Lake Como. *Lodging* 24(4):11.

Moreland, R. F. (1995). *IGT SMART system*. Las Vegas, Nevada: IGT, 1–10.

Mullen, Liz. (1999). A two-billion-dollar marketing tool. *Sports Business Journal* 1(41):26.

Oppermann, Martin. (1999). Database marketing. *Journal of Travel and Tourism Research* 37:231.

Plume, J. (1999). Ad ruling breaks ground, opens abyss. *Casino Jounal* 12(1):66.

Roberts, P. (1992). Fasten your seatbelts . . . It's tournament craps. *Casino Player* IV (2):20–21.

Rudd, D. (1980). *Veterans needs survey.* Las Vegas: University of Nevada, 21.

Rudd, D. (1993). Marketing to senior conventioneers. Proceedings from the Convention Expo Summit IV, Las Vegas, Nevada.

Rzadzki, J. (1995). Slot Clubs. *International Gaming and Wagering Business* 16(2):30.

Tournament listings. (1994). *Casino Player* V (10):48–49.

Weld, W. (1998). Preparing for the wave. *Lodging* 24(1):29.

Chapter 11

Casino Financial and Accounting Control

OBJECTIVES

- Examine the procedures necessary to ensure casino financial stability.
- Develop an understanding of casino credit and its applications.
- Review the laws and procedures for casino credit and collection throughout the world.
- Develop an understanding of the major principles of casino finance.

HISTORY

Accounting can be defined as the process of recording, classifying, reporting, and interpreting the financial data of an organization (Walgenbech, 1977). The casino and gaming industry consists of a number of different types of operations that provide different products and services to their patrons. The casino industry provides lodging, food and beverage operations, entertainment, and recreational activities to the casino patrons. These customers can be local residents or travelers from afar.

The birth of accounting and financial procedures can be traced back to the ancient Egyptians. On the tombs of the ancient pharaohs, elaborate accounting procedures were depicted for the transactions of trade between the pharaoh's temples and neighboring countries. During the height of the Roman Empire, the Romans would deduct 1/18 of the value of a building for each year that the building remained functional. This procedure was the forerunner to modern depreciation. In the late 1400s, a Franciscan by the name of Paciolo from Venice developed the first form of double-entry bookkeeping. Although accounting has advanced much since then, it is still predicated on the principles and fundamental concepts developed by this fifteenth-century monk.

There are many different types and sizes of casinos and gaming operations, from a small bar with video and slots to the mega-casino offering table games, slots, video lotteries, keno, and sports booking, but one thing remains constant within them: a necessity for accurate and up-to-date accounting and financial information.

The casino and gaming industry is relatively labor intensive. Major industries across the United States, including the automobile and aircraft industries, have been able to reduce their basic labor need by improvements within technology. However, the casino industry remains intensely labor oriented. Labor intensity is not the only factor affecting the casino industry.

The industry itself is fixed/asset oriented. An example of this is the new MGM Casino, constructed at a cost of $1 to $1.25 billion. Like all assets, the building will be carried as a fixed asset and will be depreciated over time. The costs associated with the casino are relatively the same whether it is full or not. A casino or a casino game should be looked at as a perishable product: If the game is not played that day, it can never be played on that day or time again. The revenue that would have been generated is gone forever. Even if the casino doubles the amount of drop for tomorrow, the drop for that day has been lost forever. These are some of the factors that provide the accountants and financial advisors within the casino industry with their most difficult tasks.

In the past, the casino industry has faced major problems in acquiring capital for investment within the industry. Financial undertakings within the casino and gaming industry presented a moral as well as a high-risk potential. High construction costs and inflation have made the financing of casinos and entertainment complexes extremely difficult. The recent reduction in interest rates has substantially lowered these risks.

In the past, the sharing of accounting and financial data among casinos was limited. However, through the control agencies within each of the states where casino and gaming operations are legal, comparative analysis of data is now encouraged.

GENERALLY ACCEPTED ACCOUNTING PRINCIPLES

To become knowledgeable about the accounting methods of casinos, one must first understand basic accounting principles. The **generally accepted accounting principles (GAAP)** provide the basis for a comparative analysis within like or similar firms for the financial community. The GAAP was developed by the Financial Accounting Standards Board. These principles have been established over time through the efforts of the American Institute of Certified Public Accountants and the Financial Accounting Standards Board (Brock, 1976). The generally accepted accounting principles are discussed below.

Business Entity

The business entity principle assumes that the business in question maintains its own separate financial records and that the funds are not commingled with another business or the owner's funds. For example, a casino owner enters the cage area and withdraws $10,000 cash from the casino operations. This cash transaction should be charged directly to the owner and not to the business. When business transactions are recorded separately from those of the owner, a true picture of the financial profitability of the casino can be seen. In addition, it is a necessity in filing tax returns.

Element of Measurement

Businesses need some basic standard of measurement to compare and contrast their financial results. Without a unit of comparison, one would be unable to compare a large casino with a small casino. In the U.S. system, the unit of measurement is the dollar. However, at certain times the dollar becomes relatively meaningless; for example, during periods of high inflation. The exchange rate allows casinos in the United States to compare their results with worldwide operations.

Going Concern or Continuance of Business

The principle of going concern assumes that the business will continue for an indefinite period. If there is concern that a business may not continue into the future, then the asset value of the company would have to be reflected as the market value. For example, if a casino could not meet its present obligations, then those items carried on the balance sheet in excess of the market value of the property would have to be deleted.

Conservatism

The principle of conservatism requires the accountant to recognize expenses as soon as possible and to only recognize revenue as it is received. If there is a choice between two alternatives, the accountant will choose the lower one.

Costs

There are five different methods of establishing the costs of assets: current costs, current market, net realizable value, present value, and the one most often used, historic cost. For example, a casino that purchased ten used slot machines for $5,000 must list the slot machines at cost rather than at the $4,000 that the supplier might have paid for them or at the $10,000 the slot machines could be sold for.

Realization

In the casino and gaming industry, the realization concept is utilized to recognize the contributing revenue center. For example, in the casino industry when the drop is made and the table calculations are complete, the difference between the two determines that game's revenue or expense. The cash at the drop cannot be considered revenue, but an exchange in units of measurements from cash to casino chips.

The Materiality Principle

The materiality principle is concerned with the cost of specific items and their relationship to the time consumed in registering them. An example of this would be that $100 tokens that are blemished might be disposed of by a mega-casino because of their relative minor importance, but to a small casino they would represent a major consideration. The basic question that is asked is, Does this item affect the total financial statement of the casino?

Matching

The matching principle pertains to the point at which revenues are recognized against their costs. In most cases, the revenue is recognized first and then it is matched with the appropriate costs. An example of this would be a casino purchasing a computer system that will benefit the entire casino. The cost would be recorded as a fixed asset and would then be written off over the computer's useful life. This is attempting to match the revenue that the computer would generate with the expenses involved with the computer. This method is generally used when the accrual accounting system is used.

Consistency

The consistency principle requires that businesses give the same treatment to comparative transactions year after year. For example, there are several ways of depreciating a fixed asset over a number of years. If a casino were using the sum-of-the-year's-digits method (an accelerated form of depreciation) and later in the life of the asset changed to straight-line depreciation (a uniform method of depreciation), the true financial position of the casino would not be known.

Full Disclosure

The casino must provide full financial statements, and these statements must reflect the true and pertinent facts of the financial condition of the company. In some cases, additional disclosures must be made through the use of footnoting (e.g., provisions of bonds outstanding, details of pension plans, or medical plans). All these statements should summarize significant financial information. The disclosure should include the accounting methods used, recurring and non-recurring items, events that have happened after the financial statement dates, and any contingency or liability that may exist.

Objective Evidence

In most cases, objective evidence would be an invoice, bill, or canceled check. If these items are not available, then the accountant must estimate the costs involved. For example, the owner of a small casino gives a car as a prize to attract business for the casino. The casino owner believes the car to be worth $15,000, but the original list price of the car is $17,000 and an appraiser appraises the car at $10,000. In this case, the objective evidence would support the value established by the appraiser of $10,000.

The Accrual and Cash Basis Accounting Principle

Utilization of the accrual basis of accounting requires that cash is recognized when it is received and expenses are recognized when they occur. The cash system is relatively simple: We recognize the cash at the point at which it inflows or outflows. Most casinos are on an accrual system, not a cash system (Gibson, 1992).

BALANCE SHEET

Casinos, like all other business entities, need financial data to ensure their continued survival. The major financial statements that casinos utilize are balance sheets, income statements, and statements of change in financial positions (cash flow).

The **balance sheet** is the statement of financial position at a specific time. It represents the balance between the casino assets, which are the resources of the firm, and claims against those assets, known as liability and owners' equity (owners' interest in the firm). At any given point, the assets must equal the combination of the debts of the company plus the owners' share, or assets equal liability plus owners' equity (shareholders). The balance sheet represents a snapshot of the investment and financial activities of a casino as of a specific moment in time. It is like a single photograph (Davidson, 1988).

INCOME STATEMENT

The **income statement** is a summary of the revenue and expenses, gains and losses, for a specific period. In most cases, the income statement ends at the date of the balance sheet. It summarizes the results of the operation for a specific

CONSOLIDATED BALANCE SHEETS   CIRCUS CIRCUS ENTERPRISES, INC AND SUBSIDIARIES

JANUARY 31, (IN THOUSANDS, EXCEPT SHARE DATA)	1994	1993
ASSETS		
CURRENT ASSETS		
CASH AND CASH EQUIVALENTS	$ 39,110	$ 43,415
RECEIVABLES	8,673	3,977
INVENTORIES	20,057	16,565
PREPAID EXPENSES	20,062	14,478
TOTAL CURRENT ASSETS	87,902	78,435
PROPERTY, EQUIPMENT AND LEASEHOLD INTERESTS, AT COST, NET	1,183,164	851,463
OTHER ASSETS		
EXCESS OF PURCHASE PRICE OVER FAIR MARKET VALUE OF NET ASSETS ACQUIRED, NET	10,200	10,563
DEFERRED CHARGES AND OTHER ASSETS	16,658	9,997
TOTAL OTHER ASSETS	26,858	20,560
TOTAL ASSETS	$1,297,924	$950,458
LIABILITIES AND STOCKHOLDERS' EQUITY		
CURRENT LIABILITIES		
CURRENT PORTION OF LONG-TERM DEBT	$ 169	$ 154
ACCOUNTS AND CONTRACTS PAYABLE—		
TRADE	14,804	11,473
CONSTRUCTION	13,844	27,762
ACCRUED LIABILITIES—		
SALARIES, WAGES AND VACATIONS	19,650	16,097
PROGRESSIVE JACKPOTS	4,881	4,827
ADVANCE ROOM DEPOSITS	6,981	4,012
OTHER	25,648	20,363
INTEREST PAYABLE	2,278	2,098
INCOME TAX PAYABLE	3,806	708
TOTAL CURRENT LIABILITIES	92,061	87,494
LONG-TERM DEBT	567,345	308,092
OTHER LIABILITIES		
DEFERRED INCOME TAX	77,153	64,123
OTHER LONG-TERM LIABILITIES	1,415	740
TOTAL OTHER LIABILITIES	78,568	64,863
TOTAL LIABILITIES	737,974	460,449
COMMITMENTS AND CONTINGENT LIABILITIES		
STOCKHOLDERS' EQUITY		
COMMON STOCK $.01-2/3 PAR VALUE		
AUTHORIZED—450,000,000 SHARES		
ISSUED—96,168,769 AND 95,914,143 SHARES	1,603	1,599
PREFERRED STOCK $.01 PAR VALUE		
AUTHORIZED—75,000,000 SHARES	—	—
ADDITIONAL PAID-IN CAPITAL	120,135	111,516
RETAINED EARNINGS	618,446	502,257
TREASURY STOCK (10,062,814 AND 8,663,214 SHARES), AT COST	(180,234)	(125,363)
TOTAL STOCKHOLDERS' EQUITY	559,950	490,009
TOTAL LIABILITIES AND STOCKHOLDERS' EQUITY	$1,297,924	$950,458

THE ACCOMPANYING NOTES ARE AN INTEGRAL PART OF THESE CONSOLIDATED FINANCIAL STATEMENTS.

Balance sheet. *Source:* Circus Circus Enterprises Inc.

CONSOLIDATED STATEMENTS OF INCOME   CIRCUS CIRCUS ENTERPRISES, INC AND SUBSIDIARIES

YEAR ENDED JANUARY 31, (IN THOUSANDS, EXCEPT SHARE DATA)	1994	1993	1992
REVENUES			
CASINO	$538,813	$495,012	$471,823
ROOMS	176,001	147,115	141,716
FOOD AND BEVERAGE	152,469	135,786	129,951
OTHER	117,501	92,500	89,652
	984,784	870,413	833,142
LESS——COMPLIMENTARY ALLOWANCES	(29,861)	(27,388)	(27,119)
	954,923	843,025	806,023
COSTS AND EXPENSES			
CASINO	209,402	189,499	175,771
ROOMS	78,932	68,783	64,799
FOOD AND BEVERAGE	149,267	128,689	124,093
OTHER OPERATING EXPENSES	72,802	58,917	56,565
GENERAL AND ADMINISTRATIVE	152,104	130,152	124,313
DEPRECIATION AND AMORTIZATION	58,105	46,550	47,385
PREOPENING EXPENSE	16,506	—	—
	737,118	622,590	592,926
OPERATING PROFIT BEFORE CORPORATE EXPENSE	217,805	220,435	213,097
CORPORATE EXPENSE	16,744	14,953	12,706
INCOME FROM OPERATIONS	201,061	205,482	200,391
OTHER INCOME (EXPENSE)			
INTEREST, DIVIDENDS AND OTHER INCOME (LOSS)	(683)	820	245
INTEREST EXPENSE	(17,770)	(22,989)	(43,632)
	(18,453)	(22,169)	(43,387)
INCOME BEFORE PROVISION FOR INCOME TAX	182,608	183,313	157,004
PROVISION FOR INCOME TAX	66,419*	62,330	53,656
INCOME BEFORE EXTRAORDINARY LOSS	116,189	120,983	103,348
EXTRAORDINARY LOSS ON EARLY EXTINGUISHMENT OF DEBT, NET OF INCOME TAX			
BENEFIT OF $1,885	—	(3,661)	—
NET INCOME	$116,189	$117,322	$103,348
EARNINGS PER SHARE			
INCOME BEFORE EXTRAORDINARY LOSS	$ 1.34	$ 1.41	$ 1.23
EXTRAORDINARY LOSS ON EARLY EXTINGUISHMENT OF DEBT	—	(0.04)	—
NET INCOME PER SHARE	$ 1.34	$ 1.37	$ 1.23

THE ACCOMPANYING NOTES ARE AN INTEGRAL PART OF THESE CONSOLIDATED FINANCIAL STATEMENTS.

Income statement. *Source:* Circus Circus Enterprises Inc.

accounting period. Income statements reflect the revenue, which is the inflow of assets; the expenses, which are the outflow of assets; the gains, which are the increase in assets; and the losses, which are the decrease in assets for a specific period. In casino operations, the income statements may be prepared weekly or monthly for management's use and quarterly or annually for outsiders, such as creditors and government agencies (Gibson, 1992).

STATEMENT OF CHANGE IN FINANCIAL POSITION

The statement of change in financial position, better known as the **cash flow statement,** details the source and use of cash during a specific period. The cash flow statement shows the effect on cash of businesses' investments, financial activities, and operations. In the casino industry, the casino manager is extremely interested in the daily cash flow statement because of its use in determining the ability of a casino to meet its current obligations and its ability to predict future net cash flows.

Each of the above-mentioned financial statements is useful to the casino manager, owners, and shareholders in specific ways. The balance sheet depicts at a specific point in time how well the company's management has invested the casino's resources in specific assets and how these assets are financed by loans, bonds, or shareholder's equity. The income statement shows the managers and owners the amount of income a casino earned during a specific period. The shareholder's equity statement depicts the change in ownership during a specific period. It also shows the accumulation of any income that might be retained within the business. And last, the cash flow statement shows the casino's cash receipts and cash payments during a specific accounting period. In addition, it provides information to management and owners about the casino's operating investments and all other financial activities during a specific accounting period. All activities that affect cash in any way must be summarized on this statement. It provides the investors with information helpful in determining the company's ability to manage its cash, pay its liabilities, pay its dividends, and generate future cash flow to the casino (Needles, 1990).

Each country and each state has different and distinct regulations requiring casinos to account for their revenue. The primary concern of these regulatory agencies is the collection of gaming taxes and fees. In most instances, the regulatory agencies' largest concern is the same as that of the casino: the safeguarding of its assets, the reliability of its financial records, and the consistent and timely recording and execution of transactions, according to the authorization of management. This allows the regulatory agencies to compare and contrast a casino's internal financial data from one accounting period to the next and an external comparison by the agencies of all gaming operations under their control. Most of the control agencies require internal control systems for the drop counting procedures, fill and credit procedures, revenue accounting, and, most of all, cage or casino control operations. These procedures are covered under regulatory requirements and modern casino operations.

To better understand the operations within a casino, an illustration of a typical cycle within a casino operation will be given. The casino cage that houses the house bank roll consists of cash, chips, and change for the gaming operations. For a game to initiate on the floor or in the pit (a pit being a group of games within a casino), usually four crap tables, or twelve other tables, make up a management section (the larger the casino, the more pits it will have). Chips have to be transferred from the cage to the tables. To do this, a fill slip is prepared. The **fill slip** records the transaction and the amount of chips that are being transferred. A request for a fill slip requires the pit boss's signature. This is a two-part form; the original is sent to the fill bank and the duplicate remains on the table until the fill arrives. When the chips arrive at the table, they are accompanied by the fill slip. The amount is checked and initialed by the pit boss, and the fill slip is given to the dealer. The dealer signs his/her name and license number, if appropriate, after agreeing on the accuracy of the fill slip and duplicate. The floor person is then handed the slip for his/her signature and license number. The floor person returns the original to the dealer. The dealer drops the duplicate slip into the drop box and the original fill slip is returned to the cage (St. Clair College, 1993).

The **drop box** is a box attached to each table game through which receipts and cash are placed. A player at the table will either purchase chips from the cashier window or from the table with cash, traveler's checks, or credit. All these are immediately deposited in the drop box. If the player decides to play with cash, as soon as the table has won any cash, it is immediately deposited in the drop box. When a customer plays for credit, the pit boss presents him or her with a credit voucher, which is a promissory note that he or she signs and one copy of which is deposited in the drop box, one of which is retained on file at the originating pit, and one of which is returned to the cage. A credit slip is then issued to the table and placed in the drop box. The credit voucher is then returned to the cage, where it remains in the custody of the cage for accountability. When the credit customer has completed his/her play, he/she may redeem the credit instrument at the casino cage. In some casinos, the instrument may be repaid right at the gaming table rather than at the cage. At the end of a shift or the closing of a table, all of the pit's chips are returned to the cage and a credit voucher is issued in the amount of the chips that were received. The contents of the drop box are then counted. To determine the win or loss, the total amount of cash and credit instruments issued and credit received for chips returned to the cage are added together and the fills received from the cage are deducted. This amount represents the table win or loss. All fill slips and credit slips must contain the following information. First, they must be date and time stamped. Second, they must contain the shift at which time the fill took place or the credit was issued. Third, they must contain the game, table, and pit in which the transaction took place. Fourth, they must contain the total value of the fill or the credit that was issued to the player. Fifth, they must contain the total value of each denomination of chip; for example, red are normally five, green are twenty-five, and black are one hundred. Sixth, they must contain appropriate signatures; normally casinos require four signatures on a fill slip and three signatures on a credit slip (Friedman, 1992).

At a number of casinos, the gaming tables do not return their chips to the cage. They maintain an inventory level similar to a cashier's drawer. The starting balance is subtracted from the ending balance, and the difference represents the inflow and outflow for the day. All transactions that take place at the table or in the casino cage are documented, providing a paper trail for auditing and accounting procedures. Win or loss for a casino represents either an increase or a decrease in the casino's assets as a result of specific gaming.

GAMING TABLE TRANSACTIONS

The win or loss is demonstrated in the following example.

Cash in the drop box		$24,000	
Credit issued and outstanding		$12,000	
Total drop			$36,000
Minus: Beginning table inventory	$56,000		
Chips transfers			
Fills		$20,000	
Credits		($4,000)	
			$72,000
Ending table inventory	$44,000		$28,000
Win			$8,000

At the end of the shift or the closing of tables, a computation of the win or loss amount is done by table, by game, or by pit for every shift. This data is then recorded on a shift sheet, which is the master game report document. The results are then totaled for each game by shift, and the daily totals are calculated from these (American Institute of Certified Public Accountants, 1984).

CASINO SLOT ACCOUNTING

The basic business cycle for slot machine operations or VLTs starts with the filling of the hoppers on each of the machines. Each machine receives a predetermined amount of coins in whatever denomination the machine accepts; for example, nickels, dimes, quarters, half-dollars, dollars, and tokens (a token is a coin that is substituted for a specific dollar amount). This is referred to as the hopper load. The first or subsequent slot fills can be obtained either from the slot booths or from the main cage. Fill slips similar to those used in the pits provide accountability for transfer of coins from the cage to the slot booths to the slot machines.

As customers use the machines, the hoppers fill up with the coins that are inserted by the customers. When the hoppers are full, these coins drop into the drop bucket. When a customer hits a jackpot or receives a payout, the coins come from the hopper. If a number of large payouts are made, the slot's hopper will need to be filled. If a customer hits a large jackpot and there are insufficient coins within the machine to pay the jackpot, the jackpot is then paid by the change person, who receives payment from the change bank, cashier, or the casino cage (Ortiz, 1992). At this time, a numerically kept jackpot payout slip is filled in. In most casinos, jackpots over a specific amount, for example, $500, require the approval of a supervisor on duty. A large number of casinos now offer their customers the opportunity to play quartermania, megamania, and exotic games. Jackpots at these games can run into the millions of dollars. Donna Casesse, slot manager for the Luxor hotel, was the slot manager on duty the night the Mirage Hotel hit the megamania for $3 million. She stated that "Approval for payment had to come from God himself."

At a specified time each day, a **hard count** is taken from the drop buckets located securely under the slot machine. The coins from each of the machines are collected and are counted or weighed to determine the slot drop, which is then recorded within the slot records. When the hard count is taken, the slot and VLT meters on the machines are read. With some of the newer machines, the readings are taken electronically. The older machines are visually read. From this electronic or meter information, the actual hold percentage is computed and compared to the theoretical hold percentage for each of the machines. The recorded drop meter readings are compared with the actual drop to determine whether there is a discrepancy. If there is, an investigation is initiated. The win/loss for the slots is computed by machine and then by denominations. It is then added and totaled. Similar to that of the floor games, the slot machines' and VLTs' win or loss is equal to the drop minus the fills and any hand-paid jackpots.

The cage provides the accounting department with the slot summary sheets and any supporting documentation such as the hopper fill slips, credit slips, and jackpot paid slips. An audit is then performed using the following calculation to determine the gross slot win:

$$\text{Win} = \text{Drop} - \text{Jackpot tickets} - \text{Jackpot payouts} + \text{Hopper fills}$$

The coins that are carried within the slot operation are looked on as gaming tools, but are carried as part of the cage's cash inventory.

KENO

Keno is a game that casinos love. The statistics are heavily in their favor, providing them with a 25 percent advantage. The accounting for keno in most places is operated using a common bank. The keno cashiers issue a set amount of money to each of the keno runners, who in turn bank the games. At the end of each shift,

K E N O

Keno is simply a game of guessing numbers. In each game, 20 balls with distinct numbers are randomly drawn out of 80 in our Keno Lounge. Those numbers are flashed on various Keno boards throughout the casino, studio cafe and Keno lounge areas.

To make a wager on the game, obtain a Keno ticket and mark the numbers you wish to play with a bold "X". Write the amount you wish to bet on the top right-hand corner of your ticket, and below it, the number of spots you have selected.

After picking your lucky numbers, present your Keno ticket and wager to one of our Keno Runners, or at the window of the Keno Lounge. The Keno Writer or Runner will register your ticket and return an authorized game ticket with the number of the game you are playing in the top right-hand corner. Your ticket is good for that game only, and winnings must be collected before the start of the next game.

Keno Talk

Way or Combination Tickets – An exciting variation of Keno which lets you play several number combinations on just one ticket. These more sophisticated tickets are fun and challenging and greatly increase your odds on some winning combinations.

Multi-Race Keno – This is another fun way to play your favorite tickets. Ask your Keno Writer or Runner to explain this option to you. This will allow you to enjoy yourself throughout the property without interruption.

For more information and detailed instructions on Keno, ask one of our Keno Writers or Runners, or pick up a free Keno brochure.

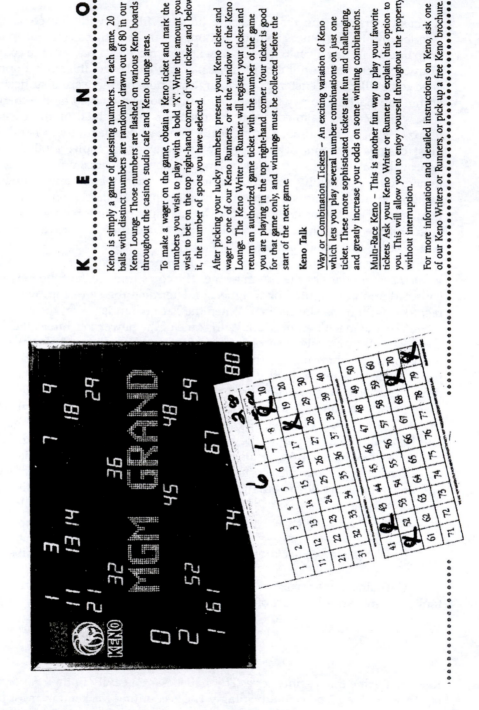

Keno. *Source:* Circus Circus, Las Vegas.

the banks are closed out and the difference between the opening bank and the closing bank is the shift's win or loss. Then this amount is returned to the cage. There are some advantages and disadvantages to this. The common bank allows for ease of operation. However, if there is a loss, it is difficult to pinpoint the keno runner who is responsible. In the majority of the newer casinos, a bank is issued to each individual runner and tallied by individuals rather than a common bank. The accounting procedure is similar to that of slots and floor operations, in that the keno runner fills out a fill slip, which in this case normally contains the name of the employee and the opening bank. The keno runner takes the customers' tickets and cash and gives change. These tickets are submitted, processed, and returned to the customers. The game is checked by the keno runner and prizes are paid if appropriate. If the prize is larger than the runner's bank, the keno cage provides the payments. At the end of a shift, the keno supervisors conduct an audit to determine the win percentage. The shift report processed by the supervisors contains the date and time of the shift and signatures of at least two people. It is obtained by taking the value of the closing keno banks minus the opening keno banks minus the fills to keno; this equals the keno shift win. In most states where keno is legal, gaming operations utilize it to its fullest extent (Freidman, 1974).

INTERNAL CASINO ACCOUNTING

At the conclusion of each shift, casino cage personnel do a reconciliation of all cash and cash equivalents that they hold within the cage. These are normally summarized for the shift's operation, the day's operation, the week's operation, and the month's operation. This reconciliation includes the cage's total inventory of all cash equivalents, such as gambling chips, credit instruments, coins, and currency. These are compared to the balance at the beginning of the period of time (e.g., shift, day, week, or month). The basic business of the casino is cash and cash equivalents. It is a direct function of gambling activities. It is affected by the amounts contained within the drop boxes, payments received for markers and credit instruments, and the transfer of excess cash above that which is needed to bank. When the inventory of chips is taken, many casinos find that they are short chips. In some cases, this is due to the chip float, a large number of customers at casinos take chips home as souvenirs; these chips are never returned but represent a potential liability to casinos and must be carried as such.

A growing percentage of gambling at casinos today is done on credit. To receive credit at a casino, a guest must apply through the casino credit department and provide it with credit information and identification. Normally this is done prior to the arrival of the customer at the casino. In most casinos, check-cashing and credit policies are established by management. The credit systems at the majority of the casinos are computerized. The computer processes the data when a guest cashes a check or obtains credit from a casino. The system provides verification and requires the date, time, amount of the transaction, and an identification code from the employee entering the data into the computer system. The amount of the transaction is deducted from the guest's established credit line. If the transaction were in excess of the guest's established limit, an executive would be required to override the system and issue further credit. The system has within it an automatic float system that clears transactions after a given period of time. Executives within the casino have the authority to override the system (Newman, n.d.).

It is in the casinos' best interest to grant credit to customers. By doing so, they increase their drop and their potential win. The creation of credit enhances the guests' ability to interact and facilitate with gaming activities. The collection rate for credit in the casino industry is relatively high. In some casinos, from 50 to 60 percent of their total table drop is credit. In *Casino Credit and Collection Laws* Anthony Cobalt states that a casino's attorneys become involved in the collection of gaming debts only after all reasonable attempts to collect from gaming patrons have failed, and the casino determines that the patron has the ability to pay but, for whatever reason, refuses to honor his or her obligation.

In the United States, most states have adopted the British statutes involving the enforcement of gambling debts. These prohibit the enforcement of gambling debts collection in the United States and in Britain. Presently a number of states are changing these laws because of gambling activities located within their states. Those states that have casino and gaming operations within them will be adopting resolutions to protect the individual gamblers as well as the casinos.

To maintain the customers' loyalty, it is in the casino's best interests that credit only be extended to those guests who can afford to pay it back, and in a reasonable amount that will ensure the continued patronage of their clients. Casino executives are not doing their job if they grant credit to a guest and the casino does not receive payment (Cobalt, 1989).

In addition to all these other activities undertaken by the casino cage, the casino cage is responsible for keeping the general ledger. Ledgers are files that contain all the accounts within an accounting system. In large casinos there may be subsidiary ledgers, but a general ledger must be maintained to summarize these ledgers. For example, cash itself may be contained within the subsidiary ledger, with separate subsidiary ledgers maintained for each type of cash. However, the general ledger's cash account would include the total balance of all these subsidiary accounts. The economic effect of all the transactions of the casino is captured within this general ledger, and the financial story of the casino begins (Danos, 1991). The general ledger should agree with the cage's daily summaries. If not, the auditors have their work cut out for them.

REVIEW TERMS

accounting	fill slip
balance sheet	generally accepted accounting principles (GAAP)
cash flow statement	hard count
drop box	income statement

REFERENCES

American Institute of Certified Public Accountants. (1984). *Audits of casinos.* New York: AICAP, 1–77.

Brock, Horace. (1976). *Accounting: Principles and application.* New York: McGraw-Hill, 9.

Cobalt, Anthony. (1989). *Casino credit and collection laws.* International Association of Gaming Attorneys.

Danos, Paul. (1991). *Casino supervision: A basic guide.* California: Panzer Press, 126.

Davidson, Sidney. (1988). *Financial accounting.* New York: Dryden Press, 7–9.

Fay, C., Rhoads, R., and Rosenblatt, R. (1976). *Managerial accounting for the hospitality service industry.* Iowa: William C. Brown Publisher.

Friedman, Bill. (1974). *Casino management.* New Jersey: Lyle-Stuart, 220.

Friedman, Bill. (1992). *Casino management.* New Jersey: Lyle-Stuart, 338.

Gibson, Charles. (1992). *Financial statement analysis.* Cincinnati: South-West Publishers.

Needles, Belverd. (1990). *Principles of accounting.* Boston: Houghton Mifflin, 732–735.

Newman, William. (n.d.) *Current information systems developed in the gaming industry.* Informational paper. Reno, Nevada.

Ortiz, Darwin. (1992). *On casino gambling.* New York: Lyle-Stuart, 190.

Schmidgall, R., Tarr, S., and Fay, C. (1982). Michigan: Educational Institute of the American Hotel Motel Association.

St. Clair College. (1993). *Blackjack dealers procedures manual.* Ontario, Canada: St. Clair College.

Walgenbech, Paul. (1977). *Financial accounting.* New York: Harcourt Brace Jovanovich, 4.

Chapter 12

Security and
Surveillance

OBJECTIVES

- Explain the function and procedures of security in the casino and gaming industry.
- Familiarize the reader with the computer and technological advances that have taken place in the security and surveillance industry.
- Examine the establishment and maintenance of e-files.

SECURITY

Security for a major casino today involves far more than the protection and surveillance of gaming operations. The security of the premises is a considerable undertaking. The MGM Grand Hotel must protect its 5,100 guest rooms, 500 suites, convention facilities, a 36-acre amusement park, parking lots, restaurants, theaters, and a $1.25 billion investment. This is the primary function of the security director. In many instances, the security, surveillance, and internal auditor for the hotel work closely together, investigating and uncovering covert and ingenious plots to embezzle or steal funds from the casino.

Prior to the opening of the MGM Grand Hotel, now called Bally's Casino, the director of security stated that the MGM Grand Hotel would have more security personnel working in the hotel than the entire city of Las Vegas had employed to protect the city. Security and surveillance is one of the main concerns of operators of casinos and gaming establishments. Casinos are well aware that when individuals handle vast amounts of currency, there is an overwhelming temptation for many of them to steal. A casino's ultimate profit is derived from a very small win percentage. This win is based on a huge volume of currency passing over tables and through slot machines. When an ingenious thief devises a way to siphon funds from the operation, it takes a large volume of currency to replace this small loss. Many casinos throughout the world have gone into bankruptcy because their security and management teams were not effective in preventing this type of theft (Denos, 1991).

Technology and science provide a varied range of physical security means and measurements that can help the hospitality, casino, and gaming industry reduce its potential risks and diminish its losses. The people factor is ever important in the security and surveillance of the hospitality and gaming industry. It is people that must deal with people; it is employees coming in contact with guest property and casino assets that are the prime responsibility of the security director.

It is the prime responsibility of a gaming establishment to protect its guests and their property, but in many cases guests contribute to or are responsible for losses or damage to assets and property at casinos. They do not limit themselves to the theft of ashtrays, soapbars, or towels; anything that is not nailed down becomes fair game. Security problems within the casino gaming industry must be recognized for what they are, and solutions must be forthcoming. Problems that are ignored will not disappear, nor will they solve themselves. A quick solution is no solution at all. The modern security director emphasizes prevention rather than prosecution. In this manner, a limited amount of guest interference takes place and employees are not restrained in the performance of their duties. From a financial and social viewpoint, it is far more economical to prevent a problem than it is to identify, apprehend, and punish those who are responsible for it (Burstein, 1985).

A comprehensive and sound loss prevention policy will improve operational efficiency, enhance the casino's image, and generate additional working capital without providing exorbitant expenses to a hospitality and gaming concern. Security is more than one of the management functions. It is a valuable tool, and one that must be utilized by management.

Security can be broken down into five major areas. First is physical security, which deals with the physical makeup of the hotels, restaurants, and casinos. It delves into the perimeter of the property, the internal design, electronic devices, storage and protection, and the grounds security itself.

The casino and gaming complex must be capable of being physically secured, particularly at night. The term *physically secured* means that it is improbable that unauthorized persons can enter a property without being observed, or without the use of force or physical violence. It is the function of security to provide a means whereby guests and their valuables and the assets of the casino can be protected simultaneously. Under physical security, things that are relevant are the location of the gaming property, police protection provided by the local and state authorities, and the size of the property. The size of the property increases the problem when there are a large number of entrances and exits. The availability of staff will directly affect the security operation of the casino, because security itself is a 24-hour-a-day operation. The value of the property itself and the assets within bear a direct relationship to the security requirement. The basic question is how much the gaming property is willing to spend to limit its exposure to theft.

Second is guest security. Guest security looks at the protection of guests, conventions, and groups. A casino and gaming operation is concerned with the safety of the guests, whether they are in their assigned rooms, hallways, public facilities, or in the casino itself. In addition, casinos invite the general public to use a portion of their casino complex. Although the law does make a distinction between the responsibilities to a guest staying in a facility and to an invited patron, the gaming concern should strive to avoid any injuries or possible unpleasantness for any of its customers. Security and the guests' safety go hand in hand. Guests are the most important commodity that a casino has, and the safety of these guests is the primary function of the director of security (Buzby, 1978).

The third area is administrative and operational security. This deals with human resources, food and beverage departments, public relations, computer operations, and front office. As noted earlier, sound physical security effort will prevent unauthorized personnel from gaining access to the casino's property and stealing a gaming concern's property. However, the securing of the physical property will not solve problems caused by employees who are in unauthorized areas and embezzling or stealing assets of the gambling concern. To effectively combat these problems, it is necessary to develop a system of administrative policies and procedures, implement them, and ensure that they are followed. Physical security helps to protect the casino's real property, but to prevent the loss of other assets, the physical and administrative security must be combined. There is a concern within the casino operation for the security of cash, not only on the casino floor, but in the food and beverage, and front office operations. Because the front of the house is where the sales take place and where cash changes hands, it is there that a higher percentage of pilfering on the part of the employees takes place. This same pilfering takes place in the bar operations and in restaurant operations if adequate controls are not maintained. In the back of the house, where guests never go, security systems can be set up all over without regard to the aesthetics or the effect on the subtle moods that restaurants attempt to establish (Security World, 1979). The single, most important factor in any organization's loss prevention efforts is the human one. Modern technological security devices are only as good as the people who run them. Thus, a casino's personnel practices and procedures, from preemployment screening, hiring, training, and termination, are of paramount importance to the success of any security system. The security division is concerned with the computerized gaming systems within a gaming concern; however, the operational system of the casino is another aspect that is sometimes overlooked. The two are related but different, and failure to protect both the software and hardware used for various operational systems and management functions could have a disastrous effect on any casino operations using an in-house computer system. In most casinos today, the computerized system coordinates and controls the accounting, auditing, safety, forecasting, and even the wake-up calls within the hotel division. The benefits and the savings from the systems are enormous. However, the assumptions that these computer operations need neither security nor physical protection can be disastrous. The system itself and the backup data and terminals need physical security (Burstein, 1985).

Fourth is emergency security. This deals with fires, bombs, and natural disasters. The emphasis on fire prevention and control has escalated since the disaster at the old MGM Grand in Las Vegas, Nevada. The last thing an emerging industry such as the casino industry needs is the roaring fire and billowing black smoke on the front pages of the *New York Times*. It is the duty of the security department to ensure that the gaming property is protected from fire and natural disasters. The training of employees and staff in preventive techniques and procedures has become a central part of the security and human resources training programs during employee orientation and subsequent employee reorientation. When an emergency does occur, the difficulty is not gaining the employee's attention but rather having the employee act appropriately and immediately to a stressful situation. In most cases, the employees' reaction would be a simple one; notify the police, call the fire department, etc. Even though the reaction is simple, these actions may not be taken if the person panics. The clear cure for such potential panic is training that will allow the employee to act correctly on an instinctive basis. This is not orientation training; this is continuous training (Palmer, 1990).

The fifth area deals with the security department and involves the training, supervision, responsibilities, and authority of the security department. In the casino industry, no position other than the general manager's entails as much variety or such a range of activities and responsibilities as that of a security director. The security director is responsible for the security staff, facilities, and equipment within the property. Personnel within the security department may include watchmen, guards, security officers, and assistants; and each would have a unique role to play in providing security within the gaming concern. The security director is directly responsible for training and supervising personnel. Cooperation between the security department and other departments in the gaming concern determines the effectiveness of its security department.

Every day tourists throughout the world are demanding more security and asking their travel agents whether a property is safe. Security is not limited to foreign countries, but is becoming a necessity within the United States. For most hoteliers in the United States, the question is not whether they can afford to provide reasonable security for their guests; after all, that is the minimum required by law. The question is how much security must the hotel provide to keep its guests happy. Experts in the tourism industry agree that safety and friendly hospitality are the two attributes most important to travelers today (Marshall, 1994).

An Example of Hotel Security

To observe a security department in action, the authors went to see Mr. E. J. Vogel, Director of Security for the Excalibur Hotel in Las Vegas. He is a former Cincinnati police officer and Boulder City Chief of Police and is a member of the Gaming Control Board of Nevada. He stated that there are a number of differences between civilian operations and gaming operations, and that in reality gaming operations are easier than civilian operations because of the lack of incarceration and procedures involving arrest and prosecution. Years ago, hotel casino security forces were as large for one hotel as they were for the entire city of Las Vegas. The Excalibur Hotel has a relatively small number of uniformed officers, 113, in addition to 5 plainclothes officers and 15 supervisors. In the old hotels, security was not as efficient. Burglaries within the hotels had been rampant. Now, security I.D.s are required for all personnel and guests using the elevators. Burglaries were one of the main problems that casinos faced. The improvements in elevator security have reduced this problem drastically. The hotel does screen its new employees extensively. Executive and casino personnel must undergo screening by the Nevada Gaming Board, and all other employees must have a valid Las Vegas I.D. card. A number of hotels use drug testing, but polygraph testing is not routinely administered to employees in the casino hotel operations. The Circus World Hotels operate independently, but there are joint operations, such as Slots of Fun, Circus Circus in Las Vegas and Reno, Luxor, Excalibur, Silver City, Colorado Belle and Edgewater in Laughlin, and part interest in the Windsor Casino in Windsor, Canada. For example, both the Excaliber and the Luxor work together in certain areas of security and management.

Hotel and casino security officer training involves a forty-hour training program, report writing, personnel tracking, firearm training, a six-week on-the-job program, and a course in commonsense security for personnel interaction with customers and guests. During the six-week on-the-job program, the security guards are graded and observed. In addition to normal yearly training, all security personnel are firearm qualified every six months. The green security procedural manual is 280 pages long; it provides the basis for promotion including oral, written, and competitive examinations. Twice a year all security personnel are evaluated by their superiors. Mr. Vogel stated that a number of casinos are allowing card counters to participate in casino games. These individuals are merely highly skilled players. Mr. Vogel also stressed that the primary purpose of the security department was the safety of the customers and guests, and the protection of company assets and liability. Mr. Vogel also pointed out that a different unit was involved in surveillance, and the surveillance department worked in close alliance with the security department. The security department is involved mainly with the guests and the hotel operations. Surveillance, on the other hand, is principally involved in the gaming aspect of the casino. If people within the casino are caught cheating or manipulating machines, they are turned over to the

Nevada Gaming Control Board, who then prosecutes them through the District Attorney's office. If individuals are involved in theft or stealing within the hotel or casino, they are turned over to the Las Vegas Police Department and are prosecuted by them.

Some of the major problems that casinos face today are guests losing personal items. With the emphasis on family vacations to Las Vegas, the presence of children and underage persons within the casino and on the gaming floor is another serious concern. Most casinos do not want to risk losing their licenses, so they enforce stringent regulations regarding children on the gaming floor. The difficulty is readily apparent when, in walking from the front desk to rooms, guests must pass through the casino.

To patrol the vast property, a twelve-person bike unit and four vans are utilized in three eight-hour shifts per day. Security problems within the casino involve people called scoopers. These are individuals who steal coins from the slot machine trays of other people playing the machines. Women, when involved in the rush of slot gambling, often leave their purses unattended. Professional pickpockets cruise the casino looking for likely victims. In some cases, surveillance teams up with security and notifies them of these problems.

One of security's functions is to ensure that money is taken from the tables in the form of drop boxes and is safety escorted to the counting room, where it is counted or weighed. In most Las Vegas casinos, change is weighed to determine the value. Private corporations such as Brinks provide pickup of funds from casinos. In addition to escorting money, security provides escort and supervision of repair personnel within the casino and hotel area. Someone has to watch the repair personnel fixing the slot machine, roulette wheel, crap table, and so on.

One of the areas of interest within the casino is known as risk management. This is essentially guest relations operation. It provides protection against liability for guest injuries that occur within the casino or hotel. Security personnel take pictures and statements, and attempt to make a settlement before the action goes to court.

There are two basic philosophies in the hotel industry for the handling of guest injuries. The first one sees guests as a source of liability; therefore, if guests fall, don't pick them up but let them crawl out, because anything that you might do will only aggravate the situation. Under the second philosophy, the hospitality unit does everything in its power to provide for the guests; house doctors are used, and x-rays and statements are taken from the guests, providing the guests with a feeling of concern. In addition, the facility receives firsthand data on the accident so that it can utilize it in future litigation.

Casino and gaming complexes spend millions of dollars on security systems. The protection of the casino's assets is the responsibility of all employees, not just the security department. If management believes in the importance of security procedures and develops a positive security philosophy, the security of the property is ensured.

SURVEILLANCE

The casino and gaming **surveillance** department's primary functions are to prevent theft and provide security for guests and employees of a property. In most cases, the people involved in surveillance are retired police chiefs or police officers, because management believes that these individuals had been trained in all types of surveillance activities. The director of surveillance should coordinate and provide assistance to other departments within the casino. Fortunately for the surveillance department, the public believes that the eye in the sky catches all (see next section). In reality, the surveillance department is only as good as the personnel that monitor the equipment or the informers that provide information. This information can be provided by monitors, computers, alarm systems, telephones, or informers. A good surveillance department must be aware of all that is happening throughout a gaming property, not just in the casino itself. Like the

Surveillance cameras. *Source:* Harrah's Hotel and Casino, Las Vegas.

security department, the surveillance department has a procedural manual to guide and direct its surveillance efforts. This manual provides the basis for a successful surveillance operation. In general, people are honest, but dishonesty is close at hand. For example, at the casino change booth, a customer asks for dollars and hands the cage personnel a $20 bill; in return he or she receives $100 in change. How many people would say, "Take 80 of this back, I only gave you a 20"? Or, the customer is at the slot machine and the payoff is three cherries or $10, and he or she receives $100 in tokens. How often do they turn the service light on and inform the change person that they have been overpaid by $80? The guest is playing blackjack, the dealer has 18 and the guest has 18 yet the dealer pays the guest as a winner. Does the guest normally say no, I don't get paid because it is a tie? Working with large sums of money, including chips and tokens in a casino, it becomes very difficult for individuals to remain honest. That is the point of the eye in the sky. If the guests and the employees believe that the eye in the sky can catch them in a dishonest act, they will probably not commit that act.

Imagine the following: A man walks up to the entrance of a casino's money room. He pauses at the door and his eye is scanned, and he is authorized admittance. The door is then automatically opened. This is not a Reeves movie (*Matrix*)—technologies like this are used in a number of casinos." And as crooks become more sophisticated in their methods for bilking cash from casinos, security and surveillance professionals have likewise turned to state-of-the-art equipment in order to level the playing field. New digital cameras, identification technology and advanced recorders are just some of the tools casinos now use to catch criminals and deter potential scam artists" (Parets, 1999).

Eye in the Sky

The **eye in the sky** is there to protect the casino's assets and to ensure that guests receive equitable and fair treatment while in the casino. It is a surveillance system located above the casino tables and in some cases it utilizes cameras. In some cases it is necessary for security and the internal auditor to work with surveillance to undercover and apprehend potential thieves. When the internal auditor detects a discrepancy within the paper trail, he or she notifies the security department, which in turn may work with the surveillance department to evaluate and correct these discrepancies.

Even though surveillance may use closed-circuit televisions installed throughout the building, their use can save but not eliminate the salaries for surveillance personnel. Regardless of where or by whom the monitoring is done, for optimum effect there must be a readily available response capability from security or surveillance. The surveillance department must not install more equipment than can be monitored or responded to within a realistic time (Burstein, 1985).

The surveillance department must balance the guests' feelings of invasion of privacy with the necessity for monitoring hallways and public access areas.

The installation of closed-circuit systems provides a possible employee/labor-relations problem. It is common with the installation of video equipment that employees feel that this equipment is installed to monitor their working habits and represents an invasion of privacy to them.

Many casino surveillance operations rely heavily on agents. **Agents** are those individuals who are sent out into the casino to spot thieves, cheaters, dishonest employees, and embezzlers. They provide a vital link and a method of verifying possible problems within the system. The agents must understand their function and understand the directions and the goals of specific operations. The agents are cautioned not to get involved in possible conflicts and to follow procedure. Sometimes an agent acts as an outside man. An **outside man** observes the game from outside the game.

Within the gaming and casino industry, employee files are normally maintained by the human resources department; however, when incidents within the casino operation occur, surveillance may establish **e-files.** Normally these files are only established when a serious incident or a breach of procedure has taken place. The surveillance department becomes involved in tracking these people. These investigations normally remain confidential and the files are maintained in locked cabinets. If no incriminating information is obtained and subsequent incidents do not occur, the e-file is destroyed.

In today's modern casino and gaming operations, it is necessary for the surveillance department to continually upgrade its equipment and its personnel. Continual training and the improvement of procedures is of primary importance to the successful completion of the surveillance department's missions and goals.

REVIEW TERMS

agent	outside man
e-file	security
eye in the sky	surveillance

REFERENCES

Burstein, Harvey. (1985). *Hotel security management.* New York: Prager Publishers, 4, 24, 84.

Buzby, Walter J. (1978). *Hotel security management.* California: Security World Publishing, 81.

Denos, Peter. (1991). *Casino supervision.* California: Panzer Press, 82.

Marshall, Arther. (1994). At Your Risk. *Hotel Motel Management Magazine* 209:1.

Palmer, John. (1990). *Principles of hospitality engineering.* New York: Van Nostrand Reinhold, 17.

Parets, D. (1999). A sharper eye in the sky. *International Gaming and Wagering Business* 20(2).

Security World Publishing. (1979). *Restaurant and bar security book 2.* California: Security World Publishing, 13.

Vogel, E. J. (1994). Interview by author, August.

Chapter 13

Modern Casino and Gaming Operations

OBJECTIVES

- Develop an understanding of the modern casino and gaming operations.
- Understand the phenomenal growth within the casino and gaming industry.
- Understand the organization and operation procedures of casino management.
- Understand the financial structure of the casino industry (the process of checks and balances).

INTRODUCTION

In modern casino management, each of the major hospitality units is looked on as a profit center. All are expected to generate specific shares of profit, including rooms, food and beverages, entertainment, keno, table games, slots, poker, sports booking, and casino operations.

The era of the modern casino began in Las Vegas with the entrance of mega-corporations into the gambling market. With Howard Hughes's purchase of five hotels in Las Vegas—the Sands, the Castaway, the Landmark, the Frontier, and the Silver Slipper—the casino industry took one of its first steps toward modernization and reorganization. Hilton's purchase of the International Hotel was one of the succeeding steps in the modernization of the casino industry. Prior to this, high rollers and grind-customer orientation were prevalent and paramount to the casinos' success. Casinos concentrated on maintaining their client base, and profits were derived solely from gambling operations. Entertainment, hotels, and restaurants merely provided support activities for gaming revenue. Guests were encouraged to come to Las Vegas through reduced airfares and incentive packages, which included air, hotels, and meals; rooms, entertainment, and restaurants were expected to break even or even lose money.

Gambling in one form or another, no matter how diminutive, is legal in every state in the United States (except Hawaii and Utah) and all provinces of Canada. Twenty-two states have legalized some form of casino-type gambling. Thirty-seven states and the District of Columbia are presently operating lotteries. Charitable gambling in one form or another is legal in forty-five states. To date, six states have legalized riverboat gambling. The success of these operations in the states that feature riverboat or dockside casinos has convinced other jurisdictions to approve or seriously consider riverboat gambling.

Three basic premises are at the center of the recent expansion of gambling around the world:

1. The continuing deterioration of the finances of countries, states, counties, and local governments.
2. The public's changing views of casino and gaming from that of a vice to an acceptable form of adult entertainment.
3. The view that neighboring areas are reaping the benefits, so why shouldn't we?

It appears that gaming operations will continue to spread across the country at an ever-increasing rate, and the industry is expected to generate $50 billion by the year 2000 in the United States alone. This indicates a growth rate of 7 percent or more for the next decade. Casino gaming should continue to lead the industry with a 13 percent increase in the next decade (Rohs, 1994). In 1998, Las Vegas hosted 30.6 million visitors; more than 175,000 people were directly employed in the hotel, gaming, and recreation industries; tourists and conventioners spent approximately $24.6 billion; a total of 3,999 conventions were held; the percentage of international visitors was 13 percent; citywide hotel occupancy was 85 percent; and the percentage of first-time visitors to Las Vegas was 25 percent. The projected visitor volume for 1999 is approximately 32 billion (Shock, 1999).

The only factor that could change this picture of continued growth would be for the industry to reach a saturation point by constructing too many casinos or gaming outlets or by invoking a major scandal, which would cause the public to reevaluate its assessment of gaming and casino operations as an acceptable form of entertainment.

DEFINITIONS

In casino operations, there are two types of transactions:

1. The customers purchase chips to gamble with.
2. The customers gamble with cash.

In the event that a gambler wins, he or she will always receive chips that can be cashed in at the cage.

> Drop: The **drop** is the collective amount of money the casino receives from the customers. The drop allows the casino to measure the skill of the dealers by tracking revenue per game and per dealer.
>
> Win: Each table starts with a predetermined number of chips. The **win** is calculated by subtracting the amount of the bank from the drop.
>
> Hold: The percentage of the drop that the casino wins is called the **hold.** A casino can expect to hold a certain percentage of the drop over a given period. The expectation varies greatly for each type of game in different casinos, because the expected hold percentage is a function of the casino advantage on each bet and the customer's wager. The typical hold for a strip crap table is 20 percent.

Management can use all of the above components in its evaluation of the casino's success. However, the drop is management's most useful tool in evaluating credit and marketing policies, because it includes chips, cash, and credit slips.

Many casinos offer large shows to increase the number of people visiting their operation in hopes to increase revenues. For example, in 1968, Frank Sinatra performed at Caesars Palace in Las Vegas. Caesars' management hoped that this show would bring in more gamblers and, therefore, increase the casino's winnings. The first three days of the show, Caesars Palace lost $1 million. In terms of a win, this was a disaster. However, when the drop figures were calculated, they were the largest in Nevada's history. From the three-day drop figure, Caesars anticipated that at the end of Sinatra's four-week engagement it would win back the $1 million plus a substantial profit. This was because more customers were brought into the casino, which increased the drop figures. The win over the first few days did not accurately predict the financial picture for the casino; however, the drop did. The large drop figures were able to predict that the casino would make a large profit over time (Friedman, 1990).

The win is a poor indicator of the amount of business a casino is doing due to the fluctuations of the statistical variations of the cards and dice. In the short run, the win is erratic. However, in the long run, management can maximize its expected win by training the entire casino staff to strive to produce the largest possible drop.

Win and hold are calculated as follows:

1. Total chips issued to the table during the shift
    − Total chips on the table at the end of the shift
    _____
    Total chips missing from the table equals a hold

    Drop (All the customer cash in the table box)
    − Total chips missing from the table for the shift
    _____
    Win

2. Win/Drop = Hold (percent)

CUSTOMERS

There are two types of customers at a casino, grind customers and premium customers. A **grind customer** is someone who bets in small amounts. He or she will buy approximately $20 worth of chips and make $1 wagers. Eventually the casino will "grind" the $20 out of him or her, $1 at a time. A **premium customer** is a person who bets in large dollar amounts. These customers are also known as "high rollers."

Because there are far more grind customers than premium, casinos that market toward grinders tend to have a more stable hold percentage from shift to shift. Although premium casinos can achieve similar win figures because of the higher dollar values involved, their hold percentages can greatly vary between shifts.

CASINO FINANCIAL STRUCTURE

With few exceptions, all casino monies eventually flow through the cage. It is the financial hub of the entire operation. The accounting controls must be effective and closely monitored.

The cage serves several basic functions:

- supplies customer credit information to the casino
- makes difficult customer credit decisions
- conducts large financial transactions with the casino departments and customers
- records practically all gaming department transactions

Cage Personnel

Cage Manager. He/she is responsible for the smooth operation of the cage, which records every dollar that flows through the casino complex. The cage manager generally reports to the accounting department.

Cage Shift Manager or Head Cashier. He/she reports directly to the cage manager and executes his/her policies. The head cashier is the cage manager's assistant.

Cashier. He/she is responsible for most cage duties, including the following:

Responsibilities to the Customer
- exchanges chips
- issues credit
- provides safe deposit
- issues transportation slips (for authorized customers)
- approves walking money (when premium customers lose all their credit and chips, the cage may give them **walking money** to cover the expenses for the remainder of their stay, excluding gambling money)

Responsibilities to the Casino
- issues money drawers to each casino register and conducts all reporting procedures
- issues all chips and money used
- issues casino banks
- issues casino credit
- issues special keys

CONTROL

To reemphasize the importance of establishing controls as soon as the casino is opened, we should look at the following example.

Deadwood, South Dakota, has gambling similar to the type of gaming proposed for the Niagara Falls region, especially in terms of limits on the types of gaming allowed. Additionally, the majority of gambling won't be done at hotels. Deadwood originally anticipated its gaming operations to remain small and for the use of its citizens. In November 1989, there were fourteen licensed gambling operations. The people of Deadwood estimated a modest $2 million a year to be wagered, bringing the city $100,000 in revenue. This estimation proved to be incorrect. In 1990, there were eighty-four gaming halls, and in eighteen months approximately $335 million had been wagered (*International Gaming*, 1994).

This example shows that legalizing gambling, even on a limited basis, is literally like rolling the dice. When the city of Deadwood discovered a $4.2 million surplus in 1990, it had to be certain that the surplus was used properly and accounted for accurately. With large windfalls, it is often too easy to overlook stealing and poor accounting practices. This is why the accounting controls and strict cash flow systems must be established prior to the implementation of gambling. The distribution of the money should also be established prior to implementation. Allocations should be in percentage of drop figures and not necessarily the net amount of win. This will ensure that skimming is not occurring and that revenue is properly distributed.

SOCIAL ISSUES

Even if all regulations are in place, the area still must consider the social problems that have accompanied gambling in cities such as Las Vegas and Atlantic City as well as such towns as Deadwood, South Dakota. Recognizing the fact that gambling brings some problems into an area is the first step toward minimizing or preventing them. "Lured by the promise of easy money, economically depressed areas are trying to cash in by legalizing some form of gaming" (*International Gaming*, 1994). Gambling has brought jobs and more money to the areas it legally takes place in. Along with increasing employment and pumping up local economies, gambling can be followed by increased crime rates, addiction, misuse of allocated gambling revenue, and possible adverse effects on children. Deadwood, South Dakota, suffered some of the above effects after gambling was legalized in 1990. Gambling has brought more money into the town of Deadwood, but in other ways it has changed the lives of these small-town residents forever. The population of Deadwood plummeted from 1960 to 1980. Because of this, the tax base declined and various city services, including highway maintenance, deteriorated (*International Gaming*, 1994). Summer tourists on their way to Mount Rushmore simply did not spend enough money in Deadwood to compensate for the decreasing tax base.

Deadwood was listed as one of America's eleven most endangered historic places in 1991. Many small businesses were sold to real estate developers, causing the community to go without services. More specifically, a drug store, a couple of hardware stores, and a department store were among those that became casinos and souvenir shops. Arrests increased 250 percent, reports of child abuse and neglect increased, and a local chapter of Gamblers Anonymous was founded. Many families chose to move away rather than subject their children to the many changes occurring in Deadwood. Parents were particularly disturbed by the fact that a drug store, one hundred feet from the town's middle and elementary schools, was converted into a casino. Parents worried about their children witnessing gambling firsthand, but they were also concerned that winners, in their elation, and losers, in their despair, may not be conscious of the children's safety when entering or leaving the casino. The debt and addiction that gambling has brought to the area are also a concern (*International Gaming*, 1994). The National Center for Responsible Gaming 1998 Annual Report indicates that in spite of higher rates of gaming, only the adult segments of the general population have shown an increasing rate of gambling disorders.

Atlantic City, New Jersey, has also experienced social problems related to gambling. This seaside resort is visited by approximately thirty-three million people annually. The local population has declined by 20 percent and residents continue to migrate to the suburbs as a result of gambling. According to the Atlantic City Consolidation Plan 1995 Executive Summary, the city reported that 61 percent of the households were identified as low income or very low income. Based on statistics, it is estimated that 34 percent of all households in Atlantic City are subject to a cost burden greater than 30 percent of the gross monthly income. Severe cost burdens exist when gross housing costs exceed 50 percent of gross income. Based on the information provided by the city, it is estimated that 21 percent of the households in Atlantic City face severe cost burden. Although Atlantic City consists of over 7,600 acres, only about 2,500 of these acres, or roughly one-third of the city, is capable of being developed. The lack of available land and high land costs combined with excessively high construction costs have directly impacted the availability of affordable housing in Atlantic City. When land costs in Atlantic City are compared to other areas, they are found to be significantly higher, and the cost of developing projects in Atlantic City is substantilly higher (Rudd, 1999). Atlantic City has 7,472 casino hotel rooms, but its housing stock is down by at least 15 percent. There are roughly 18,103 slot machines in the city, but one is hard pressed to locate a car wash or movie theater and there is only one grocery store. The police department's budget has more than tripled at $24 million, but Atlantic City's crime rate is the highest in the state (Painton, 1989).

The casinos have created forty-one thousand new jobs; however, the welfare rolls have also increased and the number of overnight guests at the rescue mission have risen dramatically. The revenues from the casinos do assist the local taxpayers by contributing to the funding of public education (Painton, 1989).

Riverboat gambling has become popular in states such as Mississippi, Illinois, Louisiana, and Iowa. These states are discovering that the gaming and wagering business talks in big figures, but it cannot always deliver what it promises.

Lotteries have become an important source of revenue for many states. Lottery funds in Florida and California were targeted for public education as well as other needs. These states, and others, have discovered that gamblers are not very good fortune tellers. "Dropping revenue in California, where 34% of lottery proceeds go to education, have contributed to major problems with the state's education system, which faces possible layoffs of thousands of school teachers"

(Atkins, 1991). The Iowa Gaming Commission noted that revenue for riverboats operating on the Mississippi was well over projected figures, but per capita spending by gambling visitors was as much as one-third below projections (Atkins, 1991).

Some people contend that gambling contributes to broken homes, depression, and suicide as well as prostitution, drunkenness, and organized crime. Americans placed legal bets worth more than $638 billion in 1997 (Harrah's, 1997). This is well over the $274 billion that was spent on public elementary and secondary education (National Center for Education Statistics, 1997).

Somewhere between eight and ten million people in the United States are compulsive gamblers. Claims have been made stating that legalized gambling particularly victimizes women, youth, and minorities. Although over 90 percent of the members of Gamblers Anonymous are men forty years of age or older, a New York State study found that 36 percent of problem gamblers are women, 32 percent are nonwhite, and 33 percent are under thirty years of age (Neff and Giles, 1991).

REGULATIONS

When gambling is legalized in an area, the social problems mentioned previously must be taken into consideration. City officials must develop a clear picture of how gambling revenue will be allocated. Government also must set up controls to ensure that allocations are made according to plan. The area must also examine its infrastructure to determine whether changes need to be made to effectively combat increases in crime, prostitution, and child abuse and neglect and to provide counseling for people with gambling problems. It seems as though a good deal of the natural charm such places as Atlantic City and Deadwood had prior to being bitten by the gambling bug has disappeared. These areas have a good deal to offer tourists, and it would be a shame to not attempt to preserve what they currently have while still trying to improve the economic situation by introducing gambling to the area.

Regulations are a necessary tool to ensure the success of casino gambling in these areas. Successful markets have learned how to maintain a balance of regulation. If regulation is too lax, crime and corruption may flourish; if regulation is too strict, a profitable operation is extremely difficult to achieve. When an anticipated gambling region develops the regulations and control for its gaming operations, consideration must be given to a variety of factors including the following. First, a reporting system must be developed. A gaming commission must be established to ensure that a proper reporting system is developed. A system of checks and balances should be incorporated into such a commission. One possibility is to develop three separate agencies as members of a gambling commission. The first of these agencies would have the final authority over all legal matters concerning gambling and provide final approval for gambling licenses. The second of these agencies would advise the state on gambling policy and inform the industry of those policies. The third agency would carry out the actual enforcement of all regulations and policies.

When a gaming commission develops its regulations, it considers the following areas:

- quality
- public space requirements
- layout of facilities
- accounting records
- table and slot drop counts
- credit procedures
- game rules
- employee licensing

Quality

The standards of quality regarding the facility itself and its maintenance should be high.

Public Space Requirements

Public space requirements must follow local zoning regulations.

Layout of Facilities

This should include on a square-foot basis the number of games that can be placed in any room. It should also include a specific breakdown of the types of games allowed. For example, for every five thousand square feet of space there cannot be more than three craps tables, twenty slot machines, and so on.

Accounting Records

Accounting records be standardized prior to implementation of gaming operations. For example, "Each casino licensee shall submit to the commission a description of its system of internal procedures and administrative and accounting controls. Such submission should be made at least ninety days before gaming operations are to commence . . ." (Nevada Gaming Commission, 1990).

Table and Slot Drop Counts

The area of drop counts should include an inspector and two locking devices for the cash boxes. Additionally, the rooms where the drop amounts are counted and

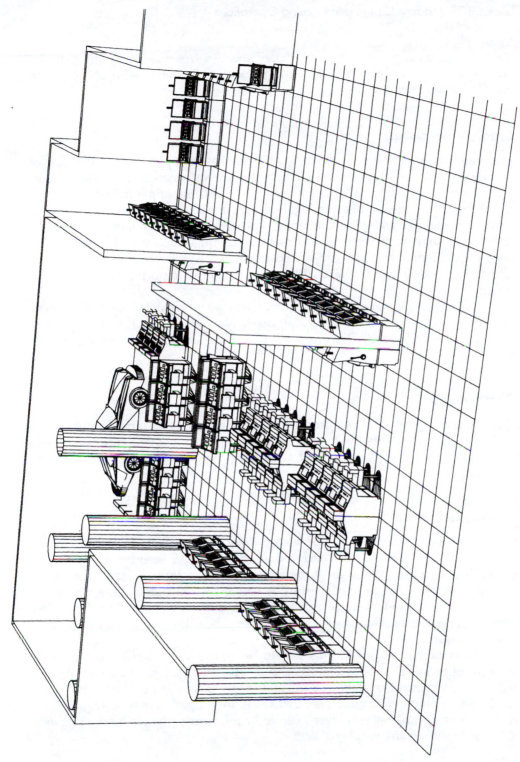

IGT's slot layout. *Source:* International Gaming Technologies.

the procedures used should be extremely specific. In some areas, this includes rules such as wearing only full-length, pocketless garments with openings for only the arms, feet, and neck.

Credit Procedures

The gaming commission must look at check-cashing procedures, the use of money orders, credit cards, treasurer's checks, and traveler's checks. Credit must be established by obtaining a bank report on the applicant from either a credit-reporting agency, another legal casino, or the applicant's bank. Persons issuing credit must also be examined. Credit should be authorized only by casino executives in the credit department under the direction of the credit manager. Credit issued at tables can be recommended by casino executives but not authorized. Additionally, the credit manager should report only to the controller.

Casinos are becoming dependent on credit; 40 percent of all casino action in Las Vegas is based on credit. The Asian markets are even higher, with 90 percent of all play being on credit. Every year casinos write off a tremendous amount of losses.

Game Rules

A full and complete listing of the rules for each casino game must be published. It should be consistent between casinos; therefore, it should be developed by the gaming commission. The published rules must be available to every customer upon request.

Employee Licensing

Each employee involved in a supervisory capacity empowered to make discretionary decisions that regulate casino operations should be licensed. To obtain such a license, the applicant must meet minimum standards for the job or position he/she wishes to be employed in. A personal history disclosure should be available to stockholders, directors, and necessary managers within the casino upon request and on file for the gaming control board, gaming committee, and gaming commission.

Photographs and fingerprints should be handled by a division of the gaming control board. The board should conduct an investigation for each applicant, including a review of criminal records and credit history at the federal and local levels. Based on the preliminary review, a field investigation may be required for further disclosure of key employee licenses or follow-up when incriminating evidence is found for any employee license.

GAMBLING PROFILE

Because the casinos get so many varied types of repeat customers, they can easily develop a computer database profile of groups. The casinos can then determine which of their patrons are profitable and market exclusively to these customers. Eventually, certain groups will emerge as extremely desirable in contrast to groups that are less profitable. Research shows that independent business people have a tendency to take more risks than the norm, and consequently tend to lose a great deal of money at the tables. Casinos will increasingly use computers to compose databases on their prospective clients (Thomas, 1994).

With the advent of the new technologies, casino operators can now use incentives for the first time to reach their key market, the frequent gambler (similar to frequent flyer, frequent car renter, etc.). With the advent of the computer database and tracking systems and the ability to monitor the gamblers according to their length of play, frequency, and average bet size, casino operators can now target the lucrative but previously elusive mid-range frequent gambler. Once they have identified these players, they can encourage them to patronize a specific casino with prizes, parties, and other incentives. The tactic can solidify a casino's market share of the mid-range gambler, who can become a casino's lifeblood. The high-end gamblers are usually spread out among many casinos.

Family entertainment: MGM Grand Theme Park. *Source:* MGM Grand Hotel and Casino.

The increase in riverboat gambling and lotteries have a tendency to make the gambling experience less unique. The technology needed to track the mid-range players will represent a large investment for a specific property; however, if properly used, the information that is yielded will have a dramatic effect on a casino's profitability (Zimmerman, 1990).

HUMAN RESOURCES

Carol Thomas is the Director of Human Resources for the Excaliber Hotel/Casino in Las Vegas, Nevada. She moved to Las Vegas in the early 1990s and began work for the Excaliber in 1993. She has a master's degree in industrial labor relations from the Indiana University of Pennsylvania. Although it is difficult to get into a major casino in Las Vegas because of the policy of promoting from within, she persisted and was able to obtain a position within the human resource operations at the Excaliber.

The human resource department of the Excaliber Hotel/Casino functions similar to any other casino resort. The guest room and food service employees are unionized. Customer service is very important, as it is in any hotel or restaurant industry. Because of the uniqueness of the casino industry (running seven hours a day, seven days a week), it is necessary for the employees to adjust to this intense schedule. She estimates that the Excaliber has approximately 4,500 employees. Individuals applying for work are first processed by the human resource specialist, who makes an initial check of the application and processes the paperwork. The employees are screened by the human resources department, which forwards their records to the individual departments who make the final determination on the selection of employees. If an applicant is approved, the applicant is called in for drug testing and must receive clearance from the gaming control board and the screening by the appropriate police department, if the job requires it. If hired, the applicant must go through a two-hour property orientation, which includes a description of the Excaliber property.

Employees attempting to obtain a position in the food and beverage department must obtain a health card and an alcohol awareness card. These things are required and conducted by the state. To receive the alcohol awareness card, the applicant must participate in a program that includes viewing videos and classroom participation.

All employees are given a basic Excaliber handbook and then are sent to their departments where further training and handbooks are given to them. For example, those who are involved in the cashier's cage would be taught the proper procedures involved in distributing change, accounting, and the correct security procedures to ensure the protection of the casino's assets.

A hazardous-awareness program has been instituted to inform employees about hazardous and dangerous materials and what to do when encountering them. Safety committees made up of employees have been formed.

There is a very high turnover among employees, and casinos have attempted to screen more efficiently to weed out those employees who might not last. Ms. Thomas contacts a number of service organizations in order to meet the needs of the casino. Some of her primary sources of employment are displaced homemakers, Nellie Air Force Base, Nevada Business Services, and the University of Nevada Las Vegas.

The areas within the Excaliber that are unionized are the food and beverage department, front office, valet parking, bell service, and slots. Certain hotels in Las Vegas have utilized nonunion employees; for example, the MGM Grand is nonunionized. Ms. Thomas feels that the future for the human resources department begins with the interpretation and understanding of regulations.

Employee relations will also be important because of the changing population within the United States. She feels that part of the labor problem in the future can be handled with the effective utilization of future retirees within the Las Vegas area.

The survival and success of the human resource department into the twenty-first century will depend on its ability to process and comprehend the volumes of legal and regulatory data that will be put in place before the end of the century.

ECONOMIC ACTIVITY

Many times public policy debates the increase in income, employment, tax revenue, and tourism that casino tax revenues generate, but in truth to be successful these economic activities depend on the importing of gamblers from outside the community where the gambling activity is located. Atlantic City, New Jersey; Windsor, Ontario; Niagara Falls, Ontario; and Las Vegas, Nevada are successful because they draw their patrons from around the world. In Mississippi the economic performance of the gambling industry has strengthened local and state economies of the Gulf River and Mississippi River, while other areas have remained relatively weak (Federal Reserve, 1999). This provides the community with the opportunity to benefit from the multiplier effect of tourism. The multiplier effect allows the foreign infusion of income to remain within the community and provides a continuing benefit. The same dollar can be spent two, three, or four times before it is lost from the community in the form of leakage. Leakage is money that is spent outside the community (Anders and Siegel, 1997).

Niagara Falls Case Study

An example of the rationale behind the development and implementation of gambling in a city can be seen in the paradox of Niagara Falls. One of the major reasons for introducing gambling to the Niagara Frontier is the positive impact that the potential revenue, in conjunction with the tourism trade, will have on the economy. The Niagara Frontier is an area with many economic problems. It is the site of one of the Seven Wonders of the World. Yet, due to many factors including seasonality, changes in the manufacturing base, and the recession, the tourism industry is not strong enough to support the entire region year round. Tourism in the area is quite strong throughout the summer months; however, it declines significantly during the rest of the year, except for a five-week period from November to January during the Festival of Lights. The area's economy suffers in the winter and spring months mainly due to the lack of tourism dollars.

In the past, the Niagara Frontier did not experience as severe a decline as has been seen over the past few years. At one time, industry was strong and it flourished in Niagara Falls. Unfortunately, plant closings and layoffs have transformed the area from a booming economic profit center to a region characterized by unemployment and an increase in the number of individuals receiving welfare relief.

A few attempts have been made to increase the revenue base of the area. Retail outlets were introduced into the area to stimulate the lagging economy. With the increase in Canadian taxes, these outlets have become a popular haven for Canadians to spend their dollars. Yet, welfare and unemployment are still the norm for many Niagara residents. Something else is needed to stimulate the economy and bring the area back to a booming, thriving region.

One way to bolster the economy by creating jobs and increasing revenue is the introduction of casino gambling. It is clear, however, that in addition to jobs and money, legalized gambling brings with it some adverse effects. The best way to address these problems is to take preventive measures and learn from similar areas that have legalized gambling.

1979 New York Gambling Study

In 1979, New York State appointed a panel to study the effect of casino gambling on the state as a whole. Research was completed that identified the economic and social impacts in the sites that the panel selected as most appropriate for introducing casino gambling. The panel also estimated the "likely scale of the market for casino gambling" (New York State Gambling Study, 1979) in each area studied.

Three critical sources of data were used to estimate revenue, areas of expenditures, and number of potential markets. The sources were the panel's own survey on gaming by New York State residents, data collected by the National Gambling Commission on resident gaming in Nevada, and a continuing survey on gaming in Las Vegas, particularly the data on Los Angeles residents gaming in the Nevada city.

The actual study began with the general criteria used to determine which areas of New York State would be designated for casino gambling, should it be legalized. The panel considered three questions in making its determination of the designated gambling areas. The questions were as follows:

1. Which areas would most likely benefit from the development of casinos/hotels in terms of tourism, conventions, business, and overall economic competitiveness and activity?

2. Which areas could best absorb and support a casino industry without adversely affecting the local community's character and overall environment?

3. Which areas indicated significant local interest in casino gambling as expressed in public hearings, meetings with panel members, various communications, and the survey commissioned by the panel? (New York State Study on Gambling, 1979)

After careful review of these questions, the panel determined four areas to be designated for casino gambling: the Niagara Frontier, the Catskills, the city of Long Beach, and the city of New York. The results of a study done by Coopers and Lybrand (1993) concur with the information collected during the 1979 survey conducted by New York State.

The Niagara Frontier

The Niagara Frontier was chosen as one of the four sites because of the area's need for a positive economic impact. Although the Niagara Falls, themselves, continue to attract scheduled tours and individual tourist trade, as does the area's annual Festival of Lights, the traffic is highly seasonal.

Casino gambling would give the area a much needed economic boost. With casino gambling, the area's natural beauty, and its close proximity to two major cities (Toronto and Buffalo), the Niagara Falls region has the potential to become a major convention city.

The study also found that the issue of casino gambling was strongly supported by many business leaders, and 50 percent of the residents also supported the introduction of casino gambling in their area.

With local support of gambling, the study next determined whether there was, indeed, a market for casino gambling in the Niagara Frontier region.

The population falling within one hundred miles of the area was substantial. There were 1.8 million persons in Erie and Monroe counties. The Toronto metropolitan area provides an additional 3 million people, and communities between the border and Toronto add another 1 million. Therefore, even considering only the regional market, the study found that the area contained at least 6 million people within a two-hour drive. An estimate of potential gaming expenditures from these 6 million individuals was determined by the panel as being $545 million, on average.

This $545 million would generate an additional 28,800 jobs: 13.7 thousand in direct employment (casino/hotel), 7.8 thousand in additional potential multiplier employment, 6.4 thousand in other direct nongaming employment (outside casino complex and casino/hotel support), and .9 thousand in average construction. The study also determined that casino gambling would generate additional jobs for 29 percent of the local employment base (New York State Gambling Survey, 1979).

Gambling in the Niagara region is strongly supported by these economic facts and figures. Yet, some residents remained unconvinced. Gambling in the area was not an issue that was strongly pursued by residents or politicians. Why? The economic benefits seem clear.

When most people think of gambling, they think of organized crime and high rollers. The truth is that little organized crime is involved in the large casino gambling operations. Men like Howard Hughes and William Harrah worked long and hard to transform the gaming industry's image from tawdry to reputable. With help from authorities such as J. Edgar Hoover (then chief of the FBI, who threatened the mob with investigations into skimming gambling revenue and tax evasion) and other legitimate business people who made substantial offers to buy out the gaming operations, the image was changed (Satre, 1989).

Today, almost all large casinos are owned by publicly traded entertainment and hospitality companies. With this type of ownership, one can be fairly certain that in the casino gambling industry, organized crime is a thing of the past. This information helps dispel some of the fears of organized crime taking over. To help ensure that this indeed occurs, a study of the financial operations for each of the casinos must be done. Controls on the flow of cash, authorization procedures for credit, screening of employees, and the standardization of accounting practices must be strictly enforced to ensure legitimate casino operations. By establishing a standard format with several checks and balances prior to the implementation of casino gambling, Niagara Falls can gain a reputable and profitable casino market.

The recent report to the Ontario Casino Project submitted by the Coopers and Lybrand consulting group set forth the following strategic considerations and objectives for casinos in Ontario: first, the creation of jobs; second, the continued development of tourism; third, the community economic development; fourth, the start up of a viable new industry; and fifth, revenue generation. Upon completion of their extensive research, Coopers and Lybrand found that their conclusions were similar to that of the 1979 New York State Gambling Survey (Coopers and Lybrand, 1993).

The temporary casino in Niagara Falls opened in 1996 and has over 96,000 square feet of gaming space, with a total of 123 gaming tables and over 3,000 slot machines. In addition, the casino has five different dining rooms offering meals and beverages from fast food to fine dining. Gamblers in Ontario must be 19 years of age or older to enter a casino area. All games must be played with Canadian currency. It is one of the most successful casinos in the world (Warson, 1996).

REVIEW TERMS

drop	premium customer
frequent gambler	walking money
grind customer	win
hold	

REFERENCES

Anders, G., and Siegel, D. (1997, January). *Displacement effects of riverboat gambling in Missouri: A pilot study.* Paper presented at the North American Economics and Finance Association Annual Meeting, New Orleans.

Atkins, J. (1991). The states bad bet. *Christianity Today,* 25 November.

Coopers and Lybrand. (1993). *Report to the Ontario Casino Project.*

Federal Reserve. (1999). Econ South. Vol. 13, no. 12. Atlanta, first quarter, p. 23.

Friedman, B. (1990). *Casino management.* Secaucus, New Jersey: Lyle Stuart.

Harrah's. (1997). Harrah's survey of casino entertainment. Available at: http://www.harrahs.com/survey/ce97/ce97_revenue.html

International Gaming and Wagering Business. (1994). North American gaming report. *International Gaming and Wagering Business,* 5 July.

National Center for Education Statistics. (1997). Available at: http://www.nces.ed.gov/fastfacts

Neff, D., and Giles, T. (1991). Feeding the monster called more. *Christianity Today.*

Nevada Gaming Commission. (1990). Report put out by the Nevada and State Gaming Control Board.

New York State Gambling Study. (1979).

Painton, P. (1989). Boardwalk of broken dreams. *Time,* 25 September.

Rohs, J. (1994). Gaming industry: Why the continuing explosion? *Institutional Investor* 28(2):6.

Rudd, D. P. (1999). Casino gaming in the U.S.: Atlantic City. Edited by Cathy Hsu. Binghamton, New York: Haworth Press.

Satre, P. (1989). The future of gambling, you can bet on it. *Vital Speeches of the Day,* 3 November.

Shock, P. (1999). UNLV Convention program, 28 April.

Thomas, Carol. (1994). Interview by author. August.

Thomas, R. (1994). Looking at gamblers' profiles. *Journal of Successful Meetings* 39:5, 80.

Warson, A. (1996). "Great expectations." *International Gaming and Wagering Business,* December.

Zimmerman, N. (1990). Incentives. *Defying the Odds,* 135.

Chapter 14

Canada—Gambling in the Provinces

OBJECTIVES

- Explore the growth of the Canadian gaming industry.
- Examine present and future trends in casino gaming, lotteries, video lottery terminals, horse racing, and simulcasting.
- Assess the effect of Canadian gaming interests on Canadian citizens and on the gambling industry in the United States.

INTRODUCTION

As a result of the substantial economic benefit and stimulus to tourism offered by recreational gaming, it has been adopted by every province within Canada. The policy objectives for the creation of casino gambling are job creation, new revenue creation, tourism development, community economic development, and new industry development (Rudd, 1997b). Over the past few years, Canada has expanded its gaming industry to increase provincial revenues. The industry has grown with such abandon that many critics feel the provincial and federal governments have disregarded caution because they are caught up in the web of easy profits. Although this may or may not be so, the gaming industry in Canada is substantially different from that in the United States. In spite of this difference, or perhaps because of it, many industry experts envision Canada as the gaming mecca of the future. How much this phenomenal growth will affect the gaming industry in the United States is a matter of speculation. As a result of the substantial economic benefits and stimulus to tourism and travel offered by recreational gaming, it has been adopted in one form or another by every province in Canada (Rudd, 1997).

CASINO GAMING

In 1969, the Canadian federal government legalized casino gaming; however, only the provincial governments or nonprofit organizations could initiate such establishments. The casinos were restricted to table games, but the federal government recently included video lottery terminals (VLTs) and slot machines as legitimate gaming devices. Each province, within the broader federal law, governs how gaming may operate within its jurisdiction. The provincial governments regulate how many casinos there will be, whether or not they will be permanent, and how they will be licensed. Most of the casinos are situated in Alberta, Saskatchewan, and British Columbia, but other provinces have jumped on the bandwagon (Connor, 1993a).

The casinos in British Columbia and Alberta are operated by private management companies that contract with nonprofit organizations, which use the casino facilities to raise funds. These charitable organizations apply for gaming licenses that restrict their use of the casino to two days. Even under these conditions, the casinos are usually open every day of the year (Connor, 1993a). The exception to this is the Calgary Stampede and the Edmonton Exhibition every summer. During the summer, a ten-day special casino permit is issued, which allows each of the cities to operate between 170 and 200 gaming tables. In British Columbia in October 1994, the government services minister announced that there would be no Las Vegas–style casinos within British Columbia.

Alberta and British Columbia treat the distribution of gaming profits differently, however. In Alberta, the charities pay the casinos an agreed-upon fee for use of the facility; in British Columbia, the provincial government receives a specific fee. The province of Saskatchewan grants licenses to nonprofit organizations that assist the farming industry, but these gambling facilities only operate on a part-time basis. New Brunswick and several other provinces grant two-day licenses to nonprofit organizations (Connor, 1993a).

The provincial government of British Columbia ruled in early 1997 that there would be no Las Vegas–style gaming allowed in British Columbia for fear of cutting in on the charitable gaming that presently exists in the province. British Columbia's new gaming policies also call for the prohibition of video lottery terminals in bars and pubs. The existing charitable casinos will be improved to allow them to compete with casinos that exist in other provinces and the United States. British Columbia is the only province that does not have a province-wide VLT network. It is also one of five that does not have Las Vegas–style casinos (Ministry of Employment and Investment, 1997).

Charitable gaming across Canada represents a 70 percent return on wagers; however, there is considerable variation in the percentages among provinces and a significant variation in the prizes paid on different types of gaming within a single province. This difference can be explained by the differences in the types of charitable gaming within different provinces (Canadian Centre on Substance Abuse, n.d.).

Although riverboat casinos in the United States are on the rise, the first modern-day version of the old Mississippi steamboats came into being in Canada a little over two decades ago. A landbound paddleboat in Dawson City, Yukon, became Diamond Tooth Gerties Yukon Casino with gaming tables and slot machines that attract a large number of visitors each year. Revenue from the riverboat operation is distributed to various worthy projects by the Klondike Visitors' Association, a nonprofit organization. The casino is open seasonally in the spring and summer months (Connor, 1993a).

Through April 1993, there was only a single provincial government-operated casino in Canada (Connor, 1993a). By August 1994, several other provinces had constructed government-operated casinos and additional casinos were in the planning stages (Quebec plans, 1994). Manitoba's **Crystal Casino** in Winnipeg opened in 1989 and was watched closely by the other provinces. The casino is operated by the Manitoba Lotteries Foundation, which is planning to open two more casinos that will also be located in Winnipeg. The revenues from the Crystal Casino are used to overhaul Manitoba's health care system. The revenues from the two new casinos have not been earmarked for any specific purpose as yet (Connor, 1993a).

The casinos in Manitoba are not like those found in the United States; they are built on a much smaller and more sedate scale. Even so, the Crystal Casino attracts approximately 600,000 visitors annually who generate revenues in excess of $11 million. Although 75 percent of the Crystal's customers are from Manitoba, the remaining visitors are mostly from other provinces and the United States. This is especially satisfying to the Manitoba government because many Canadian casino customers had previously crossed the border into the United States to gamble in Native American casinos (Connor, 1993a).

Quebec, quick to notice Manitoba's success, built two casinos, one in Montreal at the site of Expo 67 and the other in the Charlevoix region (Quebec plans, 1994). The casino in Charlevoix is rather small, but the casino in Montreal boasts more than sixty gaming tables and over a thousand slot machines. The government spent in excess of $60 million on the building site, construction, and gaming equipment (Connor, 1993a).

The Quebec government built a casino in the Ottawa-Outaouais region, Casino de Hull, at a cost of almost $90 million. It holds fifty gaming tables and a thousand electronic slot machines; there are restaurants and bars on the premises.

WINDSOR

In Canada the federal criminal code states that only provincial governments may regulate or operate legal forms of gaming such as bingo, lotteries, and casino games. In Ontario and Quebec the casinos are owned and operated by the provinces. Each has a slightly different system of operation. In Ontario, the provincial government bids out the management of its casinos to private companies while retaining ownership through a publicly owned company. In Quebec the provincial government decided to give ownership of the province's casinos to a company already set up to operate lotteries (Gors, 1997).

Not to be outdone, the Ontario provincial government completed a casino in Windsor, which opened to the public on May 17, 1994 (Warson, 1994c). The casino is on the Detroit River and is about the same size as the one in Montreal. This casino is temporarily housed in an art museum overlooking the Detroit skyline. Windsor, like other Canadian cities near the United States border, has been particularly plagued by the **Free Trade Agreement** and the decline of the Canadian dollar against U.S. currency. The casino has lured American dollars back across the border to make up for some of the lost revenue (Connor, 1993a).

In 1979, Rachel Bogatin was dealing blackjack in Atlantic City, New Jersey. She attached herself to the fast track and in 1994 Ms. Bogatin became the Vice President of Casino Operations at the Windsor Casino and one of the highest-ranking woman executives in the casino and gaming industry today. Ms. Bogatin stated that the Windsor Casino is operated by a consortium of companies including Caesars, Hilton, and Circus Circus. According to Ms. Bogatin, the gaming industry, unlike many businesses in the United States, Canada, and around the world, is experiencing rapid growth, which in turn lends itself to rapid advancement for employees within the industry. The vast majority of employees within the Canadian casino industry are Canadian nationals. There is very limited foreign participation in the Canadian casino and gaming industry. She expects the industry to continue at its rapid pace at least into the year 2000. The new facility that has been erected to replace the temporary casino includes a hotel, casino, and restaurants.

A 1993 Coopers and Lybrand study indicated that visitors from the United States were expected to account for approximately 94 percent of the casino's attendess, foreign visitors for 0.4 percent, and Canadians for 5 percent. The results of the one-year operation at Casino Windsor were significantly different from the expectations. Eighty percent of the casino visitors were from the United States and other countries, 15 percent were from other parts of Canada, and 5 percent were from Windsor. This difference can be attributed to two factors: first, the nonavailability of casinos in the region at that time, and second, to a larger draw from the Niagara Falls and Toronto areas than anticipated. These figures have changed substantially since the opening of the Niagara casino (Rudd, 1997).

NIAGARA FALLS

Niagara Falls, Ontario, is another community that has suffered economically during recent years. The city attracts over ten million tourists annually who visit the spectacular Falls; the problem is that the tourists spend only a few hours in the

Windsor Casino, Windsor, Ontario. *Source:* Windsor Casino.

area and then depart without spending the night. In an attempt to persuade their visitors to stay longer and spend more money, city officials granted permission for a casino. They commissioned a cost-benefit study, and the results indicate that the province would earn revenues of approximately $120 million annually, over 70 percent of which would be generated from outside Ontario (Warson, 1994b). The Niagara Casino opened its doors on December 9, 1996, and is one of the most successful casinos in the world.

Casino Niagara

Located across from the Rainbow Bridge in Niagara Falls, Ontario, Casino Niagara has an architectural design reminiscent of the 1920s. The creative use of stucco, glass, and stone create a unique structure. Landscaped boulevards and colorful gardens enhance the natural beauty of the surrounding park lands. Inside the Falls Avenue entrance, visitors are charmed by the meticulously landscaped terraces and cascading waterfalls, all brilliantly showcased inside an 80-foot-high glass atrium. The architectural signature of Casino Niagara is located in the main foyer of the complex. A mural of the sky painted on a high-dome ceiling magically comes alive with the use of lasers and lights, simulating the various stages of the day from sunrise to sunset. Special effects such as thunderstorms and the peace after the storm passes are incorporated into the dome. The courtyard-like atmosphere is further enhanced by the three-story waterfalls that cascade down rock facades on either side of a glass escalator.

Contractors, designers, and consultants completely renovated the former Maple Leaf Village, and in some cases restored the original European-style

Casino Niagara, Niagara Falls, Ontario. *Source:* Casino Niagara.

facade. A collaborative effort among the Toronto architectural firms of Reich and Petch, Forrec, Ltd., and Directions in Design, an international company which specializes in interior casino design, created the Ontario region's second wonder. During construction, 700 workers labored on site working three shifts. Approximately 90 percent of the labor force for the project was local, and more than 95 percent of the contracts were unionized. In total, construction is expected to create 600 person-years of employment. Real effort was made to keep contracts in the Niagara region. The $160 million ongoing project, which includes renovations, training, and equipment, stayed on budget up through the present time.

Gaming Space. Casino Niagara offers a total of 96,000 square feet of gaming space. The 3,000 slot machines accept Canadian currency tokens in denominations of 25¢, 50¢, $1, $5, $20, and $100.

Some machines offer progressive jackpots, while others feature cars as top prizes. In addition, members of the Frequent Players' Advantage Club are eligible for discounts at more than 100 local attractions, restaurants, and hotels.

Casino Niagara also offer 123 gaming tables, such as blackjack, roulette, baccarat, Caribbean stud poker, let-it-ride, pai gow poker, and big six. Located on the third floor, the exclusive but not private high-limit Billionaire's Club offers full and midsize baccarat, blackjack, and single "O" roulette. Members are automatically eligible for valet parking on site (Ontario Casino Corporation).

Services and Entertainment. In keeping with the policy of working cooperatively with the horse racing industry, there will be an off-track betting (OTB) teletheater in the casino which will be operated jointly by the Ontario Jockey Club and the Mohawk Raceway. This will allow the Casino to compete successfully in the lucrative and competitive OTB market. The competition not only comes from the racing industry, but from online sports betting services (CSI Columns, June 12, 1996).

Visitors to Casino Niagara will appreciate the fourteen retail stores located in the complex which will include men's and women's high-end accessory stores, a fragrance shop, a jewelry store, and a liquor store that will showcase Niagara wines.

The observation tower offers an observation deck and includes features that will promote attractions in the region.

Interim Operation of the Casino. In July 1996, following a competitive bidding process, the Ontario Casino Corporation announced the Navegante Group had been selected as the opening operator for Casino Niagara Falls, Ontario. A total of eight companies were invited to bid. Navegante is a core group of industry executives who are internationally renowned for their experience and cutting-edge skills. As such, they are able to assist a client in the multitude of pre- and post-opening tasks necessary to develop a successful gaming project.

Navegante is led by Mr. Larry J. Woolf, most recently chairperson and CEO of the $1.3 billion, 5,000-room MGM Grand Hotel in Las Vegas, Nevada, the world's largest casino, hotel, theme park, and exhibition center. This five-year project is typically regarded as the definitive statement of what constitutes a gaming mega-resort.

Cumulatively, Navegante team members have worked in seven American jurisdictions and twelve countries to design, develop, open, and operate ten new projects and two merger/acquisitions. Navegante has also fostered an extensive and diverse network of industry specialists, many of whom may be called on to meet the specific needs of a project. Navegante will operate Casino Niagara until such time as a permanent operator is chosen. This is expected to occur in July or August of 1997.

While the OCC has contracted the day-to-day operations of Casino Niagara, ownership of the casino business and managerial authority of the casino rests with the Government of Ontario through the OCC.

Expected Gross Revenue. Casino Niagara is grossing $650 million a year, of which the Government of Ontario retains a 20 percent win tax. Navegante is then paid an operating fee based on a percentage of the gross and net revenues. Expenses such as salaries, benefits, equipment, and rent for the casino site, and the cost of leasing off-site parking and shuttle service, are also paid out of the gross revenues. Casino Niagara also pays for the additional Niagara Regional police officers who have been hired as a result of the larger crowds. The rest of the money, the profits generated by Casino Niagara, go directly to the Ontario government. (Source: John Palumbo, Public Relations Manager, Casino Niagara, Ontario, Canada.)

As a result of substantial economic benefits, and as a stimulus to tourism offered by recreational gaming, casinos have been adapted, in one form or another, by every province in Canada. The policy objectives of Ontario and the Niagara Falls Casino Statement of Goals are intertwined. Their desire is to create jobs, develop tourism (create a year-round destination), integrate the various casino products throughout the community, and generate revenue for the community and province.

Inherent within this policy for casinos in Ontario and Niagara Falls are the generation and capture of new spending as opposed to simply creating a venue for the redirection of existing spending within the province. The sources for such spending are identified as:

1. New tourist visitors
2. Existing tourist visitors who will spend more and stay longer in Niagara Falls
3. Ontario residents diverted from casinos in other jurisdictions utilizing the facilities at Niagara Falls

The 1995 Coopers and Lybrand Market and Impact Report for the Ontario Provincial Government.   The 1995 study differs from the 1993 study in that the revenue increased from $439 million to $531 million, visitors increased from 6 million to 8 million, jobs increased from 10,000 person-years of employment to 15,000 person-years of employment, and the casino square footage increased from 75,000 square feet to 90,000 square feet. The projected 560 direct construction and start-up jobs and 116 indirect positions would result in total wages of $41 million. Over 7,000 direct operating jobs and 9,500 indirect jobs would also be generated, totalling yearly wages of $508 million. The giant casino complex would also generate $67.5 million in provincial taxes and win taxes of another $63.0 million, $139 million in federal taxes, and $22.8 million in local taxes.

Casino Niagara represents an important tourism attraction for the Niagara region. For this reason, in order to develop and market Casino Niagara, it must recognized that the primary tourism goals for Niagara Falls, which, according to the Niagara Falls Casino Information Sheet, are increasing the number of visitors, encouraging a longer average stay, and enhancing Niagara Falls as a year-round visitor destination. In order to accomplish this, there are three primary markets which the Casino must attract:

1. Dedicated casino gamers whose visit to a casino is the paramount trip objective. They have relatively little interest in other activities and typically make minimal ancillary purchases outside the casino.

2. Recreational visitors for whom casino gaming is another activity participated in on a trip. For this market a casino can either be a demand generator, causing the person to visit the local area over other destinations, or it could act as an added attraction encouraging them to extend their stay at a destination which they already find attractive.

3. Non-gambling family and friends of casino patrons, including spouses, children, and other members of the casino visitors' travel parties. This group will be very heavy spenders on activities outside of the casino, particularly attractions and entertainment. The extent of attractions in Niagara Falls (and the always ongoing development of more) would be extremely inviting to this group. In addition, by having family members accompany them on their trip, dedicated casino gamers would have a greater opportunity to extend their visit to the casino.

It is the recreational visitors and non-gambling family and friends of casino patrons who will create exponential spin-off revenue for businesses outside the casino, and therefore, attention should be focused on these two markets.

The operation of Casino Niagara, including incremental tourist expenditures, will result in nearly 15,000 person-years of employment for Ontario residents, approximately 63 percent of which will be within the Niagara Falls region. The Casino will contribute over $750 million to the province in wages; of this amount, over $500 million will be earned by Niagara Falls residents.

One of the major problems that Windsor Casino faced was the transformation from a business economy to a tourist economy. The Casino attendance figures for Windsor were phenomenal. The town, the city, and the Casino were unable to handle the unprecedented public response the Casino generated. This lack of foresight on Windsor's part resulted in excessive Casino line-ups and a public relations nightmare.

Niagara Falls will not face this problem because it is an established world-class tourism destination. Niagara Falls is a veteran in tourism relations and recognizes how to attract, welcome, and accommodate the over eleven million tourists that visit the Falls each year. Niagara Falls has the necessary infrastructure that is needed to support the development and visitation levels of anticipated tourists. Casino Niagara will be a catalyst for the development of tourism and tourist attractions in the Niagara Falls region into the twenty-first century (Rudd, 1997a).

PROBLEMS GENERATED BY CASINOS IN CANADA

Canadian casinos were legalized and developed to raise much-needed revenues for the provinces and/or charitable organizations. For the most part, they have accomplished that purpose. They are not, however, without their share of problems. Some of the provinces have already come up against a particularly knotty dilemma: the issue of gaming on Canadian Indian reservations. The First Nations, a tribe of Canadian Indians based in the southeastern region of Saskatchewan, opened a casino that operated only on weekends. The province did not issue a license to the tribe. While the Indian entrepreneurs and the government were trying to iron out their problems, the casino was allowed to operate. Since then, the provincial government has devised a system that would allow the Canadian Indians to enter into gaming operations only in cooperation with the nonprofit organizations that hold licenses and the Saskatchewan government. All revenues from the casinos would be shared among the partners (Connor, 1993a).

The Indian developers of the Saskatachewan casino did not see this as a solution. They believed that the government had no regulatory power over the reservation since there was no specific legislation in place to cover this situation. Aside from any jurisdictional disputes, the First Nations tribe was not satisfied with the proposed division of profits (Connor, 1993a). Since then, however, the two groups have come to terms. Saskatachewan wants a piece of the action as do the Canadian Indians. An agreement was reached early in 1994 that would allow the First Nations to operate casinos in Regina and Saskatoon in conjunction with the government (Warson, 1994a).

Canadian Indians from other provinces are also interested in opening casinos on their reservations. In Manitoba, several small unlicensed bingo games were opened, only to be shut down by government officials. The position taken by the provincial officials is that unless gaming casinos adhere to established laws, they have no inherent right to exist. The Manitoba First Nations are permitted to operate government-owned video lottery terminals that are connected to the central monitoring system the government has established. Several tribes who exercise this legal option retain all the profits from the machines; in return, they pay a certain percentage to the government as an administration fee (Connor, 1993a).

Manitoba government officials have other concerns about Indian gaming operations within the province. They are afraid that if reservation casinos are not regulated as to number and quality, they will glut the market and bring overall casino revenues down.

Several Canadian Indian reservations in British Columbia and Alberta have also indicated their willingness to operate casinos. Not all Indian tribes, however, welcome gaming casinos on their land. A Mohawk tribe in the province of Quebec voted against a measure to allow a casino on the reservation. The chief of the tribe saw the casino as a viable means of bringing some economic stability to the reserve, but the tribe voted it down. Many of the tribe members expressed concern that the size of the projected revenues might prove irresistible to organized crime and did not want to risk that association. In addition, research conducted by the tribe's social worker found that the incidence of gambling addiction among Canadian Indians is six times greater than that of the Canadian population as a whole (Warson, 1994a).

Along with the Indian gambling issue, Canadian casinos are facing the types of problems associated with any gaming operation. Eleven days after it opened, Casino Windsor in Ontario had three professional cheaters arrested; just a few days later, a warrant was issued on a pair of international cheaters from France and Italy (Warson, 1994c). Although this type of crime was expected, another, more ominous activity is plaguing charity casinos in Toronto, Ontario. Twice in early spring 1994, armed robbers showed up at separate charity gaming functions and robbed patrons; during one of the incidents, a security guard was disarmed and beaten. As a result, the Ontario government now requires that charity casino operators hire two police officers to be present at each function. Officials hope that the presence of armed professionals will deter any further incidents of this kind (Warson, 1994b).

Alberta, after reviewing the results of a research study conducted on behalf of the government, decided to set aside gaming funds to address another problem common to gaming communities: the addiction of players to games of chance. The study revealed that approximately 5 percent of the two thousand Albertans interviewed admitted that they had an addiction problem. Some of them were categorized as pathological gamblers. Allocated funds are used to sponsor community-based programs that will offer help to problem gamblers. Government officials are quick to point out that people with this type of addiction would still gamble even if it were illegal to do so.

Even faced with the problems generated by legalized gambling casinos, the Canadian provinces will almost certainly allow an increasing number of casinos to operate. The funds gained from such operations are just too attractive to a country suffering from a sluggish economy. Canadians have been flocking to nearby U.S. casinos since they were opened, and the provincial governments have decided to fight for their share of gambling revenues. To their credit, Canadian officials and citizens alike are concerned about social and other issues created by casino gambling; many communities have already put programs in place to combat potential and existing problems. There is also great concern about overdevelopment; if more and more casinos are allowed to operate, a possible result could be reduced revenues for existing casinos. This cautious approach to a ballooning industry is both prudent and admirable. However, the entire process is still in its infancy. Only the passage of time will establish whether the casinos will continue to be lucrative enterprises.

NOVA SCOTIA

Sheridan Corporation jumped into the middle of casino and gaming operations with two big feet. In January 1995, ITT Sheridan Corporation took over Caesars World Inc. at a price tag of $1.7 billion. At the same time, Nova Scotia's government awarded ITT Sheridan Canada Limited the exclusive right to develop and operate Nova Scotia's first two casinos for a period of twenty years. Recently, the

ITT Corp. was taken over and is spinning off its casino operations. The Sheridan hotel in the provincial capital housed the initial temporary casino. The other casino was developed in Sydney on Cape Breton Island and opened August 1, 1995. The casino in Halifax features 21,000 square feet of casino gaming area, and the Sydney casino covers 16,000 square feet. Both interim casinos are open and permanent facilities are scheduled for completion in 1999 (Warson, 1995).

LOTTERIES

Over the past twenty years, Canadian lotteries have grown steadily in popularity as a result of effective advertising campaigns. The lotteries offered were the types of games people have grown used to over the years, such as instant lotteries, lotto, and sports gaming products. In an effort to counteract increasing competition from lotteries and other forms of gambling in the United States, Canadian government officials are turning to more innovative types of lotteries they hope will capture increased gaming revenues. One of the newest wrinkles in the industry is the introduction of video lottery terminals (VLTs). Even those involved in the expansion of VLTs agree that the traditional lotteries may slip as a result of the newer products (Connor, 1993b).

Video lottery terminals were introduced in New Brunswick in 1990. By 1993, over fifteen thousand VLTs were established in seven provinces, and many provincial governments want to install even more because the income from the machines far exceeded expectations. Some officials, however, are afraid that too rapid an expansion may backfire on the lottery industry as a whole, especially in the face of the public's concern over social problems that might develop. What happened in one province after the introduction of the new product lends a certain validity to their fears. In Nova Scotia, the government allowed VLTs to be installed in food stores and similar non-age-controlled establishments. Not surprisingly, underage gamblers discovered that they, too, could try their hand at winning. Store personnel soon realized that there was no effective way to prevent the minors from playing on the machines. This development generated some bad publicity regarding VLTs, and government officials swiftly removed them from all but age-restricted establishments (Connor, 1993b).

As a result of what happened in Nova Scotia, most of the other provinces have thus far allowed the machines to be set up only in age-restricted businesses such as liquor stores. Manitobans, in particular, have been very cautious as to where and how many VLTs they will allow. Two hundred fifty locations in rural areas were chosen for initial VLT installation. They were allowed to run for a year, and their operation was fully assessed before the government permitted them in metropolitan areas. Provincial officials are also of the opinion that gauging the social impact of the game is just as important as the game itself. This reflects increasing public scrutiny of all gaming proliferation. Alberta, like Manitoba, has a heightened awareness of public acceptance of yet another gaming device. And one province, as of 1999, did not allow VLTs at all: British Columbia.

Traditional lotteries are also in the market to increase revenues. By the spring of 1994, all Canadian lotteries except the British Columbia Lottery Corporation participated in a new lotto game called 7/47. This is a seven-digit lotto much like the 6/49 lotto that was introduced in 1982, except it adds one more number to the set. The new game was a gamble, because there are few successful seven-digit games in place anywhere in the world. However, the lottery was successful and continues to operate as of 1999. Some lottery officials are of the opinion that the seven-digit games failed because the six-digit games were taken off the market. Canadians have the option of choosing between the two (Connor, 1994b).

Lottery officials are realistic about the almost certain loss in revenues from 6/49. Most of them are of the opinion, however, that the revenues from 7/47 will more than make up for any losses. To some degree, they want the old game to lessen in popularity. Because more and more people are participating in 6/49, the jackpots are awarded more often; thus, the jackpot amounts are smaller than they used to be because the chance of someone winning for each drawing is more probable. If jackpot amounts are not large enough, fewer people will lay out money on tickets because the amount is not sufficiently enticing. In addition, lottery officials think that many 6/49 players will remain loyal to their game. They believe that 7/47 will attract new players and that the two games together will generate more revenues than did the old six-digit lotto (Connor, 1993b).

British Columbia has chosen not to participate in the new lotto game. Lottery officials do not want to lose any autonomy in the lucrative lotto industry. They are fearful that their decision-making ability will be lessened if they join the other provinces in this venture. They also entertain serious doubts about the format of the game itself, the increased price for playing 7/47 (three sets of seven numbers for two Canadian dollars, or sixty-six cents per play), and the terrible odds for the players (Connor, 1993b).

On June 10, 1994, Ontario was the first to offer the new game, officially called **Lotto 7.** The minimum jackpot for the weekly drawing was 2.5 million Canadian dollars. The advertising campaign promoting Lotto 7 reached a cost of five million Canadian dollars by late spring of 1994, and involved some fairly sensational marketing devices. An aircraft that wrote a huge "seven" in smoke in the sky and a biplane-riding female wingwalker are only two examples of the lengths the lottery corporations will go to acquaint the public with the new game. The same type of aggressive marketing techniques proved to be very successful in promoting Canada's lotteries in the past. Even though the odds of winning the weekly drawing are one in twenty-one million per play, sales in Ontario for the first year of operation were 175 million Canadian dollars; approximately 55 million Canadian dollars were allocated to hospitals, social service agencies, and other projects. Most of the remaining earnings were awarded as jackpots (Connor and Doocey, 1994).

The province of Quebec has two projects in the offing that may rival Lotto 7 in ambition. **Loto-Quebec** plans to enter into an agreement with an international consortium that will offer an interactive program to television viewers in their own homes. Although Loto-Quebec is presently offering over forty interactive lotteries over cable television, the new electronic distribution system could attract as much as 80 percent of all the households in Quebec. The consortium plans to expand the system to other provinces and countries at some point in the future (Warson, 1994e).

Quebec tested another enterprise in the summer of 1994: selling lottery tickets at checkout counters in the stores owned by a huge supermarket chain. Shoppers will have the opportunity to buy coded lottery tickets when they go grocery shopping. The ticket will be printed out and scanned by the store cashiers. One of the most attractive features for the shoppers is that the new system will take only a few seconds of their time. The supermarket chain, like other retail stores, will receive a commission on the ticket sales they make (Warson, 1994e).

Although traditional lotteries have been in place for a number of years in Canada and have proved to be a highly successful method of raising much-needed revenue for dwindling provincial coffers, the new VLTs and Super 7 Lotto may be the straws that break the camel's back. No matter how many projections or predictions are made, no realistic assessment of these new programs can be made until they have been in place for some time. As with most enterprises in which the potential for profit is great, so is the risk. However, almost everyone likes occasional change and so far, the public has been very receptive to the additions made in the gaming industry. If Canadian lottery officials offer the possibility of great wealth for a moderate outlay of money and at the same time address probable negative social costs successfully, they will have achieved what they set out to do. Although these are no easy tasks to accomplish, so far they have adopted a prudent and responsible attitude about dealing with difficulties they may encounter.

HORSE RACING

Up to 1992, revenues from Canadian horse racing tracks were on the decline. Only in one area did the industry see a significant improvement: bets made on races that were simulcast from the United States. **Simulcasting** involves sending a signal carrying a live horse race, or any other live sporting event, from one track or sports facility to another. The enormous potential that simulcasting holds for Canada became possible only when the federal government revoked a regulation that allowed Canadian tracks to permit betting on only forty foreign races annually (Campbell, 1993).

Quite a few tracks in the United States offer more than four cards of racing each day. Although their Canadian counterparts do not have quite that capability as yet, many of them see simulcasting as the wave of the future, especially since there are so few Canadian tracks operating at any given time throughout the country. Simulcasting can only improve winter betting when tracks are closed down due to weather considerations (Campbell, 1993).

Ontario first saw the possibilities in simulcasting in late 1992. When local live races were shut down for the season, Ontario broadcast races from California and Miami until late March when live races began again. The public's response to the experiment overwhelmed both the Ontario Jockey Club (OJC) and American track officials (Campbell, 1993).

Other tracks in Ontario experimented with a combination card. The combo card enables bettors to bet on live races and on simulcast races broadcast at the same time. Some OJT officials had feared that the public would bet on only the first few races and then grow bored with the process. However, at a small harness racing track outside of Toronto, twenty-race cards were introduced and the betting was just as lively on the twentieth race as on the first (Campbell, 1993).

Windsor Raceway, Ontario, which is situated across from Detroit, actively pursues its customers from that area. Windsor broadcasts races from Santa Anita, California, and also offers live harness racing both during the day and the night. The track's owner charges no admission fee in order to promote his facility. He and other Ontarians believe that people want options to choose from when they place their bets and that this is key to the future good health of the Canadian racing industry (Campbell, 1993).

Another shot in the arm for the Canadian racing industry came when the federal government passed a mandate that permitted **teletheaters,** off-track betting (OTB) establishments that exist solely to simulcast racing events. The provincial governments decide whether or not they will permit such facilities in their communities. Teletheaters are required to fill 75 percent of their seating capacity, and they must offer food and beverage service to their customers. A telewagering company opened facilities in northern Ontario cities in early 1993, and the OJC eagerly anticipates the opening of teletheaters in the Toronto area (Campbell, 1993). The Ontario Racing Commission operates three hundred new teletheaters situated throughout the province (Warson, 1994b). The provinces of Manitoba, Saskatchewan, Alberta, Nova Scotia, and New Brunswick also host teletheaters. In addition, Nova Scotia, New Brunswick, and Prince Edward Island formed a harness racing commission in the spring of 1993 to address the unification of racing regulations and how best to solve the problem of dwindling public participation (Warson, 1994a).

Even with the addition of simulcasting to many Canadian tracks, the horseracing industry is not out of the woods. A large racetrack in Winnipeg does not transmit to teletheaters anymore because the cost of doing so became restrictive. Tracks in Saskatchewan are encountering the same situation. The largest hurdle the industry faces, however, is the loss of revenues to other forms of gaming. With all the choices the gaming public has, racetracks will have to be innovative when it comes to scrambling for their share of the market. Some racetrack owners have already implemented the means of doing just that. One such owner offers VLTs at his track. He believes that those who do not want to wager on the races, but come with someone who does, may find more pleasure in another form of gambling available right on the premises (Campbell, 1993).

The future of horse-race wagering, just like the future of all other forms of Canadian gaming now available to the public, depends on how well gaming officials gauge the pulse of the public. They must seriously consider how much and what kinds of gaming their citizens are willing to allow in their communities. Ignoring their voice could be the prelude to a disaster. If too many forms of gaming are available, they may all suffer as a result. If Canadian officials do not market aggressively or wait too long to openly compete with their across-the-border neighbors, they might lose both Canadian and American dollars that are sorely needed to revitalize local economies. The success of the new gaming trends has been evaluated only over a very short time. To measure the financial health of these budding enterprises effectively, a longitudinal study must be undertaken.

REVIEW TERMS

Crystal Casino	player-operated sales terminals (POSTS)
Free Trade Agreement	simulcasting
Loto-Quebec	teletheaters
Lotto 7	video lottery terminals (VLTs)

REFERENCES

Alfieri Domenic Ontario Casino Corporation. (1995). Annual report 1994–1995.

Campbell, N. A. (1993). To combat decline in handle, Canadian tracks lean heavier on simulcasting, VLTs. *International Gaming and Wagering Business*, 28–29.

Canadian Centre on Substance Abuse. (n.d.) Gambling in Canada: A multibillion-dollar industry. Available at: http://www.ccsa.ca/gmbl.htm

Connor, M. (1993a). Great White North may be next casino gaming frontier. *International Gaming and Wagering Business*, 8–12.

Connor, M. (1993b). Social gaming products in development. *International Gaming and Wagering Business*, 12–26.

Connor, M., and Doocey, P. (1994). Lottery beat. *International Gaming and Wagering Business*, 30.

Gors, R. (1997). Canada's private public joint casino. *Casino Journal* 10(9): 50–52.

Ministry of Employment and Investment. (1997). Government rules out Las Vegas–style casinos and VLTs in bars and pubs. March 13.

Quebec plans to build third casino, at a cost of C$120M. (1994). *International Gaming and Wagering Business*, 54.

Rudd, D., Synonka, D., and Rudd, J. (1997a) The 7th wonder of the world: Casino Niagara. Paper presented at the eighth annual conference on Teaching Economics, Feb. 20–22, Robert Morris College, Pennsylvania.

Rudd, D. (1997b). *A comparative analysis of the economic impact of Casino Windsor on the Ontario Province*. Paper presented at the 1996 Pennsylvania Economic Association Annual Conference, and at the 10th International Conference on Gambling and Risk Taking, Montreal, May 1997, p. 1.

Warson, A. (1994a). Canadian report. *International Gaming and Wagering Business*, 48.

Warson, A. (1994b). Canadian report. *International Gaming and Wagering Business*, 16.

Warson, A. (1994c). Cheaters caught at new Windsor casino. *International Gaming and Wagering Business*, 6.

Warson, A. (1994d). Mohawks near Montreal reject casino. *International Gaming and Wagering Business*, 61.

Warson, A. (1994e). Quebec supermarket test for lottery [tickets] goes on-line this summer. *International Gaming and Wagering Business*, 30.

Warson, A. (1995). ITT wins licenses. *International Gaming and Wagering Business*, 4.

Chapter 15

International Casinos

OBJECTIVES

- List and locate the major international casino areas.
- Describe several characteristics of casinos within the regions of Africa, Europe, Asia, Central and South America, and the Bahamas and the Caribbean.
- Compare and contrast the tax levied on the casino industry of a number of European countries.
- Describe some of the current and future trends of international casinos.

INTRODUCTION

One of the main reasons for the expansion of casinos worldwide is economic. Most governments or communities who have legalized casinos have done so to reap large sums of money through taxes. Without exception, most authorities charge the casinos a licensing fee and also levy a tax on the gross revenue. On the other hand, some countries have also introduced casinos as an attempt to augment the tourism product. Regardless of the initiating reason, internationally, casinos are seen as an avenue to raise revenue.

In previous chapters, we have highlighted the growth of the casino industry in North America and on cruise ships. In this chapter we will examine casinos in Africa, the Bahamas and the Caribbean, Central and South America, Australia, Asia, and Europe. This chapter will summarize how the casinos in these countries and regions are similar to and, in some cases, different from those of their North American counterparts.

CASINOS IN AFRICA

There are casinos in at least thirty African countries. Table 15-1 lists all of the African countries with casinos and the number in each of them. The countries with the largest numbers of casinos are Egypt, Kenya, Mauritius, and Nigeria, respectively.

The African continent is large and has a variety of cultures. In general, the Muslim countries, many of which are located in the north, prohibit any forms of gambling. Where gambling does occur in these countries, access is limited to nonresidents who must present a passport or other form of positive identification to enter the casino. The minimum age for entrance in most casinos is twenty-one.

Many of the traditional games, such as blackjack, American roulette, mini baccarat, chem de fer, pai gow, fan tan, Chinese sic bo, video poker, and slot machines, are played. Usually, several languages are spoken, and numerous

Table 15-1 Countries and the Number of Casinos in Africa

Countries	Number of Casinos
Benin	1
Botswana	5
Cameroon	2
Central African Republic	3
Comoros	2
Congo	1
Egypt	10
Ethiopia	1
Gabon	5
Gambia	1
Ghana	4
Ivory Coast	1
Kenya	8
Lesotho	3
Liberia	1
Madagascar	2
Mauritius	8
Morocco	2

Table 15-1 Countries and the Number of Casinos in Africa
(continued)

Countries	Number of Casinos
Namibia	2
Niger	1
Nigeria	8
Senegal	1
Seychelles	2
Sierra Leone	1
Swaziland	3
South Africa	17
Togo	2
Tunisia	2
Zaire	5
Zambia	1
Zimbabwe	3

hard international currencies are accepted. The dress code varies from casual to elegant.

In the future, South Africa has the greatest potential for growth within the casino industry (Rzadzki, 1995). The South African government is trying to legalize casino gambling from the homelands to larger cities that have other tourist attractions. The growth is almost stagnant in the other countries.

CASINOS IN THE BAHAMAS AND THE CARIBBEAN

The expanding casino industry of the United States is important to Caribbean countries because more than 70 percent of the tourists to this area are from the United States. Invariably, American tourists expect similar or the same type of entertainment when they are traveling. This section of the chapter reviews casinos in the Bahamas and other Caribbean countries and compares these casinos with their North American counterparts.

Table 15-2 lists the fourteen countries in the Caribbean, including the Bahamas, that have casinos. Puerto Rico has sixteen casinos, which is the largest number in this region. The Dominican Republic and Aruba have thirteen and ten, respectively.

Table 15-2   Countries and Number of Casinos in the Bahamas and the Caribbean

Country	Number of Casinos
Antigua	4
Aruba	12
Bahamas	4
Bonaire	2
Curaçao	7
Dominican Republic	22
Guadeloupe	3
Haiti	3
Martinique	2
Puerto Rico	19
St. Kitts	3
St. Maartes	7
St. Martin	2
St. Vincent	1
Turks and Caicos	1

The minimum age to enter the majority of these casinos is eighteen. In Martinique and Curaçao, the minimum age is twenty-one. The **dress code** varies from casual in the tourist resorts to elegant in the Dominican Republic.

Overview of Caribbean Casinos

The first legalized casino in the Caribbean occurred in 1920. This casino was located in the Bahamas (Goombay, 1992). At first, this casino was seasonal and patronized by northern Americans. The gaming regulations did not officially occur until 1969. Slots were not introduced until 1978 in Puerto Rico. The casino industry for both of these countries was primarily for rich tourists.

Perhaps it is important to look closely at the casino industry in the Bahamas, because it may be considered the "grandfather" of the casino industry in the Caribbean. A close look at Table 15-3 reveals some interesting trends that have prevailed over the years.

Table 15-3 indicates that Bahamian residents are prohibited from gambling in the casinos. From an economic perspective, this policy has been beneficial to the country, because all of the proceeds from the casinos represent a true injection

Table 15-3 Casino Gambling in the Bahamas

Name of governing body	Bahamas Gaming Board
Initial year of casino gambling	1920; 1969, Lotteries and Gaming Act
Regulations/restrictions	• No Bahamians can gamble • 500 rooms minimum • 18 years old minimum
Types of games	Blackjack, roulette, craps, baccarat, big six (slot machines)
Tax levied	• 28.5 % of gross • 100 % duty on all gaming equipment
Type of clientele	Tourists only
Why casino gambling in the country	Part of the attraction to the islands
Languages spoken	English
Number of casinos in the country	4; 2 in Nassau, 2 in Freeport
Competition	Atlantic City, Puerto Rico, Dominican Republic

of funds into the economy. Another benefit of this regulation is that it eliminates many of the social costs of gambling.

Another noteworthy regulation observed in the Bahamas is the room requirement. The Bahamas requires that all hotels wishing to obtain a casino license must have a minimum of five hundred hotel rooms. This policy was also adopted by the New Jersey Casino Control Commission when legislation was made for gambling in New Jersey. Unfortunately, this policy was not adopted by other Caribbean countries that have introduced casino during the past two decades.

On December 12, 1998, Sun International opened their $800 million Atlantis Casino on Paradise Island in the Bahamas. This resort is the newest and largest casino in the Caribbean. The casino has 110,000 square feet of gambling space, with over 1,000 slots and 80 gaming tables. The resort casino complex contains 1,202 rooms and 11 food outlets immersed within a water theme. All of these features are used to attract both gamblers and their families. (Sun International Hotels Limited, 1999).

Compare and Contrast

On the average, casinos in North America, especially those in Atlantic City, are much larger than those in the Caribbean. The largest casino in this region is the Marriott Resort and Crystal Palace Casino. It has thirty-five thousand square feet of casino space (Bonamy, 1998). The smallest casino in Atlantic City has approximately forty-three thousand square feet of casino space (Bain, 1994).

Several of the Caribbean casinos have been recently renovated. During the renovation, they have improved their physical appearance as well as introduced different types of slot machines. With the introduction of new slot machines also came the introduction of new games. Many of the Caribbean casinos are now playing video keno, blackjack, and Caribbean stud poker. The introduction of these games can be a useful advertising strategy.

The games played in a casino attract a specific clientele. Presently, the games played in several Caribbean casinos include roulette, craps, baccarat, mini baccarat, video poker, blackjack, big six, and slots.

Casinos in the Caribbean are constantly competing for big-name entertainment. Their biggest challenge is how to attract big-name headliners to their properties. Headliners are expensive. Large numbers of peoples are needed to help defray the cost of bringing them to a Caribbean destination. If it is possible to attract them to your property, you must then compete with the sand, sea, and sun, as well as the gambling activities on the floor. Conversely, many gamblers will only visit a site if there is exciting entertainment. It may be a Catch-22 situation.

The tournaments held in the Caribbean are not as large as those held in the United States. Tournaments held on the mainland can be easily accessed by players. Conversely, those held in the Caribbean have the disadvantage of geography. To overcome this hurdle, Caribbean tournaments are usually held during the winter months when many players would be attracted to a warm vacation. These tournaments usually include a package that includes two or three days within a casino resort.

It is impossible to operate a casino successfully without having an aggressive comp program. At Caribbean destinations, comp policies must be in place prior to the arrival of a client. This practice may cause some complications. Currently, an effective method of tracking comping potential is to have some type of card or player identification. Caribbean casinos must develop an efficient strategy to overcome this hurdle.

Implementing a VIP club is one method of providing special services for premium customers. These clubs can keep valid information about clients, as well as provide them with literature about upcoming activities. Members of these clubs in the Caribbean can also facilitate travel and lodging arrangements, which are essential for traveling gamblers.

A well-organized junket system is an invaluable asset for Caribbean casinos. It is important that Caribbean junkets are punctual and dependable. Subcontracting this service can cause many casinos poor customer relations. Perhaps the most reliable way to overcome this problem is for Caribbean casinos to operate this service themselves.

The development of additional casinos within the Caribbean will continue to be stable until the end of this century. Several countries made unsuccessful attempts in 1994 to introduce a casino industry. Presently, religious factions have been successful in defeating efforts to legalize casino gambling before legislators could vote on it. Those countries with casinos will have to try to improve their current product to compete with other Caribbean or American competitors.

Some Caribbean countries are still in a quandary about the introduction of casino gambling. In a way, it is ironic, because they have several other types of legal wagering. The rationale that they use for the introduction is the creation of jobs and the improvement of the tourism product. Invariably, casinos do create additional jobs; however, it is debatable whether the social costs in the Caribbean, with its religious background, outweigh the economic benefits.

During the past thirty years, many of the casinos operating in the Caribbean have devoted very little time compared to their North American counterparts in concerning themselves with the social responsibility of gambling. A cursory research has indicated that in countries where the residents are able to gamble, very little efforts are exerted to teach them about responsible gambling. This omission should change during the upcoming decade.

There is a need for sociological research about the impact of casino gambling in the Caribbean. Casino organizations should encourage regional universities to research gambling addiction and other side effects of working within the casino industry. The results of this research should be compared with the conclusions from casinos in the United States and other developed countries.

The future success of the casino industry in the Caribbean will be determined by several factors. First, there is a need for aggressive promotion. This challenge will become greater with the increasing numbers of riverboat casinos in the southern states and the possible opening of Native American gambling in the southeastern states.

Another factor that will affect casinos in this region will be the enforcement of stringent regulations. These regulations should help to preserve the image of gambling as a respectable industry. These regulations should also help to discourage unsavory characters from being employed in the casino industry.

An important consideration for Caribbean decision makers should be a policy regarding allowing residents to gamble within the casino. One way to prevent economic leakage would be to prevent residents from gambling. This policy would also serve another purpose. If residents were not allowed to gamble, the spread of compulsive gambling and other social costs related to the casino industry would be prevented. This exclusionist policy would allow the tourists to be the only ones to contribute to the casinos' coiffures.

CASINOS IN PUERTO RICO

Casinos in Puerto Rico were legalized in 1948 (see Table 15-4). Slots, however, were not introduced until 1974. The usual casino games are now played in Puerto Rico. All casinos must be associated with a resort hotel. This U.S. territory has developed an interesting formula to tax the slot profits. Twenty percent of the

Table 15-4 Casino Gambling in Puerto Rico

Name of governing body	Gaming Division—Puerto Rico Compania de Turismo
Initial year of casino gambling	1948; 1974, slots introduced
Regulations/restrictions	• Limited hours • No cocktails in the gaming areas
Types of games	Roulette, craps, baccarat, mini baccarat, video poker, blackjack, big six, slots
Tax levied	57% slot profits goes to the government
Type of clientele	Latin Americans, North Americans, locals, Asians and others
Why casino gambling in the country	Part of the tourist product; revenue
Languages spoken	Spanish, English
Number of casinos in the country	16
Competition	Bahamas, Aruba, Dominican Republic

57 percent of revenue obtained from the slot machines is earmarked for the University of Puerto Rico. The minimum age for gaming is eighteen years.

CASINOS IN CENTRAL AND SOUTH AMERICA

Table 15-5 shows the countries in Central and South America that have casinos. Argentina has twenty-three casinos, which is the largest number in this region. The minimum age to enter these casinos is eighteen years, except in Ecuador and Uruguay. Many of these casinos charge an entrance fee. French roulette, American roulette, baccarat, ponta banco, blackjack, and slots are played in the larger casinos. The majority of casinos in this region are much smaller than the average North American casino. Many of them have a few slot machines, with several blackjack and roulette tables. The primary purpose of casinos in these countries is for tourist entertainment. Spanish is the principal language spoken.

CASINOS IN ASIA, PACIFIC RIM COUNTRIES, AND AUSTRALIA

The casino epidemic is spreading to all parts of the world. One of the next hot spots will be Asia and its Pacific Rim neighbors. The casino industry is booming in Asian countries and Australia (Connor, 1994). Although Table 15-6 shows South Korea with thirteen casinos, Australia and New Zealand have the greatest growth potential because of the attitude of the people. Australia's latest casino is expected to have approximately two hundred table games, with 2,500 poker machines with a

Table 15-5   Countries and Number of Casinos in Central and South America

Country	Number of Casinos
Argentina	23
Bolivia	3
Chile	6
Colombia	16
Costa Rica	16
Ecuador	17
Panama	13
Paraguay	7
Peru	5
Suriname	2
Uruguay	17

keno and sports booking section (Connor, 1994). The casinos also feature both Las Vegas and European style casino. The required dress varies from proper to elegant.

Before looking at the expansion of the casino industry of each of the countries listed in Table 15-6, it is important to appreciate why some of the other twelve countries have not legalized casino gambling. Several of the countries in the Pacific Rim and Asia practice Buddhism, Hinduism, and Shintoism. These religious doctrines prohibit their followers from engaging in all forms of gambling. This cultural nuance has been, and perhaps will continue to be, a hindrance to the introduction of legalized casino gambling in many Pacific Rim countries in the future.

Table 15-6   Countries and Number of Casinos in the Pacific Rim

Country	Number of Casinos
Australia	23
China (Macau)	9
Malaysia	2
New Zealand	2
Philippines	23
South Korea	13

South Korea

South Korea has thirteen casinos, which is the largest number within the Pacific Rim countries (see Table 15-6). Several characteristics about the Korean casinos are worth highlighting. First, the casinos are only for tourists, thus, the gross revenues from the casinos increase the multiplier effect of tourism. Additionally, the dress code and the age requirement encourages a specific type of clientele. The average size of casinos is six thousand square feet, which can only accommodate a small number of slot machines and table games.

The future growth of the casino industry for South Korea will be influenced by increased tourism. As trade increases with other Pacific Rim countries, there will be a need for more travel and entertainment. Currently, the operating expenses and government taxes in South Korea are high, which makes it difficult for casino operators to make large profits.

Australia

Australia has the second largest number of casinos in the Pacific Rim nations. It opened its first casino in 1973. The casinos in Melbourne and Sydney are the largest in Australia, with 1,200 and 1,500 slot machines, respectively (Kasselis and Landas, 1999). Table 15-7 gives an overview of the industry in the country "down under."

Casino gambling in Australia is perhaps the most highly regulated in the world. The Casino Control Authority is the regulatory body. Besides regulating the industry, it also levies a 20 percent tax on the gross revenues of each casino. The actual distribution of gaming licenses are left up to the individual states.

Australia differs from many of its Pacific Rim neighbors in that 70 to 95 percent of the casino clients are Australians. The casino industry also faces stiff competition from the **registered clubs,** which have an almost monopoly on the slot machines and keno clubs in the country. The concept of gambling is contrastingly different from that of the other Pacific Rim neighbors.

Table 15-7 gives a more detailed look at the regulations of casino gambling in Australia. It is interesting to note that there are no slot machines in the casinos in the province of New South Wales. Unlike the United States or the United Kingdom, Australian casinos are permitted to advertize and promote casino gambling. It should also be noted that it is illegal for casino employees to receive tips.

Traditional casino games, such as blackjack, roulette, craps, and baccarat, are played. Some **Asian games,** such as fan tan, taw sci, and pacapio, are also played. Most of these countries in the region have a minimum age requirement of eighteen years.

Philippines

The Philippines boasts that it is "Asia's friendliest casino." Gambling, both legal and illegal, has flourished within this country for a long time. It was finally legalized and regulated in 1977 (Cabot, Thompson, and Tottenham, 1993). Table 15-8 gives an overview of the casino industry in the Philippines.

Table 15-7   Casino Gambling in Australia

Name of governing body	Casino Control Authority
Initial year of casino gambling	1973
Regulations/restrictions	• No tipping • No restrictions on advertizing • Each state selects the owners of new casinos • 18 years minimum
Types of games	Baccarat, big six wheel, craps, keno, poker, roulette, red dog, sic bo
Tax levied	20% of gross
Type of clientele	Visitors and residents
Why casino gambling in the country	Pastime
Languages spoken	English
Number of casinos in the country	23
Competition	Registered clubs with slots, keno clubs

The nine casinos in the Philippines are much larger than those in South Korea. The average size is about thirty thousand square feet. These casinos have an abundance of slot machines as well as other table games.

The regulatory body for the casino industry is PAGCOR (Philippine Amusement and Gaming Corporation). This agency levies a 72 percent tax on the gross

Table 15-8   Casino Gambling in Philippines

Name of governing body	Philippine Amusement and Gaming Corporation (PAGCOR)
Initial year of casino gambling	1977
Regulations/restrictions	• Foreigners need passports to enter • 21 years old minimum
Types of games	Craps, big & small, draw poker, mini baccarat, pai gow, roulette, slots machines, table games, video blackjack
Tax levied	72%
Type of clientele	Visitors and residents
Why casino gambling in the country	Economics and entertainment
Languages spoken	Filipino and English
Number of casinos in the country	23
Competition	Australia

gaming win (Cabot et al., 1993). It also enforces the policy of foreigners using passports as a form of identification to enter the casinos.

The Philippines has been successful in securing a large share of the Pacific Rim casino industry by developing and operating junkets. These packages are offered from many other Asian countries. Some of the popular junket countries are Hong Kong, Taipei, and Japan.

Macau

There are also nine casinos in Macau. This small island country is a Portuguese colony, and regards tourism and gambling as its main industry. Table 15-9 shows that casino gambling was organized in this country in 1934 (Cabot et al., 1993).

Macau is one of the Pacific Rim nations that offers Chinese gambling games. The games of pacapio, fan tan, and tai sai are played at the freestanding casino. This practice is different from other Pacific Rim casino countries and is also noteworthy as an extra feature to the tourism product.

Malaysia

It is perhaps ironic that there is a casino in Malaysia. The majority religion in the country is Muslim, which prohibits any form of gambling. Notwithstanding the religion practice, a casino has been in the country since 1978 (see Table 15-10).

Malaysia may be used as a model for other Pacific Rim countries that are reluctant to legalize casino gambling because of religious reasons. The practice of banning the local Muslim yet allowing others to enter is creative. This country

Table 15-9   Casino Gambling in Macau

Name of governing body	Macau Tourism and Amusements Co.
Initial year of casino gambling	1934
Regulations/restrictions	18 years old minimum for nonresidents; 21 for local residents
Tax levied	N/A
Types of games	Baccarat, blackjack, boule, craps, dai sai, fan tan, keno, pacapio, poker, roulette, slot machines
Type of clientele	Visitors and residents
Why casino gambling in the country	Economics and entertainment
Languages spoken	Cantonese Chinese, English, Portuguese
Number of casinos in the country	9
Competition	Australia, Korea

Table 15-10   Casino Gambling in Malaysia

Name of governing body	N/A
Initial year of casino gambling	1978
Regulations/restrictions	• Malaysian Muslims are prohibited • Minimum age
Types of games	Blackjack, French boule, baccarat, keno, mini dice, roulette, slots, tai sai
Tax levied	N/A
Type of clientele	Visitors and residents
Why casino gambling in the country	Part of the resort's entertainment
Languages spoken	English, Chinese
Number of casinos in the country	2
Competition	Philippines, Australia, Korea

has demonstrated that it is possible to have a tourism attraction and not infringe on the cultural values of the people.

New Zealand

New Zealand is the latest Pacific Rim entry into the casino industry, with two casinos. Several factors have caused this decision. One of the reasons for legalizing casinos was to expand the number of tourist attractions. Another reason was to try to avoid the leakage of large sums of money that was been spent by New Zealanders who gambled in other Pacific Rim nations. Some legislators also say the casino industry will create a number of jobs.

CASINOS IN EUROPE

There has been an increase in the number of European countries legalizing casino gambling with the change from communist to free trade economy. In Table 15-11 several of the former Soviet states are listed as having casinos. Many of these casinos were opened to attract **hard currencies** from tourists. (The U.S. dollar, the British pound, the Japanese yen, the German marc, and the French and Swiss francs are considered hard currencies.) The required age to enter almost all of the casinos is eighteen years. The Slovak Republic is the only country that has an age requirement of twenty years.

Table 15-11 Countries and Number of Casinos in Europe

Country	Number of Casinos
Austria	12
Belgium	8
Bosnia and Herzegovina	3
Bulgaria	7
Croatia	22
Cyprus	5
Czech Republic	16
Denmark	5
Estonia	2
Finland	2
France	130
Greece	9
Hungary	21
Italy	4
Latvia	2
Luxembourg	1
Macedonia	4
Malta	1
Moldova	1
Monaco	4
Netherlands	8
Poland	13
Romania	2
Russia	23
Slovak Republic	2
Slovenia	4
Spain	22
Sweden	13
Switzerland	18

Table 15-11   Countries and Number of Casinos in Europe
(continued)

Country	Number of Casinos
Turkey	70
Ukraine	1
United Kingdom	128
Yugoslavia	9

Many of the European casinos are located in resort/spa areas. Some of them are seasonal and have specific **entry requirements.** Jackets and ties are required to enter many of the casinos. Another entry requirement is a passport or some other form of identification.

Membership is required to enter casinos in Great Britain (Table 15-12). Membership applications require a twenty-four-hour waiting period to be approved. Equally different, in the United Kingdom, there is no live entertain-

Table 15-12   Casino Gambling in Great Britain

Name of governing body	British Gaming Board
Initial year of casino gambling	1968
Regulations/restrictions	• Must be a member/guest to gamble • 18 years minimum entry age • 24 hours to apply for membership • Two slot machines per casino • Maximum slot jackpot £150 • No tips • No credit to gamble • No advertising permitted • No live entertainment
Types of games	Table games, two slots per casino
Tax levied	18%
Type of clientele	Middle and upper class
Why casino gambling in the country	Elite entertainment
Languages spoken	English
Number of casinos in the country	118
Competition	Morocco, Turkey, Egypt, Spain

ment nor is alcohol served at the casino table (Bain, 1994). Gambling in the United Kingdom is regarded as the most highly regulated in the world. Regardless of the size of the casino, it is only allowed two slot machines.

TAXES LEVIED

One of the main reasons why any government legalizes casino gambling is to generate taxes. Some governments levy a lump-sum tax, whereas others tax the casinos by the machines, tables, or even square footage. In the main, the taxes levied in European countries are the steepest in the world. Table 15-13 shows that Germany and Greece tax their casinos 80 percent, whereas the United Kingdom in contrast taxes its casinos only 18 percent. Some of the taxes collected from casinos are earmarked for specific social or charitable causes, whereas some countries place the revenue in the government's treasury.

AMERICAN INFLUENCE ON THE INTERNATIONAL CASINO INDUSTRY

Nevada was the first state in the United States to legalize casino gambling in this "modern" gambling era. Nevadans made gambling regulated and sophisticated. They spent millions of dollars in technological research and marketing. Addi-

Table 15-13 Taxes Levied on European Community Casinos

Country	Percentage
Germany	80
Greece	80
Italy	72
Sweden	60–70
Denmark	65
Luxembourg	48
France	45
Spain	42
Belgium	38
Netherlands	35
Portugal	20
United Kingdom	18

tionally, they spent large sums of money to attract big-name entertainment stars. The American standards of junkets, tournaments, and comps have essentially forced other casino destinations to follow suit in order to remain competitive.

Americans have also had a tremendous impact on the regulations and design of the international casino industry because of American human resources. An American can be found in management positions in almost every casino worldwide. Because there are so many casinos in the United States, they have the ability to export managerial personnel. They have been successful both as management companies and as owner-operators.

The other area Americans have had an impact on the casino industry is through technology. Large electronic companies such as **Bally Gaming, International Gaming Technology (IGT),** and **Universal** have dominated the distribution of slot and other types of gaming machines. These companies have placed machines and other gaming paraphernalia all over the world. The American company Casino Data Systems is renowned for its casino software, which improves the accounting and controls within a casino.

THE FUTURE OF INTERNATIONAL CASINOS

Perhaps the most important contributing factor to the growth of the casino industry internationally is the collapse of the Communist bloc. This factor has had an impact in South America, Europe, Asia, and several of the African countries. Governments have been forced to find hard currency to operate their countries and have looked to gaming as a panacea for their budgetary ills. Another contributing factor toward the widespread increase of casinos has been the increase of diplomatic relations between many countries. Neighboring countries are now opening their borders to tourists, who in turn bring large sums of spending money.

The casino industry will expand further within certain African and European continents as soon as civil unrest ceases. Presently, several of the casinos in both Africa and Europe are not operating because of political and civil unrest. It will be interesting to observe South Africa's attitude toward casinos since its recent government took power.

Regionally, the greatest resistance against casino gambling is occurring in the Caribbean. This opposition has been happening because of the strength of the religious groups as an effective lobby. Many of the religious leaders in that region object to gambling on moral and religious grounds. Nevertheless, the pressure of economic leakage of casino dollars being spent in other countries may be a catalyst to change this moral objection.

An important social concern about the casino industry is gambling addiction. Gambling is a very addictive activity. Preventative programs should be developed to combat addiction wherever there is legalized gambling. These programs should also address the issues of underage gamblers. These problems may be more complicated to treat in an international arena than in a Western country.

The security of the casino and its patrons is another concern. Casinos and gamblers are excellent targets for crime. Usually, the media of gambling is hard currency, which would have an increased value within many Pacific Rim countries. Casino patrons must feel comfortable within a country, otherwise the casino and tourism industry can be ruined.

Although casinos are expanding internationally, there is a serious concern about the collectibility of gambling debts. The farther a gambler gets away from the United States, the more cautious he or she becomes about both receiving and repaying credit. There is a need for stringent policies for collecting international casino debts. Perhaps an international information center may be the answer. In the U.S., there is concern about the expansion of international Internet gambling. Senator Jon Kyl maintains that virtual casinos are the "hard-core cocaine of gambling." The Kyl bill would prohibit gambling on the Internet by extending the 1961 Wire Act prohibitions on interstate sports gambling conducted by phone or wire to gambling on the Internet. It would also outlaw other forms of Internet gambling, including cybercasinos (Clausino, 1999). The stage is set for a conflict between gambling, which historically has been subject to strong government regulation, and the new (borderless?) world of cyberspace (Cabot, 1998).

The authors feel that there are several issues of concerns for the international casino industry. First, it is important to develop impartial casino regulatory agencies. Another concern is the need for regional casino training schools that are licensed by a regulatory agency. Additionally, because money laundering will continue to be a concern for all casino destinations, the casino operators should work with law enforcement agencies as well as international agencies to help stymie this practice.

REVIEW TERMS

Asian games	hard currency
Bally Gaming	International Gaming Technology (IGT)
dress code	registered clubs
entry requirement	universal

REFERENCES

Bain, J. H. (1994). *Casinos: The international casino guide.* Port Washington, New York: B.D.I.T., Inc.

Besher, A. (1991). *The Pacific Rim almanac.* New York: HarperCollins Publishers.

Bonamy, V. O. (1998). Personal interview. Director of Casino Accounts, Marriott Crystal Palace Casino. 15 December.

Boxall, F. (1994). Macau: Casinos, Matter of chance. *Asia Travel Trade* 25 (7): 40–41.

Cabot, A. (1998). Internet gambling report II. Las Vegas: Trace Publications.

Cabot, A. N. (1990). *Casino credit and collection law.* Las Vegas, Nevada: International Association of Gaming Attorneys.

Cabot, A. N., Thompson, W. N., and Tottenham, A. (1993). *International casino law.* Reno, Nevada: Institute for the Study of Gambling and Commercial Gaming.

Clausino, J. Senator unveils new effort to bar Internet gambling. *New York Times,* 23 March.

Connor, M. (1994). 94 international outlook. *Gaming and Wagering Business* 15 (1): 26, 46–49.

Goombay—*Bahamas Air In-Flight Magazine.* (1992). Gaming industry an asset to Bahamas' economy 9(4):153.

Kasselis, P. A., and Landas, P. D. (1999). Gaming in the Asia Pacific—joining the international bandwagon. Available at: http://www.hotel-online.com/neo/Trends/Andersen/asia_gaming.html

Kelly, J. (1994). Australia's open largest "temporary" casino. *Gaming & Wagering Business* 15 (8): 3, 52–53.

Kenney, M. (1994). International gaming credit, due diligence and enforcement: How can the risks be mitigated? *Gaming Research and Review Journal* 1 (1): 77–87.

McQueen, P. (1994). International gaming at a glance. *Gaming and Wagering Business* 15 (10): 14–18.

Rzadzki, J. (1995). More gaming opportunities emerge in Africa. *Gaming and Wagering Business* 16 (1): 42–44.

Sun International Hotels Limited. (1999). Royal Towers Atlantis, Paradise Island. Available at: http://www.sunint.com/atlantis/press/archive/royaltowerfact.html

Worldwide casino directory. Available at: http//www.casinocity.com/countries.html

Chapter 16

The Future of the Casino Industry

OBJECTIVES

- Identify several economic and social changes that indicate a growing future for the casino industry.
- Describe the growth within the casino industry.
- Identify specific corporate responsibility for the casino industry.
- List and discuss the technological changes in the casino industry during the next decade.
- Identify some of the human resource challenges within the casino industry.
- Recognize several ethical considerations in the gaming industry.

INTRODUCTION

The origin of gambling is unknown, and the exact impact it will have in the next millennium is also unknown. When we look at the twenty-first century, one thing seems inevitable, there will definitely be more casinos in the future than there are now. There will be an increase in gaming venues and activities in all of the continents. This growth will have both positive and negative effects on the host communities.

Somebody once said, "the future is now." If we look into various regions of the world, growth and expansion is already here. In 1998, we already saw an increase in the number of casinos, in contrast with 1997, in all of the continents of the world. We are also observing an increase in the venues of casino activities. In addition to the venue changes, we also see an increase in the number of games and gaming devices.

In this chapter we will discuss future trends within the casino environment, social concerns, human resource concerns, educational concerns, regulations, geographical expansion, Native American gaming, riverboat gambling, technological trends, and ethical concerns.

CASINO ENVIRONMENT

Casinos do not exist in a vacuum. Their success or demise is a factor of many social realities. People are living longer, working fewer hours, and retiring earlier, and hence have more leisure time. Additionally, there has been an increase in the number of three- and four-day weekends. This abundance of leisure time enables the average citizen to use it in a variety of ways.

The casino industry is a multibillion dollar industry. In the United States, in 1998 it was estimated that at least 92 million Americans visited a casino establishment to gamble (Harrah's, 1996). This statistic surpasses the number of persons attending Broadway, symphony, and arena concerts.

In the United States, the average age of these gamblers was forty-five years. Fifty percent of them were white collar, with almost an equal amount of blue-collar and retired persons. These individuals had a higher level of education than the average population. Approximately 55 percent of them had attended college, which was higher than the nation's average of 48 percent. Casino patrons had a median income of $38,600, which was higher than the population's average (Fine, 1994).

The gamblers of the next decade will perhaps be different in many ways. These authors believe that casino patrons of the future will be younger and have an even higher level of college education. The casino patrons of the future will be a product of the "now generation." They will have been conditioned by television to obtain instant, or almost immediate, gratification. Where else can financial gratification be obtained legally? In the casinos, of course.

Previously, legalized gambling was conducted only in Nevada in the west, and for a long time only in Atlantic City in the east. Now, it is possible to engage in some form of legalized casino, riverboat, Native American, limited-stake, and cruise ship gambling in almost any state. Individuals wishing to gamble will soon have a gambling venue within a three-hundred-mile drive. They will also have greater accessibility to a variety of gambling activities.

SOCIAL CONCERNS

Just as gambling is expanding, so are the social concerns. In North America, many constituencies have voiced their opposition to all forms of gambling because of the disproportionate number of minorities, low-income, and underage individuals who are becoming addicted to gambling. This number will increase as the accessibility of casino and other types of gambling increases.

The social cost of gaming will continue to be a concern in the future. The costs include tardiness or absence from work, crimes to support one's habit, and treating the gambling addiction itself. The implication is that all these costs will be increased as legalized gambling becomes more widespread (Wildman, 1998). Currently, the United States has only two states where gambling is not legalized. Many states continue to hold referenda to legalize gambling. In many cases the social cost of gambling has been used as a defense against gambling.

In the other parts of the world, especially within the Muslim countries, religion will continue to play an important role in determining whether gambling will be permitted. In the next decade, it is important to watch the receptivity of lotteries and casinos in China, India, and Indonesia. These highly populated countries are being seriously courted by large North American casino conglomerates.

The next decade will also see a greater corporate responsibility for gambling-related problems. Part of the corporate citizenry will be to identify chronic gamblers, and just as there are programs for alcoholics, there will be a similar program for gamblers. Additionally, casinos will enforce their regulations to prevent underage gamblers. It is foreseeable that more casinos will follow the footsteps of Harrah's and implement their own version of Project 21.

In the future, casinos opening in new areas should look at the social concerns in a proactive manner. Strategies should be developed to assist individuals with clinical gambling problems. Perhaps funds should be set aside specifically for treatment and rehabilitation. Moreover, all states with any form of legalized gambling should legislate treatment centers.

Even Las Vegas has changed its image. It is now promoting itself as a family destination. All of the larger casinos are providing elaborate themes and activities for the entire family. The larger casinos are also sharing the same roof with conventions for the Boys Scouts and church groups. These conventions in the "temples of chance" legitimizes the casino activities and in a way encourages the youngsters to gamble in the future.

HUMAN RESOURCE CONCERNS

Although the casino industry in the United States may be prospering economically, it has its share of human resource problems. Several charges of sexual harassment have been filed within this industry. Women feel they have been harassed both by clients and employers. These charges have forced casinos to implement stricter sexual harassment policies to handle infractions of company policies by both employees and patrons.

Employee turnover within the hospitality industry has always been extremely high. The casino industry is not exempt from this albatross. This problem will increase as the number of casinos also increase. Casino operators will have to improve their human relations skills as well as their benefit packages. Employees who do not feel that they are being treated fairly or making an attractive salary will invariably leave. Managers must now motivate their employees to provide superior customer services to the already fastidious casino customers.

Casinos have also developed creative **Employee Assistance Programs (EAPs)** for their staff. It was discovered that many casino employees also suffer from a variety of addictions, which include drugs and gambling. In the long run, it is more cost effective to rehabilitate an experienced employee than to try to recruit and develop a new one. This practice will definitely increase in the future within the casino industry.

Another problem that will haunt the casino industry during the next decade is the shortage of human resources. Currently, there is a limited number of experienced, qualified gaming personnel in the world. It is a foregone conclusion that the casino industry is expanding. This unfortunately will bring about a personnel shortage. This will mean good news for some professionals who are currently in the industry. These individuals will have opportunities for promotions and advancement. On the other hand, this shortage will cause a large number of casino professionals to change jobs. Equally important, during this period of shortage, casino operators must exercise extreme caution that the integrity of the gaming industry is not compromised.

EDUCATIONAL CONCERNS

One of the biggest concerns for the casino industry will be the acquisition of qualified personnel to work within the industry. The multibillion dollar industry requires individuals with a higher level of education than a high school diploma. Previously, individuals who played cards or shot dice felt they could make a career in the casino industry. It was not felt that there was a need for any training, much less a university degree. The industry is almost demanding its managers have a college degree. During the past five years, there has been an increase in the number of casinos attending career fairs and also offering internships to attract college students. They are looking for sophisticated managers who understand finance, marketing, law, and customer service.

In 1989 it was possible to count the number of tertiary level institutes that offered a course or curriculum in casino operations. One decade later, at least fifty programs or courses are being taught. These programs are rather popular in the community colleges. It is now possible to obtain both undergraduate and graduate degrees in casino management. Efforts should be made to offer casino management courses as continuing education for supervisory and management personnel.

A large part of the education and development of the casino industry will also be the responsibility of the casinos. Many of them are either sponsoring in-house private training academies or contracting their training to specific private casino schools. The introduction of these new games will force the casinos to maintain an ongoing training program. These programs should also include the social and ethical impact of gambling.

REGULATIONS

If a host community or casino patrons do not believe a casino is properly regu-lated, the casino will fail. All casino jurisdictions have a governing body. These three- to seven-member bodies serve as regulators and police for the casino industry. The regulations will remain strict in the future. However, there will also be continuous lobbying as was seen in Atlantic City, New Jersey, to ease many of the requirements to operate a casino.

Countries considering legalizing gambling must be cognizant of the infil-tration of criminal elements into the industry. One way to safeguard against these elements would be through stringent regulations. These regulations must be reviewed and enforced more closely. Unfortunately, this vigilance will bring about an increase in the cost of background checks as well as an increase in the amount of time taken to conduct them. The only consolation for the regulating bodies would be "it is better to be safe, than sorry." Sometimes, the cost of an irreproachable reputation can be expensive. The integrity of the casino industry will remain intact only if the regulations are strictly enforced.

There will be a need for more observation by the regulatory agencies for these newer games. As more Asian games are being introduced in the casino industry, more research must be done to ensure that fraudulent activities are not occurring. The same vigilance that occurs on land-based casinos must also be enforced on riverboats and cruise ship casinos. During the past five years, a number of nontra-ditional casino table games have been introduced on riverboat casinos.

Keno is another game that is having, and will continue to have, a tremen-dous impact on the casino industry. The game originated in China to raise funds. Although it is similar to bingo, the house has the largest advantage of any casino game. Notwithstanding, since the tickets are inexpensive and the jackpots can be over $250,000, gamblers play it incessantly. Previously, this game was played only in Nevada. Keno is now being introduced in all casino venues. It also con-tinues to grow in other parts of the world.

GEOGRAPHICAL EXPANSION

Presently, all but two states in the United States have some legal form of gambling. If we look at the continents of Asia, Africa, Europe, or South America, we see the same expansion occurring. Casino gambling is also expanding in the Caribbean and the Pacific Rim. Every corner of the world will be affected by casino gambling.

Currently, riverboat gambling is popular in the United States. At the end of the century, there will be a noticeable increase in the number of riverboats both in the United States and other parts of the world. The blueprints of regulations are now being planned. After a decade of riverboats, the trend will proliferate in other parts of the world that have navigable rivers. There will also be an increase in the number of "cruises-to-nowhere" in international waters in other parts of the world.

The space currently used for casino gambling on cruise ships has already begun to expand. Some of the Carnival and Royal Caribbean cruise ships are expanding the size of the casino area from the average eight thousand square feet to eighteen thousand square feet. Many cruise lines will follow Carnival and actively participate in Comp-A-Cruise programs. Moreover, frequent gamblers will receive even more complimentary items to keep them gambling on cruises.

NATIVE AMERICAN GAMING

Within the United States, perhaps the largest future growth within the casino industry is in Indian gaming. Scores of tribes are negotiating compacts with various states to allow them to become involved in class III gambling. It is estimated that Indian gaming is worth more than $5 billion. If more of the 557 Indian nations were to receive their compacts, this number will increase. The passage of Proposition 5 has left tribal leaders in California jubilant. It will be a source of huge revenues for both Indian and non-Indian gaming entities, and many say that this will make California a billion-dollar gaming market (Connor, 1999).

The Native American tribes that do not have a class III compact with their states will continue to pursue the profitable market of bingo. Many of the tribes have numerous bingo halls. Some of these halls have nightly jackpots that range from $10,000 to $50,000. Some tribes are making efforts to operate bingo games via satellite links. The jackpots have been steadily increasing over the past five years.

RIVERBOAT CASINOS

The historic excitement of riverboats will be an attraction for many residents to gamble. In the past, several states were overzealous in distributing casino licenses. In the future, the states with pending riverboat legislation should develop a strategy that will not cause an oversaturation of boats on their rivers. Presently there are nearly one hundred riverboat casinos operating within the United States. This number is expected to almost double by the end of the decade (Catch the New Wave, 1994). Several states, such as Massachusetts, Maryland, Ohio, Pennsylvania, South Carolina, Texas, Virginia, and West Virginia, are still trying to introduce legislation that would permit riverboat casinos. When riverboat gambling becomes legalized in all of these states, the total number of floating casinos would perhaps double.

TECHNOLOGICAL TRENDS

Many futuristic technological innovations have already been introduced into the casino industry. One of these innovations is the introduction of **virtual-reality games.** The experiences with these machines are so real that it is extremely difficult for people to differentiate between reality and the game. These video games are also very addictive to problem gamblers.

Touch screens are another technology that has now been introduced into the casino industry. These screens were first introduced into the gaming industry in 1990 as a part of the video lottery terminals (VLTs). Later, other states also approved video lotteries. Now the transition has been completely made directly in the casinos (Ragonese, 1994). It is now possible to play a number of games by touching the screen. A recent study showed that more than 90 percent of the participants showed a preference to starting out their games by using touch instead of the traditional button (Ragonese, 1994). These machines will also become more popular to manufacturers because they will enable a variety of games to be played on one machine, and the entire processing is quicker.

The Internet will have one of the biggest technological impacts on the casino industry. Presently, it is worth almost $2 billion. It is estimated there are at least sixty casinos operating on the net. In 1995, there was only one. The number of Internet casinos will continue to grow, and the economic and social impact will require much research.

The technology is already in place to experiment with on-flight gambling thirty thousand feet in the air. In the very near future, it will be possible to engage in gambling on a video screen, lap-top version of slot machines and other casino games. Flyers will be able to access a video screen with their credit cards, which would enable them to gamble using a touch screen (Connor, 1993). This type of interactive entertainment will perhaps be implemented only on three-hour or longer domestic and international flights.

Computers will perhaps play the most revolutionary role in the changing face of the casino industry. Casinos of the future will not be able to operate without a computer mainframe. Presently, they are already playing a significant role in gaming. They have become invaluable in producing both internal and external reports. These reports provide financial information as well as marketing data about clients. The reports also help to keep track of large cash transactions. Also, in the future they will become more valuable in providing and maintaining credit records, which could be transferred to selected properties. Computers and their related technology will also become essential in maintaining ship-to-shore interface for the new super cruise liners and the new riverboats.

Besides the mechanical technology, there will also be more architectural marvels. Already, we are seeing casinos being built with specific themes in mind. The last **mega-casino-hotels** have set a trend. When one thinks of MGM, Luxor, Treasure Island, and the Mirage, the first thought is not of gambling but Disney, ancient Egypt, and fantasy, respectively (Andersen, 1994). Afterwards, we think of gambling in these edifices. Newer casinos, be they in Nevada, Atlantic City, or any other part of the world, must compete with these types of imagery.

ETHICS IN THE CASINO INDUSTRY

It is not common to discuss the issue of ethics within the casino industry. Perhaps, because the morality and legitimacy of gambling has always being a delicate point, many persons prefer to sweep the issue under the rug. As hospitality educators, it is important to expose the future industry leaders to important issues.

Ethics is important for both the internal and the external customers of the casino industry. Is it ethical for management to purposely exclude persons of a different race, sex, or national origin from working in specific positions? Is it ethical for management to encourage a patron to continue to gamble when he or she may obviously be intoxicated? Another ethical concern would be to permit teenagers to gamble.

All of the above issues are ethical considerations for future casino managers to think about. On the other hand, what should managers do to ensure that the casinos are operated with the highest integrity? Do they go the extra mile to ensure that clients have not been cheated by employees? Are managers concerned with the activities outside of the casinos? During the upcoming years, these ethical issues may come closer to the spotlight of the glamorous casino world.

CONCLUSION

"Nothing in itself is bad." Gambling may indeed be a part of adult entertainment. However, anything in excess may be harmful. In the next millennium, one of the major concerns for the casino industry will be regulation and control. Casino operators will continually fight the image battle. They will also be challenged to increase their corporate citizenry regarding problem gamblers.

Perhaps the largest growth of the casino industry will occur in Asia and the Pacific Rim countries. They have a large population, and many of their economies are growing. The second greatest area of expansion would probably be Europe. Many of the European countries already have casinos in selected locations. The disintegration of the Soviet Union will also bring about the establishment of many casinos. In these countries, it is possible to see the introduction of different games than those played in the United States.

The corporate structure of casinos has already begun to change. Many of the casino giants are now publicly traded on the stock exchange. Partnerships are also becoming more frequent. Several of the Las Vegas giants are forming partnerships with government to operate their casinos. In the future, non-gaming amenities will be the cost for casino resort growth. In Las Vegas and elsewhere, tourists were spending—and will continue to spend—less on gaming and more on restaurants, shopping, and shows (Berns, 1998). International companies like Sun International are also forming partnerships with Native American tribes as well as etching out a market for themselves both in the United States and the Bahamas. Moreover, several countries are requiring that a specific percentage of the ownership be composed of local residents. Austrian and Malaysian companies are also striving to become financial globetrotters within the casino world. Most new casinos in the world will use casino management personnel that contract with the owner to operate these casinos (Ruben, 1995).

The casino industry in the United States is now being viewed as adult entertainment and not gambling. Included in this concept of adult entertainment will be the provision of all types of entertainment that will be appealing to both adult gamblers and other members of the family. Many casinos, especially within North America, are now developing theme concepts and packages that are attractive to all members of a family. This type of positioning will definitely increase the casinos' market shares within the entertainment world. Mega-resorts like the Venetian Little Italy recreate famous landmarks that provide the tourist with more than casino action (Henderson, 1999). This promotional concept will continue.

The multibillion dollar casino industry will continue to grow throughout the world. In the future, efforts must be exerted to preserve the social, economic, and ethical integrity of the industry. The integrity will only be maintain if both lawmakers and corporate decision makers continually regulate and review the current regulations. Even if casinos are considered adult entertainment, they must still be properly overseen.

People will continue to gamble as long as they see it as a way to overcome poverty and gain something for nothing. On the other hand, people will also continue to gamble because they regard it as entertainment.

REVIEW TERMS

Employee Assistance Programs (EAPs)	touch screens
mega-casino-hotel	virtual-reality games

REFERENCES

Andersen, K. (1994). Las Vegas, U.S.A. *Time* vol. 143 (2): 42–51.

Catch the new wave. (1994). *Gaming and Wagering Business* 15 (9):2.

Berns, D. (1998). Non-gaming amenities. *International Gaming and Wagering Business*, winter.

Connor, M. (1993). The latest gaming frontier? The sky's the limit. *Gaming and Wagering Business* 14 (11): 1, 57.

Connor, M. (1999). In the spotlight. *Indian Gaming IGWB*, winter.

Eade, V. H. and Eade, R. H. (1997). *Introduction to the casino entertainment industry.* Upper Saddle River, New Jersey: Prentice-Hall.

Fine, G. (1994). Who are we? *Casino Player* V (9): 6.

Gros, R. (1993). Past, present & future. *Casino Player* IV (9): 20–21.

Harrah's. (1996). Harrah's survey of casino entertainment. Available at: http://www.harrahs.com/survey/ce96/ce96_index.html

Henderson, A. (1999). Little Italy. Nevada Magazine 59(3).

Ragonese, J. (1994), Touch-screen technology; gives casino flexibility. *Gaming and Wagering Business* 15 (5): 20–22.

Ruben, M. (1995). *Managing casinos.* New York: Barricade Books.

Sympson, R. (1994). Place your bets. *Restaurant Business* 1 November, 54–68.

Warson, A. (1994). Cheaters caught at new Windsor casino. *Gaming and Wagering Business,* 15 (7): 6.

Welles, C. (1998). America's gambling fever. *Business Week,* 24 April, 112–120.

Wildman, R. (1998). Gambling: An attempt at an integration. Canada: Wynne Resources, p. 263.

Chapter 17

Casino Gambling on the Internet

OBJECTIVES

- Discuss the history of the Internet casino.
- Identify at least five major Internet casino companies with their addresses.
- Describe the process of using an Internet casino.
- Locate and identify at least five countries where Internet casinos are based.
- Discuss the legal concerns of gambling on the Internet in the United States.
- Identify at least five Internet terms.
- Discuss the social concerns of the Internet casinos.
- Describe future trends of the Internet casino.

INTRODUCTION

Casinos have reached the **Internet** for three main reasons. The first reason is accessibility. Approximately thirty to forty million Americans are connected to the Internet. Moreover, in the closing years of this millennium, more people are using their computers as an entertainment center. A second reason the casinos have reached the Internet is because of its convenience. Gamblers no longer have to leave their homes to experience the thrill of gambling. Right within their homes in their pajamas, individuals can gamble. The home and the computer are not perceived as a threatening environment. Casino gambling is now being viewed as adult entertainment. Perhaps the last explanation of how the casino has entered cyberspace is just people's greed and desire for excitement.

In 1995, Internet Casinos became the first Internet casino online. Currently, there are approximately sixty operational Internet casinos accessible to almost 160 countries. Approximately 75 percent of the Internet users are Americans. These numbers are astounding when we consider the casino Internet industry is less than a decade old, and it has already grown to a $10 billion industry (Rutherford, 1997).

Warren Eugene may be regarded as the "Bugsy Siegel" of the Internet. He developed the idea from working with a specialty pay cable channel. The idea of a casino on the Internet matured during 1994, and in May 1995 he formed Sports International Limited in Antigua. Later in August, Internet Casino became operational with wagering over the Internet.

In this chapter, we will review the history of Internet casinos, identify several of the major Internet companies, describe the process of accessing the Internet, identify the countries hosting Internet sites, discuss the legal concerns of the Internet in the United States, identify several Internet terms, and also describe future trends of the Internet casino.

LOCATIONS OF THE INTERNET CASINOS

The majority of the Internet casinos are located within the Caribbean; the only Internet casinos located within the United States are on Native American reservations. The following places have Internet casinos:

Amsterdam	Ireland
Antigua and Barbuda	Liechtenstein
Australia	Manchester
Belize	Monaco
Canada	Native American reservations
Costa Rica	Spain
Dominica	St. Kitts and Nevis
Dominican Republic	St. Martin
Greece	St. Vincent and Grenadines
Grenada	Turks and Caicos Islands

Internet casinos do not operate from within the United States because of three laws. The **Interstate Wire Act** (18 USCS 1084) of 1961 stipulates, "It is a crime for any one in the business of gambling to use a telephone line which crosses a state or national boundary to transmit information assisting in the placing of bets." This legislation further states, "In order for defendant to be convicted of violating 18 USCS 1084 (a), a court must be convinced beyond reasonable doubt that defendant, while being in business of betting and wagering, knowingly used wire communication facility to transmit information assisting in placing of bets and wagering." This was designed to help enforce the public policy of the states about forty years ago. Individuals caught transmitting wagering information would be "fined not more than $10,000 or imprisoned not more than two years, or both." This law makes it illegal for Americans to place a bet on the telephone to another country.

The second law that attempts to prevent Americans from gambling over the Internet is the **Professional and Amateur Sports Act,** which was enacted in 1992. This law was designed to prevent the spread of the state lotteries and the wagering on sports events. It made it illegal for any person to sponsor, advertise, promote, or operate any betting or wagering on any professional sports. This law would also make Internet casino activities prohibitive (Brown, 1997).

A third law, the **Interstate Transport Act,** prohibits the transportation of any wagering paraphernalia. The purpose of this act was to prohibit individuals from knowingly sending or carrying paraphernalia or other devices designed to be used in illegal gambling. Many legislators are arguing that Internet casino Web site is used as a "device designed for use" in illegal gambling. In July of 1998, the senate voted to ban Internet gambling (*Los Angeles Times*, 1998).

MAJOR INTERNET CASINO COMPANIES

The growth within the cyber world continues daily. The number of Internet casinos are continually growing. Table 17-1 shows the names and Internet addresses for ten of the more established Internet casinos (Rutherford, 1997).

Table 17-1   Names and Internet Addresses of Internet Casinos

Name of Internet Casino	Address
Acropolis Casinos	www.acropoliscasinos.com
Casino Fortune	www.casinofortune.com
Casino On Net	www.casino-on-net.com
Casino Royale	www.funscape.com
Grand Dominican Resorts	www.granddominican.com
Gold Club Casino	www.casino.com
Golden Palace Online Casino	www.goldenpalace.com
Interbet	www.interbetcasino.com
Intercasino	www.intercasino.com
Virtual Vegas	www.virtualvegas.com

The majority of the casinos listed in Table 17-1 encourage their users to play as many as eighteen games. Some of the games played on the Internet casinos include slots, roulette, poker, keno, lotto, and bingo. Many of the games are displayed in either two or three dimensions with creative sound effects. Some of the sites provide as many as six different languages for their users.

ACCESSING THE INTERNET CASINO

Previously we mentioned that one of the reasons the casino has entered the Internet is because of its accessibility. The following equipment is needed to gamble on the Internet (Zabel, 1997/1998).

1. Computer
2. Modem
3. Internet service provider
4. Long-distance provider
5. Browser
5. Sound blaster
6. Monitor

These items are no longer expensive. Many households or workplaces have them. It is suggested that you use an Intel Pentium 90 microprocessor or higher (Rutherford, 1997). The computer should also have a minimum of two gigabytes (Gb) of storage space on the hard drive. Because these software packages are rather large, the computer should have at least sixteen megabytes of random access memory or active memory. The random access memory (RAM) is the available space for the computer to manipulate the software programs. The larger the RAM, the more operations the computer will be able to handle. The computer will also need an efficient sound blaster with an audio card to reproduce quality sounds. Also included with the computer would be an eight-bit color super video graphics array (SVGA). These monitors are capable of producing 256 colors.

The computer and monitor alone would not enable a user to access the Internet. The next important device is a modem. This device connects the computer to the telephone, a long-distance provider, and an Internet service provider (ISP). The modem should be at least 28,800 bits per second. The faster the modem, the quicker and better it is for the user.

The browser is the last item a potential Internet gambler would need to have. A browser is a software that allows a user to see and access a specific Internet site. Presently, Netscape Navigator is the most popular, followed by Microsoft Internet Explorer.

After all of the above items have been assembled and connected, users can follow the steps below and gamble to their heart's content.

1. Determine which Internet casino you wish to gamble with. For example, the address for Intercasino is www.intercasino.com.
2. Type www.intercasino.com.
3. Download the software.
4. When the home page appears, follow the prompted instructions or options.
5. Set up an account in the user's name by depositing a specific amount of money in an account.
6. Obtain a password.
7. Using the mouse, select the game of choice.
8. Participate in a free trial game.
9. Play the game making wagers.
10. Exit from the computer.

After completing the above steps, within minutes an Internet user can be involved in a three-dimensional virtual casino. Some sites are so sophisticated that the actual sounds of a real casino are heard.

There are, however, a few concerns. Perhaps the greatest concern about Internet gambling is the issue of confidentiality. Many users are worried that hackers will obtain their credit card number and use it fraudulently. Many of the online providers have installed encryption software to prevent such abuse. **Encryption** is the process of using a code to prevent other individuals from accessing an individual's account.

SOCIAL IMPACT OF THE INTERNET CASINO

One of the important social concerns about the Internet casino is that it can be easily abused by all of its users. This abuse is particularly a concern for underage gamblers. Although there are a number of software packages available to block specific sites, it is difficult for parents to be aware of all of them. Today there are approximately sixty, tomorrow there will definitely be more.

Underage gamblers are not the only users to be concerned about. Invariably, the use of an Internet casino is a solitary activity. Problem gamblers can lose large sums of money on the Internet without anyone being aware of the problem. One advantage of the other forms of gambling is that the participants must travel to the venue. Because a computer is so accessible, this abusive habit can be nurtured almost anytime of the day or at any place. Because most of these casinos are scattered all over the Caribbean and Europe, it will be difficult at best to police them. At this time, attempts are being made by the industry to self-regulate.

At the moment, the Interactive Gaming Council has been the primary spokesperson for self-regulation. It has been advocating the registration and auditing of all cyber operations. The catalyst for the self-regulation is to nurture consumers' confidence in the industry. An advantage of the traditional casino is that a customer is able to see the casino personnel and obtain immediate feedback if they have any concerns. It is not so easy on the Internet. Many of the cyber casinos have customer service and fraud departments. However, there have already been a number of online rip-offs (Haring, 1998). A *USA Today* article reports of defrauding by both Web sites and customers.

FUTURE TRENDS IN THE INTERNET CASINOS

Sebastian Sinclair of Christansen/Cummings Associates of New York estimated that in 1998 gaming on the Internet was $440 million. He further projects this figure in the year 2000 will increase to $8.6 billion (Haring, 1998). This figure is too lucrative for the gaming giants to remain out of the cyber casino industry. Invariably, during the next decade a number of them will enter. By that time the wars of litigation will have subsided.

During the next decade the cyber casinos software will become more sophisticated with 3D virtual reality as the norm. The programs will also become more user friendly. The time for downloading graphics will increase. There will also be faster interaction and fewer transmission problems. During the upcoming years, the level of encryption will become more refined and reliable.

Perhaps one of the biggest changes in the future will occur in the regulating of the entire Internet casino industry. Too much American money is being spent outside of the country without being taxed. The solution is not to prohibit it, but rather to develop a system that would enable the government to also profit from this burgeoning industry. The Internet Gambling Prohibition Act of 1997 introduced in the house by Senator Jon Kyl, R-AZ, is not the solution. This bill was introduced to stop online bettors and fine them at least $25,500 or jail or both. This bill will probably be repealed within the next five years.

Native Americans will also become beneficiaries of the Internet casinos. During the next millennium, there will be an increase in Internet casino gambling operated by Native American reservations on their reservations. If the laws do not change, they will continue utilizing their class II exemption to circumvent the law. Similarly, Native Americans will hire more skilled individuals to operate their operations on the reservations.

CONCLUSION

Network Wizards projects that during the next three years the number of Internet users will double every 12 to 15 months (Zabel, 1997/1998). The more users, the greater the possibilities of Internet users. The Internet users will be better educated, have a larger income, and also have a larger amount of disposable income. There is a substantial latent demand for in-home gambling services. These are presently being met by the one hundred small Internet gambling sites, but this could change with further integration of corporate giants like ATT, Hilton, Harrah's, and MGM (Cabot, 1998). The technology used in Internet casinos will improve, and the legal battle will be resolved with a compromise.

REVIEW TERMS

encryption

Internet

Interstate Transport Act

Interstate Wire Act

Professional and Amateur Sports Act

REFERENCES

Brown, P. (1997). "Gambling: New laws and regulations." Available at: http://www.ljextra.com/Internet/1087gamblinglaws.html

Cabot, A. (1998). Internet gambling report II. Las Vegas: Trace Publications.

Haring, B. (1998). "Gambling: A high-stakes Internet game." *USA Today.* Available at: http://www.usatoday.com/me/cyber/tech/ctb9/8htm

Leshin, C. B. (1997). *Internet investigations in hospitality, travel, and tourism.* Upper Saddle River, New Jersey: Prentice-Hall.

Los Angeles Times. (1998). Senate votes to ban Internet gambling. 24 July.

Rutherford, J. (1997). The newest casinos. *Casino Player* VIII (4): 36–41.

Zabel, D. (1997/1998). Integrating the Internet into the hospitality curriculum: More than a listing of "cool" web sites. *Journal of Hospitality and Tourism Education* IX (4): 66–73.

Glossary

Action. The amount of money or chips wagered or the total amount of a player's wagering over the cost of his/her play.

Apron. A dealing apron worn in the front of the pants to help prevent wear on the clothes. Each house issues its own, with an embroidered design on it.

Atlantic City. Legalized gaming in 1978 under strict regulations to help failing economy, especially the area's senior citizens. This was the first place outside of Nevada to have legalized table games.

Baccarat. A card game whose object is to get as close to nine as possible. It is housed in a separate pit and played for high stakes.

Bankroll. The amount of money/credit that players are willing to use to gamble. They may not use their entire bankroll, but often do.

Baseman. One of two dealers in the back of the crap game. He/she books all line bets, field, come, don't come, place, lay, and buy bets. Each of these bets pay different odds.

Bet. The actual wager on any given hand of cards or roll of the dice.

Big red. The number seven on a crap game.

Big six. A game in which the dealer spins a big wheel, and if the player has played on whatever dollar denomination lands, he/she wins. For example, if the wheel lands on the $10 bill, and the player had bet on it, he/she wins ten times the bet. This is probably the worst odds game in the house but is extremely simple.

Big six/eight. A bet on six or eight in the corner (of the crap table) that pays even money.

Black and whites. A term for the black pants and white shirts that dealers commonly wear.

Black in action. When a $100 check is in play. This is an approval call by the floorman.

Blackjack. The object of the card game is to get as close to twenty-one as possible without going over twenty-one. The dealer will hit his/her hand until he/she has seventeen or more. If the dealer goes over twenty-one, anyone with cards left will be paid. If the player goes over twenty-one, he/she automatically loses. Each player is initially dealt two cards and the house is dealt two cards also. One of the house's cards is exposed. The house plays its hand after all the players are through. The players can take a hit, stand, split, or double with each hand. The players play in clockwise order.

Bookmaking. The taking of bets on a specific event, such as a sporting event.

Box cars. Rolling twelve in a game of craps.

Boxman. A lower-level management position. This is the man/woman who wears a suit and sits down and watches the crap game.

Break-in. A novice dealer. A dealer is considered a break-in for the first year he/she is dealing.

Busting. When the player goes over twenty-one by drawing too many cards.

Buy in. The amount of money a player uses to purchase chips or the amount required to enter a poker game.

Card counting. A system that the players use to have an advantage over the house. The player assumes a weighted average to each card face to determine when the game is favorable for the player to bet.

Caribbean stud poker. This game is played on a twenty-one-type table and is based on five-stud poker with the added attraction of a progressive jackpot.

Cashier's cage. Commonly called the cage. Every casino's own mini-bank. The cage exchanges cash for chips (checks) and chips (checks) for cash, distributes pit fills, cashes checks, takes credit cards, approves markers, and alike.

Casino advantage. The advantage, or edge, the house (casino) has over the player in any game.

Casino checks. The chips that actually have a value printed on them and can be exchanged at the cage for money. Commonly in the denominations of $1, $5, $25, $100, $500, $1,000, and $5,000.

Casino chips. Roulette chips of no value at the cashier's cage. These chips stay on the game and are exchanged for checks when the player leaves.

Casino manager. In charge of the total operation of the casino. He/she is responsible for hiring/firing of casino staff, oversees daily operations, and is held accountable for the casino's win percentage.

Casino win/loss. This is the actual amount won/lost, calculated after every shift, and in many cases, for each individual game.

Catwalk. The area above the casino, surrounded by surveillance personnel who observe the casino floor.

Change of personnel. A termination given to a probationary employee.

Change only. A call in the crap game to signify that the money thrown in by the player is not a bet; it is specifically for change.

Checks play. Any bet over $50 that is announced to the floorman.

Come. It is a game within a game on craps. Once the point is established, a player can put money in the come and a seven or eleven wins; two, three, or twelve loses. If any other number is rolled, the money moves to that number and the shooter must roll that number again before a seven to win.

Comp. This is a complimentary meal, room, or whatever given by the pit, usually to rated players; however, some pit bosses/floormen that have "power of the pen" will write comps for other reasons.

Compulsive gambler. A progressive behavior disorder in which an individual has a psychological uncontrollable urge to gamble.

Corner red. Big six/eight.

Counting cards. This is any number of strategies players use to gain edge by reading the cards in twenty-one and assigned a plus or minus value. For example, in one strategy all of the tens and aces count as -1, all the twos, threes, fours, fives, and sixes count as $+1$, and sevens, eights, and nines count as zero. When the count is higher than $+3$, divided by the number of decks used, a player will significantly increase his/her bet. Every casino has a house counter and several dealers who can count cards. If unusual betting is spotted, the house counter will often come on the game or watch to determine whether the player is counting cards. They will then be backed off from twenty-one, and their picture will be circulated among the various casinos.

Crap. The numbers two, three, and twelve on a crap game.

Craps. A dice game that is dealt by three dealers at a time. The object is either to throw a seven or eleven on the come-out roll to pass. Two, three, or twelve will lose on the come-out. If a point is established, then the same number must be repeated before a seven rolls to win.

Credit manager. This person approves or denies a player's credit line application. He/she will also determine the amount of credit that can be established for an individual player. In many cases, casino managers have the power to raise the limit if it is a known player.

Croupier. Fancy term for a roulette dealer.

Crystal Casino. A new casino located in Montreal in the former French Pavilion of the World's Fair.

Day shift. This is 10 A.M. to 6 P.M. or 11 A.M. to 7 P.M. This is usually the grind shift. They are busy but do not see nearly the action/play of swing or graveyard shifts. Typically many family people work this shift. It is characterized by tedious steady work.

Dealer. Anyone dealing a pit game, such as blackjack, roulette, craps, or baccarat.

Don't come. The reverse of the come line on craps. Once the point is established, a player can put money in the don't come and a two or three wins, seven or eleven loses, twelve is a push. If any other number is rolled, the money moves to that number and the shooter must roll a seven before whatever number his/her money is behind.

Don't pass line. The reverse of a pass line bet in craps; two or three wins on the come out, seven or eleven loses on the come out and twelve is barred. Once a point is established, the object is to get a seven before the point is rolled again.

Double down. This is a play in blackjack. It is a double or nothing on one additional card. For example, the player who has a six and five totaling eleven can turn the cards face-up and double his/her bet on one additional card. The player then has to stand and play against whatever the house draws.

Down behind. A losing don't come bet on a crap game. This call by the baseman alerts the boxman that they are removing the bet.

Drop. The amount of money actually collected in the "cans" after each shift. This is counted by soft count, and used to calculate the percentage.

Edge. *See* casino advantage.

86. A player who is barred from entering the casino or playing the games.

Exotic bets. These bets are such bets as quinellas (betting on first or second place of a race), perfectas (betting on first or second place based on the order on which they are placed),

and exactas (betting on first, second, and third place in the order in which they finish).

Extra board. This is not a steady shift. These are the newest dealers hired into a prospective casino. They work as fill-ins on any shift and do not have insurance. Their probationary period does not start until after they get a full shift. So a person who is on extra board for one year has no benefits. They are considered part-time even though many work full-time.

Eye in the sky. The term for the surveillance people and the cameras who are constantly watching the games.

Faro. Faro comes from the name Pharaoh, from one of the kings in the old French deck of cards. The object of the game is to place your bet on a card. If that card is matched the first time, the bank gets the money; if the card is matched the second time, then the player gets the money.

Field. Two (pays double), three, four, nine, ten, eleven, and twelve (pays double), a one-roll bet in craps.

Fill slip. When the hoppers are filled each day, a fill slip representing the amount of funds utilized is completed.

Fix. This is an illegal game. It can be loaded dice, a cooler in twenty-one, or many other things. This is an item out of the past and not seen in legalized gaming today, for the most part. At least from the house's point. There are tight gaming control boards in both Atlantic City and Nevada that control the activities; any casino caught cheating would automatically lose its license. In Nevada, gaming is a privilege, not a right.

Floorman. This is one step higher than a boxman. This person watches either a crap game (standing behind the game) or several pit games. He/she makes all decisions concerning problems with players.

Front money. Bank checks, cash, or other form of payment deposited with the casino to establish credit for a player who bets against that money.

Gambler. A man/woman who really bets strong, usually a minimum bet of $100 per role. Otherwise the person is considered a player.

Generally accepted accounting principles. Twelve principles that provide the basis for a comparative within like or similar firms for the financial community.

Graveyard shift. Usually 2 A.M. to 10 A.M., or 3 A.M. to 11 A.M. in the casino industry. This is the slowest time of the night and most of the cleaning is done during these hours. A lot of the really heavy action occurs during these hours, because the casino is at its quietest.

Green in action. When a $25 check is in play. This call is usually not necessary except in break-in houses.

Grind. The amount of small-bills drop, less than $100 bills. This number is not counted by the pit, but estimated by the overall action of the casino; the soft count comes back with the actual amount the next day.

Hand. An individual game of cards in twenty-one, or the length of a streak in craps until a seven-out. Some records have been set at three-hour hands in craps, where the house loses a tremendous amount of money. These are usually referred to as monsters.

Handle. The total amount wagered by players at a casino.

Hard count. It is taken from the drop box beneath the slot machines. These coins are collected and each of the machine's coins are weighed or counted to determine the slot drop.

Hardway(s). Double twos, threes, fours, or fives in craps. The double that is bet on must roll before either a seven or that number rolls easy. For example, for the number ten, (6 and 4) or (4 and 6) are easy rolls and (5 and 5) is the hardway. The hard four or ten pay 8 for 1, and the hard six or eight pay 10 for 1.

Helps hall. A buffet set up for the on-duty employees. These are free of charge and served 24 hours a day.

High roller. This is a man/woman whose average bet is well above $100. High rollers are catered to by junkets and the like and are given free suites and meals.

Hit. The motion of taking another card in blackjack.

Hold. The hold is the win divided by the drop.

Hold card (blackjack). The dealer's unseen card.

House. Casino.

IGT. International Gaming Technologies, Inc.

Jackpot (slots). These are the big jackpots, the top line paid out on a slot machine. Can be from $50 to over $20,000,000. If the jackpot is over $1,200, the winner must produce legal identification and Social Security card to collect. The IRS receives a form with the player's winnings. If the jackpot is over $10,000, the IRS takes its percentage off the top, and it is held by the casino.

Jai alai. A game played with a ball and a wicker hand mitt that is used to receive and throw the ball. It is played by two or more players. Wagering is on individuals or teams.

Juice. The term for knowing someone in an important position who can help you get/keep a job.

Junket. A chartered flight of high rollers, given free rooms, meals, and often airfare according to the level of their play.

Keno. Like a lottery game. A player marks two to twenty spots on a ticket and turns it in before a game. The numbers range from one to eighty. Twenty balls are drawn, and players who get better than 50 percent right on their numbers will win something. The more numbers right, the higher the payout. It can reach $100,000 for a $1 bet if the player gets ten out of ten or eleven out of eleven and so forth.

Large. $100 bills that are kept track of by the floorman.

Las Vegas Strip. Las Vegas Boulevard; it is where all the fancy hotels and casinos are located and is about five miles long. The other large gaming area in Las Vegas is the downtown area.

Limit. The maximum wager a casino will allow at any one time.

Limit play. When either money or checks are being played to the posted table limit.

Loose (slots). A slot machine that pays out liberally to customers and reduces the house advantage.

Marker. This is either a credit marker or a call bet. A credit marker is established ahead of time with the casino, and the player is extended credit in which to play. Players either pay back the marker, or it is owed at a later date. These are commonly the bigger players. A call bet or temporary marker is only for the hand being played and must be immediately paid back.

Mini baccarat. The same game as the larger version; however, this game is housed in the regular twenty-one pit and usually played for less money.

Money play. This is a call on any of the games to alert the floorman that cash is being placed as a bet (instead of checks, which are much more common).

Mucker. An assistant to a roulette dealer on a busy game. He/she is also trained as a roulette dealer, and his/her job is to clean up the chips into their assorted colored stacks, and hand the dealer the payoff. (Many roulette dealers consider this the favored position, because this is the only dealing position that you do not have to deal with any customers.)

Natural. Two, three, seven, eleven, or twelve on the come-out roll in craps.

Natural (blackjack). An ace and ten value card during the original hand.

Odds. Pass line/don't pass bets and come/don't come bets in craps can have odds placed with them. Most casinos allow up to two times the flat bet, but it is not mandatory. Odds pay true odds according to the probability of the dice. For example, take the number four on two dice. it can be made three ways (1 and 3), (2 and 2), or (3 and 1) and there are six ways to make a seven. So the odds on the number four (or ten) would pay 2:1. The five and nine pay 3:2, and the six and eight pay 6:5.

Pai gow. A Chinese domino tile game in which the object is to make two separate hands out of four tiles (two tiles each hand) that either make a pair or count as close to nine as possible. They are played against the house's hand. A player must win both hands to win or lose both to lose; otherwise it is a push. Because this is an even game, a vig is charged on all winning hands. Players can "bank" and stake the whole table. Then the other players, as well as the house, play against the player who is banking. This is one of the most difficult games to learn and play.

Pai gow poker. A much more common game than the pai-gow tiles. This is a version of poker that uses seven cards to make a five-card high hand and a two-card second best hand. These hands are played against the house's hand. A player must win both hands to win or lose both to lose; otherwise it is a push. Because this is an even game, a vig is charged on all winning hands. Players can "bank" and stake the whole table. Then the other players, as well as the house, play against the player who is banking.

Pari-mutuel. A system of betting on sporting events where the winners divide the total amount wagered per event among themselves.

Pass line. *See* Craps.

Pit. A group of games within a casino, usually four crap tables or twelve other tables, that make up a management section. The larger the casino, the more pits it will have.

Pit boss. He/she is in charge of an entire pit. (Almost no women are in this position.)

Pitch game. Single- or double-deck blackjack in which the dealer pitches the cards from his/her hand.

Place bet. Any nonnatural number can be placed on a crap game. The four or ten pays 9:5, the five or nine pays 7:5, and the six or eight pays 7:6. These are paid when the number is rolled, and on a seven any of these bets lose.

Player. A small-time gambler.

Point. Can be the numbers four, six, eight, nine, or ten in craps. It is dependent on whatever number the shooter rolls on the come out if it is not a natural.

Premium player. A gambler who is rated and qualifies for complimentary (comps) service by the hotel/casino.

Progressive slots. The jackpot is like a lottery; it keeps on going up a small percentage for every dollar played until it hits, and then it starts over at its base.

Prop bets. *See* Proposition bets.

Proposition bets. These are the bets handled by the stickman on a crap game. They are the hardway bets, a one roll yo, or crap. Other set-ups include the horn, whirl bet, 3-way craps, hop bets, etc.

Qualified player. A rated player, less than a premium player, who still is eligible for meal comps, but not usually room comps.

Race book. A business that accepts wagers on race events.

Red dog. A card game in which the dealer deals two cards and the third must be in the middle of the first two cards to win.

Reg 6-A. The Federal Banking Secrecy Act of 1985, which requires casinos to record and get positive ID from all players buying in more than $10,000 in a twenty-four-hour period.

Roulette. This is a game in which the dealer spins a ball around a wheel that contains the numbers 0.00 and 1 through 36. These numbers are red, black, or green (the 0 and 00 are green). The players can bet their money in several different ways. Outside bets are red, black, 1 to 18, 19 to 36, odd or even. These bets pay even money. Column bets and section bets pay 2:1. All the other bets are inside bets. Straight-up (1 number bets) pay 35:1. Split bets (2 number bets) pay 17:1. Street bets (3 number bets) pay 11:1. Corner bets (4 number bets) pay 8:1. Double street bets (6 number bets) pay 5:1. The zeroes play as any other bet and are paid the same odds if bet. Each player is given his/her own color, which is marked up to whatever value (over the table minimum) that the player wants. Chips are usually worth anywhere from 25¢ to $25 apiece.

Score. When the dealers pick up an unusually large share of tokes for the day.

Seven-out. A losing roll on a crap game.

Shift boss. He (deliberate exclusive he) is in charge of all the live table games for a given shift. If the casino manager is not present, then he is in charge of the entire casino.

Shift for shift. When each shift divides tokes for itself.

Shill. A person hired by the casino to sit at games to attract business. Shills usually get up as soon as any real players sit down. This is a dealer's nightmare, dealing all night to the shill. However, most places only have baccarat shills.

Shoe. Four, six, or eight decks of cards are placed in a plastic shoe. Commonly used in twenty-one and baccarat.

Shoe game. This is either four- or six-deck blackjack using a shoe.

Shooter. The player in a crap game who is rolling the dice. He/she has the dice until seven-out, then the dice are given to the next player rotating clockwise.

Shuffle. An alert call to the floorman that a dealer is shuffling in a shoe game. This is for gaming protection.

Shuffle-check. When the dealer is done shuffling a shoe, some houses require a shuffle check. The dealer leaves the cards laced, and the floorman approves the shuffle before the shoe is loaded.

Sic bow. A dice game in which players can guess at what combination the dice will roll.

Sick tokes. Because dealers do not receive any sick pay, some casinos give sick tokes for extended illness or hospitalization. These are voted on by the dealers; less than half of the houses have sick tokes.

Simulcasting. The simultaneous transmission of sporting events providing the bettor with the opportunity to bet on more than one game at a time.

Skimming. Taking part of the profit (the boss or owner) before it is recorded, thus making it nontaxable. This is illegal.

Skinny dugan. Seven-out on a crap game.

Slot machine. Coin- or bill-operated gambling device using mechanical or electronic machines for the opportunity to win a prize, playoff, or jackpot.

Slot win. The amount of win in the slot department for a given shift. It is usually recorded by amount and percentage of the coins dropped in the machines, similar to the accounting systems used on the live game.

Split. Any two cards of like value can be split in blackjack. The player puts the amount equal to his/her bet next to each, and the hand is made into two separate hands. For example, a ten and a jack have the same value and can be split and made into two separate hands. Commonly aces and eights are split. With a pair of aces, two cards are placed face down, one on each ace. Any other pair that is split, the player can have as many cards as he/she wants on each hand. On the new hand, if the player gets another card on the first hit that is the same as the already split pair, he/she can resplit into as many as four different hands. (If you ever play blackjack, don't ever split tens—very poor strategy.)

Stickman. The dealer in the center of the crap game with the bamboo stick. He/she is responsible for calling the dice and handling all the proposition bets. In addition, he/she also watches the end opposite the shooter for accuracy in that dealer's pay offs.

Sweat. The term used to describe a boss who is worried if the house is losing money. Some bosses act as though it is their personal life savings that are at stake.

Swing shift. The busiest time in the casino: 6 P.M. to 2 A.M., or 7 P.M. to 3 A.M. These dealers have the reputation for partying and are out late at night, since they get off work in the late-night hours.

System bettor. Any player using a system to bet. The house allows systems because it always has the ultimate edge.

Table drop. The amount of money in each table's "can" at the end of the shift.

Table for table. When each crap crew goes on their own.

Table limit. The posted house limit on any game; can be, for example, $5 to $1,000. The dealer has the authority to book all bets in this range, usually with the approval of the floorman if the bet is over $100 for the first time. If the bet exceeds the limit, the casino manager has the right to book the bet; otherwise it is no bet.

Table win/loss. The amount each table actually won or lost at the end of a shift.

Third base. The seat furthest to the right of the dealer.

Three-card monte. This game is only played with three cards. The object of the game is to pick which one of three cards down is the queen and avoid picking any aces.

Toke committee. The dealers who are elected to represent each shift for the rules and problems. They often are the toke cutters, but don't have to be.

Toke cutters. The group of dealers who are voted on by their shifts to count and divide the daily tokes into individual shares. They are given extra money for this duty and are responsible for the money.

Toke rules. A list of rules established by the dealers as to how the tokes are to be divided up. Some of the more tyrannical houses do not let the dealers decide; they decide for them.

Tokens. Artificial coins used as a substitute for money. They come in many denominations.

Tokes. Tips received directly from patrons in the form of dealer bets or handed in. Most of a dealer's income is derived directly from tokes. Tokes are pooled among dealers in a variety of ways, but no dealer keeps his/her own tokes.

24 hours. This is an entire house pull on tokes. All dealers in a 24-hour period share tokes. This is by far the most common way of dividing tokes.

Twenty-one. Blackjack.

Vacation tokes. Tokes cut for an individual dealer while he/she is on vacation.

Video lotteries. These lotteries are played on computerized terminals and allow the winner instant verification of win or loss.

Vig. Some bets in pai gow, pai gow poker, craps, baccarat, and mini baccarat charge a 5 percent commission.

Wager. The amount bet on a single hand.

Walking money. Money given by a casino to a player who has lost all of his/her funds in order to return home.

Win. The win is equal to the drop minus jackpot tickets minus jackpot payouts plus hopper fills.

Yo. The number eleven on a crap game. If bet on a one-roll proposition bet, then it pays 15 to 1.

Index